M O

# HOT CHOCOLATE FOR THE MYSTICAL SOUL

---

## 101 True Stories of Angels, Miracles, and Healings

---

## Arielle Ford

A PLUME BOOK

PLUME
Published by the Penguin Group
Penguin Putnam Inc., 375 Hudson Street, New York, New York 10014, U.S.A.
Penguin Books Ltd, 27 Wrights Lane, London W8 5TZ, England
Penguin Books Australia Ltd, Ringwood, Victoria, Australia
Penguin Books Canada Ltd, 10 Alcorn Avenue, Toronto, Ontario, Canada M4V 3B2
Penguin Books (N.Z.) Ltd, 182–190 Wairau Road, Auckland 10, New Zealand

Penguin Books Ltd, Registered Offices: Harmondsworth, Middlesex, England

First published by Plume, a member of Penguin Putnam Inc.

First Printing, September, 1999
10  9  8  7  6  5  4  3  2  1

"Paramedic: A Call from the Other Side" by Jan Barron, from *Earth to God, Come in Please*, Book 2, Harold Klemp, series editor. Reprinted with permission of Eckankar, P.O. Box 27300, Minneapolis, MN 55427. Copyright © Eckankar, 1997.

"Malaria Pills" by Sri Harold Klemp, from *Stories to Help You See God in Your Life*, ECK Parables, Book 4, by Harold Klemp. Reprinted with permission of Eckankar, P.O. Box 27300, Minneapolis, MN 55427. Copyright © Eckankar, 1994.

"Love and Power" from *The Unimaginable Life* by Kenny and Julia Loggins. Copyright © 1997 by Kenny and Julia Loggins. Reprinted by permission of Avon Books.

"Dream House" by Mary Carroll Moore, from *Eckankar Journal*, copyright © Eckankar, 1994. Reprinted with permission of Mary Carroll Moore and Eckankar.

"The Angel Bus Driver" by Ron Paul, reprinted by permission from *Divine Guidance: How to Have Conversations with God and Your Guardian Angel* by Doreen Virtue, Ph.D. (Renaissance/St. Martin's, 1998).

"Can You See the Light of God—Even If You're Blind?" by Eric Troup, from *Eckankar Journal*, copyright © Eckankar, 1996. Reprinted with permission of Eric Troup and Eckankar.

 REGISTERED TRADEMARK—MARCA REGISTRADA

LIBRARY OF CONGRESS CATALOGING-IN-PUBLICATION DATA:
Ford, Arielle.
    More hot chocolate for the mystical soul: 101 true stories of angels, miracles, and healings / Arielle Ford.
        p.     cm.
    ISBN 0-452-28069-9
    1. Angels.   2. Miracles.   3. Healing—Religious aspects.
I. Title.
BL477.F675   1999                                                    98-54932
291.2'117—dc21                                                       CIP

Printed in the United States of America
Set in Palatino

BOOKS ARE AVAILABLE AT QUANTITY DISCOUNTS WHEN USED TO PROMOTE PRODUCTS OR SERVICES. FOR INFORMATION PLEASE WRITE TO PREMIUM MARKETING DIVISION, PENGUIN PUTNAM INC., 375 HUDSON STREET, NEW YORK, NEW YORK 10014.

*For Brian,*
*my soul mate*

# Contents

## V. Magical Love                                   155

## VIII. Spiritual Awakenings                                              273

# Acknowledgments

The surprising success of the original *Hot Chocolate for the Mystical Soul* inspired my insightful editor, Danielle Perez, and Clare Ferraro, president of Dutton Books, to order up this newest collection of mystical stories, and for that I am deeply grateful.

My deepest thanks to all of the contributors who generously shared their personal, mystical stories. It takes courage to go public with these unusual and unique experiences. Their willingness to do so is a gift to us all.

This book would not have been possible without the help of the following people:

Ling Lucas, my amazing literary agent, who guides me through the publishing maze.

Stephanie Gunning, whose skillful editorial talents and genuine enthusiasm for the mystical made this book a lot of fun to work on.

Jack Canfield and Mark Victor Hansen and the entire *Chicken Soup for the Soul* family, for their ongoing support and encouragement.

Laura Clark and Katherine Kellmeyer, for their impressive publicity skills on this book and all of the books represented by The Ford Group.

Heide Banks, Brent BecVar, Anthony Benson, Christen Brown, Julie Hill, Divina Infusino, Judy Martin, Charles Richards, Ben

Woodson, and Jeremiah Sullivan, for their friendship and for helping me gather so many stories for this book.

My parents, Howard and Sheila Fuerst, my sister, Debbie Ford, and my brother, Michael Ford, for their amazing love, support, and enthusiasm for this and all of my unusual and strange projects.

My readers who took the time to read and score each and every story so that only the best possible stories would appear here: Laura Clark, Rita Curtis, Pearl Fisk, Anne Ford, Ashley Ford, Debbie Ford, Sheila Fuerst, Jason Hill, Peggy Hilliard, Barbara Horner, Katherine Kellmeyer, Peggy Olson, Alisha Schwartz, Shelly Schwartz, Randy Thomas, Doreen Virtue, Freda Woldorf.

The divine mother, Ammachi, who teaches me the true meaning of unconditional love.

A very special heartfelt thank you to my husband, Brian Hilliard, who demonstrates unconditional love on a daily basis and who has shown me that "big love" really does exist.

# 1

# DIVINE INTERVENTION

# Angels and Pianos

## Nancy E. Myer

I am in Wilmington, Delaware, to work on a murder case. I've worked with these detectives before; I know them well. When a baby-sitter is not available for my four-year-old daughter, Heidi, they ask me to bring her along and they look out for her while I work. Heidi has been spoiled royally all morning by the detectives. She knows how to charm them, and they love her for it.

We are finished by eleven a.m. Heidi and I are walking down the street looking for a place that sells hot dogs, her favorite food, so that I can feed her before she gets cranky. She jabbers away as she trots alongside me. "Yeroy give me dis candy see." I glance down to see a well-loved piece of candy clutched in her little fist. Detective Leroy Landon is a favorite of hers, and not just because he always has candy in his pockets.

"Yeroy is my good friend. He yikes me lots. He said so." She prattles on happily as I search for a place that might carry her favorite menu item.

A *huge* voice in my head demands, "Pick up that baby and run across the street!" Without hesitation I grab Heidi in my arms and flee to the other side. I've been protected all my life by this loving voice. It never lies to me, and it has saved me from injury many times. When it is raised and loud, the situation is immediate and urgent.

As I scoop up Heidi's protesting little self, I feel hands on my back pushing me right into traffic and across the street. I run, the helping hands pushing me until I reach safety on the other side. Stunned, I turn to look back at where we had been walking in time to see a grand piano being lowered from the building we were in front of. The main cable on the piano breaks loose, and down it comes. Right where we would have been.

The piano hits the sidewalk with an awful crash. The keys shoot straight out on both sides. Piano wires snake out in all directions as the lovely instrument dies with a last sad jangle of its keys.

If I had continued on without the angel's help, Heidi and I would have been killed when the piano broke free and plummeted. A silent prayer sweeps up to the angel that watches over me and mine. "Thank you, dear angel, for saving us."

Heidi stands quietly by my side, surveying the mess on the other side of the street, coming out of her shock. "Hey, bad boys over dere!" she hollers at the movers who dropped the piano. "You not supposed to drop big things on people's heads, you know." She stands with her little hands on her hips, stamping her foot in obvious irritation. "If my mommy's angel hadn't moved us, we be squished dead now. Bad boys you are!"

Her blond curls bobbing in disgust, she shakes her little finger at them, as she often does to her brothers when she decides they are being "bad boys." A crowd has gathered to watch. They laugh with approval at Heidi's upbraiding of the moving men.

The foreman crosses the street to talk with us. "I'm sorry, little lady." He bends down in front of my irate daughter. "I didn't know the cable would split."

Not the least bit daunted by this huge man squatting down in front of her, Heidi crosses her arms on her chest and points in anger at the mess he'd made. "You better not do that again, because other peoples don't have my mommy's angels to take care of them. Right now they'd be hurted bad."

The man looks solemnly at this pint-sized irate child and apologizes once again. "I am so sorry, little lady. I would not have hurt anyone for the world!" Then he looks at my angry eyes and pales.

"Where are your warning cones, sir?" I ask, as my protective maternal fury rises in me. "You should have blocked off the sidewalk."

"You're right. It won't happen again. Is she right about the angel?" he asks me nervously.

"If she weren't, you'd be scraping us off the pavement right now. We would have been directly under that piano when it dropped if my angel hadn't warned us."

He crosses himself quickly. "I guess we both owe that angel a lot!"

"You have no idea how much I owe that angel," I say, looking down at the youngest of my three treasured children. "My angel has saved me many times."

Heidi is still glaring at this man. She has no intention of letting him off easily. "Do you know how to sing 'It's a Small World'?"

Oh no, not that again.

"If you sing me dat song, I forgive you for being a bad boy."

Some of the other men from the crew have joined us. "Go on, Dave, sing to the little lady," they urge him, enjoying his discomfort.

He takes a deep breath and starts singing softly to Heidi. After two choruses he stops. "I don't remember how the rest of the song goes. Can you help me out?"

Heidi happily obliges and so do the people in the crowd. There we all are, singing on a sidewalk after a near miss with death.

Standing beside Heidi and singing with a voice only Heidi and I can hear is the beaming angel that saved our lives. She is enjoying this whole performance by my little blond bombshell. She leans forward and whispers softly into Heidi's ear. There is a little nod of blond curls. "Mommy's angel says I can forgive you now. She says you don't mean to be a bad boy."

The teasing from the other men stops. The foreman's face

goes white. "It's still here? The angel, I mean," he says, look-ing inquiringly at me.

"Of course the angel is still here. How can she protect us if she leaves?" Heidi answers in disgust before I have time to say a thing. "Mom, don't they see her?" Heidi asks me, looking confused.

"No, Heidi, they don't see her. But we do, and that's what's important." Now I know for sure that Heidi can see angels too. It is nice to know that someone besides me shares the beauty and love of the angels.

Leaning carefully toward the big foreman, Heidi plants a sudden, sloppy kiss on his cheek. "There," she says imperially, "I forgive you. But I think it would be a good idea if you get an angel to work with you so when you do dumb things you don't hurt anybody. Okay?"

He winks at me and says, "I think that's a great idea. Could you put in a good word for me, Heidi?"

"What he saying, Mom?"

"He wants you to ask the angel to help him too."

Heidi looks back at the foreman sadly. "Don't you know you gots to ask God for that by yourself?"

Everybody laughs at this serious little girl patting the huge man on the cheek and explaining God's rules to him.

"Dis not a joke," she says disgustedly. The laughter dies immediately. "If you don't gets you an angel, you could get hurt." Taking my hand, she decides this conversation is over. "Mommy, where is dat hot-dog place. I'm hungry."

Off we go with our luminescent angel pointing to a place down the street that does turn out to have really good hot dogs.

# Soul Connections

## *Micki East*

"The biological clock is running out for you, Micki," my doctor told me. "You have multiple small fibroid tumors in your uterus. If you're going to have children, you need to do it soon." Yes, I wanted children, but where was that soul mate to have them with?

Several months passed, and I finally decided I could wait no longer. I called a friend of mine who is a physician and told him I wanted to adopt a child. Before I could finish the sentence he announced, "This is incredible! I just had a young woman in my office who is pregnant and wants to place her baby up for adoption." My mind was racing. I was picturing an older child, yet the universe seemed to be responding with a baby.

That evening, Cindy, the birth grandmother, called me. She was thrilled that I was interested in adopting her grandchild and arranged a time for me to meet her daughter Laura. Laura was eighteen and knew she wanted to go to college. She had come to this decision on her own, and her mother was supportive. Our meeting went well, and Laura decided she would like me to adopt her child. I was elated!

Over the next month, Laura and I discussed names for the baby. The boy's name that kept coming to me was Gray. One night I dreamed that I bought a gray barn-wood cabinet. As I was leaving the store, I realized that this was not what I wanted—I had been picturing oak. I tried to return the cabinet, but the clerk told me that the item was not returnable. She said my only option would be to take it back to the couple who had made it. Their workshop was in a gray, womb-shaped, barn-wood building. I confronted them with my dilemma. They explained to me that they'd made the cabinet with a great deal of love and it could not be returned. I pleaded, but they refused to take it back.

I awoke with a jolt. *Did this mean I should not adopt this baby, or was it just that Gray was the wrong name?*

The next day I received notice from my employer that I was being laid off. I began to have serious doubts about the adoption. *How am I going to support a child if I don't even have a job?* I decided to meditate and explore my options. I closed my eyes and immediately got an image of an adorable baby boy lying on my lap. He looked up at me and said, "My name is Matthew and you are not supposed to be my mother!" My heart sank.

Still wanting to believe that this adoption was the right decision, I consulted a counselor I know and asked, "Is this just the pre-adoption jitters, or is this the wrong child for me?" She said, "Micki, the universe is screaming at you not to adopt this baby." I hung up feeling an unexpected sense of relief coupled with sadness. Reluctantly, I called Laura and explained that I could not continue with the adoption. Laura confided that although she had had her heart set on me, she really wanted her baby to be in a two-parent home with an older sibling.

Two months passed, and one day I ran into Laura at a restaurant. She told me that she had found the perfect couple to adopt her baby and that her child would be their second adopted child. Things were working out exactly as she had hoped. As I walked away, I felt an intense wave of loving energy coming from her unborn child, and a strong sense of peace enveloped me.

Around the baby's due date, I spoke with Cindy. She told me that Laura had given birth to a healthy baby boy and that his adoptive parents had named him Matthew! She added that her grandson looked just like her, with dark Hispanic coloring. Matthew had found his parents.

Many times over the next four years I found myself grieving the absence of a child of my own. Sensing that somewhere there was a child who longed for a mother, I decided to call my friend Jody, who works for an agency that does foreign adoptions. She told me that she had just received information on a very sweet five-year-old boy in a Russian orphanage. She added that at least once a week he asked, "When will my American family come for me?" That night I dreamed I was pregnant and gave birth to a healthy boy.

When I received the information packet and pictures from Jody, my heart skipped a beat. Looking back at me from the picture was a boy I had seen in a meditation nineteen years earlier. I had long forgotten about this meditation, but I was sure this was the child. After an extensive search, I found my old meditation journal. In 1979, I had written: "I just saw an image of my future son. He has straight brown hair and sparkling brown eyes that turn down at the corners when he smiles. He has the East chin, looks very sweet, and reminds me of my nephew Mark. I get the impression his name is Alex."

I closed the journal and picked up the picture again. The description definitely fit. Then I noticed the boy's name written at the top of the picture: Aleksei. *Aleksei is Russian for Alex! This is the boy I saw in the meditation!* The intensity of the thought made me sit down. I quickly completed the necessary paperwork and sent it off to Jody.

On February 25, 1998, I met Aleksei for the first time. The moment our eyes met, I knew deep in my heart that this precious little boy was my long-awaited son. The orphanage staff was amazed at how quickly he took to me and the fact that he looked like he could be my biological son. "You even have the same chin," said one of his caretakers. "Russian children usually have round faces."

When it came time to leave the orphanage, Aleksei hugged his caretakers good-bye, took my hand without hesitation, and said, "Pashlee, Mama," which means "Let's go, Mom" in Russian.

# Mountain Angel

## *Azita Milanian*

That Saturday was not like any other Saturday. All the things that could have stopped me from going to the mountain to run, did happen. But something that I now know was the voice of God and my angel called me there.

Since 1980, I have been running almost every day. At seven p.m. that Saturday, I put my three Labradors—Tango, Tai, and Boo Boo—in the car, and we drove the half-mile to the mountain for an early-evening run. It was still sunny but a little on the cool side.

Right before I left the house, I grabbed my Save the Children T-shirt to wear. Save the Children has been my favorite charity for the past two years, and I have been sponsoring a needy child in Africa. In July, I will be hosting a fund-raising event for them. Since this is my favorite T-shirt, I have often worn it to the gym or other public places where it would be seen. Until that Saturday, though, I never wore it running. In hindsight, the choice seems prophetic.

For five years, I had always started my run at the same entrance to the mountain. However, just a month earlier, I had decided to shift my route to a location that did not begin at the main entrance to the public, thinking it would be a nice change of pace.

The dogs and I began to run. I was feeling depressed about my fund-raising efforts. I was tired of people ignoring me regarding Save the Children, and people not returning my calls about my fund-raising event in July. While I ran, I was talking to God in my head, asking Him for advice about business and my personal life. I would like to have a child, I thought, but it doesn't seem to be the right time in my life. Maybe later I can adopt one.

I felt extremely sad and did not know why; the usual endorphin high was not working. After thirty minutes of running, I thought I was getting sick. By seven fifty-five I was almost at my car. I was feeling intense anxiety, but I couldn't explain where it was coming from. I know now that it was because a newborn baby was being buried at that time.

Just before exiting the trail, I heard a catlike noise. I looked to see if it had come from my dogs. I saw all three dogs circling around a little mound of dirt with bushes on top of it. Thinking they had found a dead animal, I called out to them. They were pawing at the ground and looked very puzzled. Normally when they are pawing after an animal they are very animated and excited. This was unusual behavior.

I walked over to the dogs to grab their collars and began to investigate what they were looking at. That's when I looked down and saw something pop out of the ground. I jumped back and screamed, "Oh my God!" I was terrified and pulled the dogs away, thinking it was a wounded animal that might hurt them. I started having thoughts of scary alien movies. We ran to the car and I locked the dogs in before I went running back to the little mound of dirt and bushes to see what was there. As I looked, I could see a small leg. I was still thinking it must be an animal of some sort. Then I heard a noise so weak but yet so desperate, like the cry of someone who is taking his last breath.

God's voice in my head told me to go for it. Without hesitation, I shoved the bushes apart and began to dig with my hands. I could hear little mewing sounds. Then I saw a blue towel. I quickly unwrapped the towel, and I screamed when I realized that within this bundle was a tiny little baby! He was a mountain angel.

Then the baby began to cry. I cleaned off his nose and mouth so he could breathe. I knew he must just have been born; I could see the umbilical cord still attached to his stomach. I moved the child to a more comfortable position, ran to my car to get my cellular phone, and raced back toward the baby to protect him from the danger of coyotes. It was now very dark. We needed assistance.

I dialed 911 frantically as I ran and got a recording that told me to hold. While I was on hold, I comforted and cleaned the baby. I told him he would be okay and that I would take care of him. But when the 911 operator finally came on the line, the call was suddenly disconnected. I tried to call back, but this time I got a busy signal. I ran to the street, thinking I would get better reception there. Then I called 411 for the police department and was immediately connected to them. But as soon as I was connected to the police, I got disconnected again!

Luckily I heard a car on the next street, so I ran over and stopped the driver. I told the man to call an ambulance and the police, which he did. Then I ran back to the baby and wrapped him in a blanket. Thirty minutes later, the police had not appeared. I was freezing, so I knew the baby must also be cold. It made me extremely nervous.

I began to massage the baby to keep him warm. I told him that I loved him, even though I did not know him, and that he would be okay. The baby couldn't even open his eyes. He was weak, but strong enough to make a connection with me. He grabbed my wrist and would not let go. He seemed to be comforted by my pulse. In that moment I felt very bonded to the child and began to pray with all my heart that he would not die.

Finally the police arrived, shining flashlights in our faces. They were shocked to find the baby alive; they had assumed the report of a buried infant meant the baby was dead. They called for an ambulance, which arrived a few minutes later. The baby was suffering from hypothermia and was in critical condition. Doctors provided emergency care and calmed the child, who, it turned out, was only two hours old. Thankfully, within three days his condition was vastly improved.

I know I will meet my mountain angel again, but I don't know when. I know he came for a purpose, and I believe that purpose is to save all the children in the world. I know that only God knows exactly how, like He knew how when I used to tell my dad, "I will grow up and become someone very important and save all the poor children in the world." And my father used to smile as he'd say, "I am sure you will." Years later, I saved this child. I will never let the feeling leave me as long as I live.

The baby has now been adopted by a good family, and he is in a safe place where no one can harm him again. I didn't adopt him myself because I knew he would not be safe with me, since everybody knows about me from the publicity his rescue has received.

I know God put me there when the baby needed me. A year ago, at my first fund-raising event for Save the Children, I had spoken about how God had come to me on that same mountain and told me that my destiny and future in life was to save children. Now, a year later, when I was losing my energy and faith to fight for this cause, He put a baby in front of me to save.

Now I know that God is watching and crying while all the bad things are happening on earth. I believe that my mountain angel will find me one day, and when he does it will be special, like the first time we met. In our silence, we will talk in the language of angels. We will hold each other, and we will feel and believe in the same things. God and angels will always be with us as long as we keep our faith.

# Deepak, Call Me!

## Arielle Ford

As a publicist, I am often in a position to make decisions for my clients about which interviews they will do: "Yes" to *Newsweek*, "No" to the tabloids, "Maybe" to one of the talk shows.

For more than six years, I have represented Deepak Chopra. When we first began working together, it was virtually impossible to get hold of Deepak. He travels constantly, and at that time, he had only one assistant, who was equally hard to reach. I quickly introduced Deepak to the wonderful world of voicemail and secured him a personal voicemail number with his own secret password. This way I was able to leave messages for him day or night and he could retrieve them from any part of the world, as long as he had a touch-tone phone.

One year, during the Christmas holidays, Deepak took his family on a safari. He called me upon arriving in Africa to tell me that there weren't any touch-tone telephones available and that for the next five days he would be totally unreachable. It was December twenty-sixth, and I thought, No problem. What could possibly come up between now and New Year's? How wrong I was. Two days later, a very important television program called, asking to have Deepak as their guest on January third, the day after he was scheduled to arrive back in the States. I was certain that he would want to appear on this show, but I really needed to check it out with him. The producer gave me three hours to call back with an answer.

I tried to think of any reasons Deepak might have for not wanting to appear on this show, and the only one I could imagine was that he had changed his itinerary and was not coming back to the States as planned. Unfortunately, I had no way of knowing. For two hours and forty-five minutes I struggled with what to do. Finally, I closed my eyes and, inside of my head, silently screamed, *Deepak, call me!* Not sixty seconds later the phone rang. It was Deepak, asking me, "What do you need?" I was blown away but quickly apprised him of the situation. He agreed it would be fun to do the TV show and gave me the go-ahead.

Since that time I have used this unorthodox technique to get Deepak to call me when he is either on an airplane or otherwise in transit from one place to another. It never ceases to amaze me that we can communicate this way!

# The Dance of Babylon

## *James F. Twyman*

If you had told me a week earlier that I would be invited by Saddam Hussein to perform The Peace Concert in Iraq, I would have said you were crazy. But there I was in Baghdad, an official guest of the president, praying with the high-ranking members of the government, singing peace songs on national television, and doing what I could to bring an end to the crisis that had poisoned the world.

Around the world, in churches and in homes, in groups and as individuals, people prayed for peace—and I knew our prayers were being heard. Millions of people joined their hearts and minds together and participated in two separate prayer vigils. It was one of the most profound experiments of all time—proof, at least in my mind, that we can create a world of peace by resolutely choosing peace for everyone. Humanity took a giant step forward that week, a step that is still being felt today.

But in the three-day period between that first prayer vigil and the actual signing of the peace accord, something amazing happened. I did not realize how amazing it was until several days later. At the time I thought it was a chance encounter, one of those profound experiences that you don't notice right away. It crept up on me, like the whisper of an angel that you mistake for the wind. It is only when the wind is gone, when the air is quiet and still, that you remember you heard a marvelous message from God. Then you understand. Then you know the truth. And you are changed.

A driver and an escort had been assigned to me, for my convenience as well as the government's. I had already performed The Peace Concert at the Rasheed Theater, and it had been broadcast on national television. Since I had two days left before I was to leave Iraq, I decided to spend a day acting like a tourist. You may be wondering how one acts like a tourist in Iraq, especially with the threat of war. One need only realize that the ancient city of Babylon is a mere hour from Baghdad, and the question answers itself. As someone who has always loved visiting the sacred sites of the world, I could not miss this opportunity.

The area was nearly deserted when we arrived, and a guide stood in front of the city gate talking with three men who were also waiting to begin the tour. One of them was Stjepan Mesic, the last president of Yugoslavia before the country split apart.

It's an amazing experience to walk through the ruins of a palace you've read about in the Bible since you were a child. This was the city where the Israelites were forced to live as slaves and serve a foreign king. It was also the place where Daniel dreamed his own prophetic dreams and counseled the king about his. Each brick seemed to sing of the ancient past. I forgot about the others I was with—my escort, a friend from London, a friend from Sarajevo, and the three men from Croatia. I was lost in antiquity, hypnotized by the frescoes that had lasted for thousands of years, far longer than any of the governments or conflicts that had brought us to Iraq.

When we reached the far end of the city, an area that opened on a long and seemingly endless stretch of desert, I noticed what looked like an enormous palace on a distant hill. Since it appeared modern and new, even from that distance, I knew it was not a part of Babylon. But its size was formidable, and I asked my escort, Mr. Sabar, what it was.

"It is . . . it is a place where people stay," he said hesitantly, almost as if he meant to avoid my question.

"What do you mean by that?" I asked. "Who stays there?"

"It is where people stay when they come here. That is all I can tell you." Then he walked away, as if he didn't want to say anything more about it. Suddenly I realized what it was. There in the distance was one of the presidential palaces that the Iraqi government would not let the U.N. officials inspect. I had heard rumors of the enormous size of these buildings, the suspected hiding places of Iraq's supply of chemical weapons. But why next to the ancient city of Babylon? It seemed odd that such a place would be in the open, or next to a biblical site.

We turned down a long pathway that lined the outer rim of the city and headed toward a building near the spot where the famed Hanging Gardens once stood. The tour guide spoke in difficult English, and one of the Croats translated his words for President Mesic. I, on the other hand, was suddenly distracted by a sound of drumming that seemed to be coming from a hut only a hundred yards or so away. There seemed to be a celebration taking place. I could hear laughing and singing and, of course, music. It seemed to pull me away from the tour; I wanted to leave what I was doing and follow the sound. I looked over at my friends, who seemed to be fascinated by the description of the Hanging Gardens. But as interested as I was, something seemed to force me in the direction of the celebration, so I slipped away and walked toward the music.

As I came closer to the hut, I could see a group of twenty or thirty people dancing in a circle. They were singing and moving in a way that was obviously deeply evocative of their culture. One man—I will never forget him because his eyes seemed to look right through me—appeared to be leading the dance. He noticed me near the door and purposely diverted the natural flow of the circle, forcing it to the spot where I stood.

Before I knew it I was pulled into the dance, into the circle, and I began to move as if I had always known this exotic music and these people. The man with the strange eyes kept staring at me, and I felt a strong energy well up in my body. Just for a moment I forgot who I was, where I was, and that I was any different from the group. I noticed that they were all watching me, and they laughed with delight as I jumped up in the air and spun, just as if I had been born in Iraq.

Then the music ended. I don't know how long I had danced, only that I was filled with energy, more invigorated than I had ever been before. Without any apparent reason, the people began to leave the hut one by one. The drummers picked up their instruments, and the others grabbed their belongings. And as they passed me, each one smiled a strange and under-standing smile, as if we had all been part of a fantastic drama and I was the only one who didn't realize it.

Finally, the others were all gone, and the man with the strange eyes walked up to me. He stood there looking deep into my eyes without saying a word. I felt a pulse of light come into me, as if he were giving me an unseen gift. Then he reached out and touched my arm.

"Tell them thank you," he said to me.

"I don't understand . . . thank you for what?"

"Tell them we know what they did . . . everyone in the world who chose peace, who brought peace to my people. That is why we are here—to give thanks for the gift."

"Do you mean the gift of peace?" I asked him.

"For the gift of life." He gently squeezed my hand, then walked away. I stood there for a very long time, not sure what had just happened. Finally, as the strange energy continued to pulse through my body, I rejoined my friends.

The next day, Saddam Hussein and Kofi Annan signed the peace accord, and war was averted.

# Celtic Music

## Catherine Miller

It was a windy yet beautiful day as I ventured to my favorite place along the Niagara River, a sweet little park that is hidden away and that few people know about. This place is special to me, and I often visit a favorite "grandmother" cottonwood tree there that I enjoy climbing.

This was a challenging day for me. There was someone in my life whom I loved very much and who was causing me much pain. I'd been to the video store earlier that evening to look for a film to inspire the Celtic part of my soul. Somehow I felt that connecting to that energy would bring me strength. Well, the film I wanted was unavailable, and so I went to the park and the grandmother cottonwood with my heart full of pain, sadness, and questions.

I climbed the tree's trunk to a branch that would give me a clear view of the river and sunset. I lay on this large branch, and it felt almost as though my old friend were cradling me in her arms. I closed my eyes as tears began to pour down my cheeks. I asked for guidance . . . for a sign . . . some answer to ease my aching soul. Then a strong breeze blew and I felt a hand on my leg. I opened my eyes and looked . . . no one was there! My jeans were slightly indented, as though a hand were firmly pressed against the outside of my thigh, holding me.

As strange as this seemed, I wasn't frightened. A feeling of the love of an old friend came through me. I closed my eyes again, breathing deep to remain calm, and another hand began to stroke my head . . . I mean, really stroke it, firmly and lovingly. It felt bizarre, and with my eyes still closed, I saw light and then two angels perched in the tree with me, holding me and stroking my hair. My eyes welled up with tears that now poured even stronger from my soul.

I'm not sure how long I lay there before I heard the music . . . bagpipes. I opened my eyes. Sometime during my experience in the tree, a man had walked up to a picnic table in the park and begun playing the most beautiful music I'd ever heard pour out of a bagpipe. Even if I had doubted for a moment that there were really angels in the tree with me, the Celtic music was such a powerful coincidence that I knew it was the sign for which I had asked.

I lay there for over an hour, watching the sunset, listening to the exquisite music, and feeling the love of someone stroking my hair. Sometimes I wonder, at such moments in life, if those people who show up to affect us so deeply are guided there or if they are angels who have taken human form to inspire us.

Whoever that man with the bagpipe was, I wanted him to know how much I appreciated him. I kissed the branch of the tree, climbed down to search in my backpack for a suitable gift to give him, and found a copy of the magazine that I produce and always jest is a gift from the angels. I walked over to the man, thanked him for the music that had moved my soul, and gave him the gift. As I walked away, my heart felt as though it had been released from the pain and was flowing again, and my soul was filled with love and inspiration.

# Paramedic: A Call from the Other Side

## Jan Barron

Some years ago, I was working as an ambulance paramedic for the Gary, Indiana, fire department. I was at a point where I was wondering whether to switch to another field.

I asked Divine Spirit to help me. My problem with being a paramedic was that no one seemed to notice the good work my partner and I did. So I asked, in my nightly contemplative exercises, "Show me you're here, show me that you care." I wanted to feel the presence of Divine Spirit and of Wah Z, my inner teacher.

Soon afterward, my partner, Rick, and I were called at three a.m. to a two-car accident by the railroad tracks. It was misty outside, and a light rain was falling. When we arrived at the scene, we could see that several twenty-five-thousand-volt electrical wires had been knocked down by the cars. Two of the accident victims were on the other side of these live high-tension wires.

Rick and I knew we couldn't get to the other side—especially in the rain; the wet grass would conduct electricity. Rick went back to the rig to call for assistance while I squinted through the mist at the other car. I could see that a passerby had stopped and was helping one of the accident victims.

As I waited, a police officer walked up to my right side. He took my arm and said, "I will help you across these wires. Those men need you."

I had no fear as the officer flicked on his flashlight and began to lead the way. I didn't look at his face, but I felt his hand on my arm as we stepped across the wires. For one time-less moment I watched the wires as they arced and writhed in the wet grass. But all I felt was an unusual warmth and love. I needed to get to these people.

I put my faith and trust in this police officer and arrived safely on the other side of the wires. As I ran toward the car, I saw that one injured man was being tended to. He had a leg injury, and the passerby was doing a good job of applying a tourniquet to control the bleeding.

I concentrated on the second injured man. He had been crushed against the dashboard, and it was fairly evident he was not going to make it. Inwardly I did my best to be a clear vehicle for the ECK, or Holy Spirit.

I turned around to see several emergency vehicles pulling up. I looked for the police officer who had guided me across the wires, but he was suddenly gone, as was the gentleman who had been tending the other victim. They had both vanished!

I was confused. There was no way for them to have left, as the only road was on the other side of the wires. In that moment I realized I had been working with two spiritual adepts, ECK masters, who had come to the aid of the souls in the accident.

No one else on the scene saw either of these beings. My husband, who is also a paramedic with the fire department, was in one of the other responding ambulances. He was so upset with me for crossing the wires! My partner and every-one else at the scene really chewed me out, saying I could have been killed. I tried to explain, but to this day my husband, who does not share my spiritual beliefs, will not speak of the matter.

This experience was a great lesson for me in inner know-ingness and trust. I had sensed that the police officer–ECK master would protect me as I stood at the threshold of the wires. All I felt was loving trust and the presence of the ECK.

I think of this adventure sometimes when I am fearful or doubt that anyone really cares what happens to me. I can defi-nitely say that the ECK is here to help us. It is a tangible force when It needs to be. We are all surrounded by a saving grace much greater than ourselves. And when I doubt, I know I will be shown—maybe not always in such a dramatic way, but the proof is there when I need it.

# There Are No Accidents

## *Jim Wright*

It was Friday in Tacoma, Washington. I had finished working on my last case of the day as a private investigator and had decided to check my voicemail one more time and head home for the weekend. I was surprised to hear the sweet, angelic voice of a thirteen-year-old-girl named Tammy, who had left a simple message stating that she wanted to find her grandpa. She and her sisters had asked their daddy what he wanted for his birthday, and his wish was the same as every year: to find his father. I had never had a child retain my services before, so I knew there was something special about the timing and purpose of this call. I just didn't know what.

I called back, and Tammy answered the phone very excitedly. She and her sisters had sneaked into their parents' bedroom and were calling private detectives from the Yellow Pages, determined to make their daddy's wish come true. She and her sister Rachelle, age fourteen, and their younger sister, Kimberly, had pooled together nineteen dollars from baby-sitting to hire a private detective so that they could surprise their daddy and find his father, who was the grandpa they had never met.

One investigator told Tammy she did not have enough money. Another said to go to the library and check out a book on missing persons. Still another never called back. I felt that because Tammy had been unsuccessful in retaining other detectives, she must have been looking for me all along. I did not understand the exact reason of our not-so-chance encounter at the time, but I felt a premonition that this case was about more than a child's fantasy. And I also know how important grandpas and little children are to one another, so when she asked me to take the case, I said yes without even thinking.

My first question was if the girls' mother was in on the plan. They sheepishly answered no. I asked them to put their mother on the phone so I could clear it with her first. I told the mother, whose name was LaDonna, what her daughters had been up to, and all she could say was "What? They did?" But I could tell that she was proud of them. She confirmed that her husband, Tom, had always said that he'd felt something was missing from his heart because he'd never known his father, from whom he'd been separated as a toddler. They had tried to find Tom's father, Harold Z. Gates, throughout the country for years with no success, and they had practically given up hope. Tom's constant unanswered question was "Where is my dad?"

I told LaDonna that we might never be able to find Harold, since we had only his name to start the investigation, but that I would begin looking and call her back on Monday with any results. She asked me how much I charged, and I told her that this one was for free since I admired her girls' determination and obvious love for their father.

After searching across the country, I finally found *the* Harold Z. Gates in Las Vegas, Nevada. When I called Harold to tell him the news of his granddaughters' persistent efforts to find him, he calmly told me that he had been waiting for my call for a long time so that I could reunite him with his "new" family. Harold's reaction totally surprised me. I had expected shouts of joy or tears. But instead, it was almost as if he'd said something like "What took you so long? Let's get going!" This confirmed my intuition that a big plan seemed to be at work.

I called LaDonna on Monday afternoon to give her the good news. Tom was working and was not due home until eight p.m., she said, so that gave her and the girls time to plot the surprise. LaDonna handed the phone to my new client, Tammy, and I was barely able to tell her what had happened before she and her sisters began screaming wildly and giving each other high fives. It was a very short conversation.

The house was dark when Tom came home that night. He assumed his family was out, and he checked for a note on the kitchen table, as he always did. And there it was. He began reading the note, which said, "Your dad needs you to call him tonight at 8:00." LaDonna and her daughters had been hiding in the bathroom around the corner, watching with their heads stacked one on top of the other. Tammy told me afterward that her dad stood at the table staring at the note "all solemn." As Tom turned around, he saw his wife and daughters creeping silently down the hall, smiling from ear to ear. Tammy broke the silence by screaming, "Let's call him, Dad! It's eight o'clock!"

So that night, the granddaughters spoke with their grandfather for the very first time. Tom spoke with his dad for almost two hours about his search for the father he had missed so much and needed so badly, and about how they would be together after all those years.

That Easter at Tom and LaDonna's house, they all sat down to dinner together for the first time ever as a family. I was later invited over for one of the girls' birthday parties and was greeted by a banner that read, THANK YOU DETECTIVE JIM WRIGHT. On it, they had all signed their names and written what it meant to them personally to find Harold. That banner is now framed and hangs in my office as a reminder to me of the power of love and the need to follow opportunities that are placed in front of you. I know now there are no accidents.

News of the reunion spread, and my company ended up

reuniting several other families as well. The effects of Tammy's call were quite far-reaching, not just for her family but for others too. And it happened all because three little girls would not take no for an answer when it came to filling the only empty space remaining in their dad's loving heart.

# Absence of Fear

## *Modeste Slywka*

A tidal wave of fear was rampaging through my body, leaving a nauseous residue in my stomach, as I waited in the lobby of the Scottsdale, Arizona, municipal court for my attorney, who was late. It was Christmas week of 1986. The day was wet, cold, and bleak.

Here I was, facing a maximum of five years in an Arizona prison. I had been charged with DUI, possession of a controlled substance, resisting arrest, and assaulting a police officer. My seventy-three-year-old father was in the hospital waiting to have lifesaving triple bypass surgery, and my sixty-five-year-old mother was on the verge of going into the hospital herself. I had done much to create this dire situation.

The previous thirteen years of drug and alcohol abuse, mayhem, mental institutions, hospitals, and dishonesty had culminated in my standing alone outside the courtroom. I had ruined my life and negatively impacted the life of anyone who had come into close contact with me.

These thoughts intensified my fear. I was sick to my stomach.

Phillip, my attorney, finally showed up, apologizing for being late. We discussed my case before he met with the city prosecutor to see if a deal could be worked out. Phillip went into the office, eradicating any relief I had had in seeing him.

I was alone again. I thought of running away, hiding. Something made me stay.

Five minutes later, Phillip came out of the prosecutor's office and told me I would have to do one year in prison and two years probation. I asked him if he was confident and ready to go to trial. Phillip said he was.

I told him, "I'll plead not guilty and take my chances with the jury."

He patted me on my back and went back into the prosecutor's office.

I had never felt so alone and tired in all my life. Tears welled up in my eyes. The lobby was empty and it was raining hard. I started to shiver. Taking out a cigarette, ignoring the NO SMOKING sign, with shaking hands I struck a match. It was then that I burst into tears and cried out, "God, please help me! Do whatever You want to do with me! I give up. I can't take it anymore."

I sobbed a bit more, and then a quiet came over me, a stillness, what I now know to be a state of grace. I relaxed and went outside in the rain to smoke, realizing I had not uttered the name of God since I was a child.

When I came back into the lobby, Phillip was waiting for me. He was smiling and gave me a hug. "Plead guilty to all charges. Ninety days in the county jail and four years probation. What do you say?"

I said, "Okay."

At sentencing, I asked the court if I could start my jail time after my dad had had his surgery and was home. The judge agreed. I walked out of the court building in a state of amazement and relief, unaware of how my life would change from then on.

I no longer live the way I used to live. The emotional

wounds I had inflicted on my family and others who loved me have been healed. I am a sober, productive member of society.

My life since that day in court has not been easy. Many years of destroying my life have left a lot of wreckage. I have had to start from zero in all areas. But it has been worth it.

Sounds hokey, doesn't it? But it happened and has continued to happen for the last eleven years: whenever I cry out to my Creator for help, I receive an absence of fear in return.

# An Unexpected Journey

## *Elizabeth A. Seely*

I could not deny the nagging fear I was experiencing. I was in need of direction, and I knew that this guidance could come only from one place. Consequently, on a cold, snowy day in Ohio in late January 1997, I took the time to address my concerns.

I was at a weak point. I was currently in the midst of a job search, and was also contemplating the sale of my home. These facts alone were giving me a sense of insecurity. In addition, I had been dating a man who was quickly getting serious, but I was feeling smothered and manipulated by him. Through this mixture of emotions, I was now aware of what I should do: pray. Pray very hard. I started an ongoing prayer that I repeated all day. This was something I had never done before, but my need was real. The tears rolled down my face, each one a reminder of my intuitive fear. I strongly felt that an act of God was necessary to prevent me from continuing this relationship and possibly marrying this man with whom I was not in love. I told no one of my personal, vigilant request.

That evening, I searched through my basement for a box. Somewhere, packed in a cardboard box, were some of my childhood scrapbooks. Maybe, I thought, by showing these to my boyfriend, I would gain a better, more realistic insight as to what he really thought of me. Seeking resolution, I adamantly searched for my memorabilia.

Eventually, I came across a particularly musty box. It did not look familiar, and it had obviously been wet at some point. I carefully slit the yellowing tape and opened the aging flaps. This box hadn't been opened for over fifteen years. Inside was an odd assortment of personal items, including old books. I enjoyed sifting through the belongings that I had moved many times without noticing. As I picked up one of the books, an old water-stained postcard fell to the floor. It was a postcard of St. Mary's Church in Headley, England.

I stopped and sat on the basement steps to take a better look, happily entering a time warp going back eighteen years. I was seventeen and spending the summer in Folkestone, a small seaside town on the southeast coast of England, where as a child I used to visit my grandmother. My mother is English, and over many summers during our childhood, my mother would take my brother and me overseas to enjoy holidays with our English relatives.

That particular summer day, my mother's cousin Peter had driven down from London to see us. I had met cousin Peter on two other visits to England, the first when I was just eight years old. On this windy, somewhat sunny day, Peter obligingly took my mother and me on a small excursion. We decided to take a leisurely drive as we headed for Peter's parents' home

On the way, we arrived in Headley. Upon my mother's request, we stopped for a stretch and a look around this quaint village. My mother vaguely remembered her childhood visits to Headley. It had been more than forty years since she and her family had made the journey to Surrey.

We stopped at the village church, St. Mary's Church, to spark a memory. Perhaps we would find some old family names on the headstones in the parish graveyard. I felt a teenager's chill of excitement as we broke off in different directions. This was all new to me, a mystery in the making, searching for markers to indicate the life of a distant ancestor! With that thought in mind, I was off with ancestral names dancing in my head. As I looked over my shoulder, I saw that there was someone else in the churchyard. My mother noticed him as well.

Mother approached this elderly gentleman, who appeared to be clearing up some of the overgrowth on the various tombstones. To Mother's complete surprise, he turned out to be the son of a great-aunt my mother remembered. After a brief reunion, he invited us inside the empty church. We cautiously entered this ancient place of worship, which dated back to 1317.

Upon entering the church, I stood gaping in amazement. Looking up, I saw signs of the zodiac encircling the ceiling. My cousin Peter, obviously intrigued as well, looked in awe and, in a whisper, commented on them. A Christian place of worship and signs of astrology—something I had never seen entwined elsewhere.

In my basement, I stopped gazing at the postcard, realizing I was now quite cold. I also no longer had an interest in finding my scrapbooks. I had found something much more important. I took the postcard of St. Mary's Church upstairs and for the rest of the evening indulged thoughts of that summer eighteen years before.

The next day brought with it the usual routine: getting my daughters off to school, preparing cover letters for my job search, and scheduling a career placement meeting. Once again, I looked at the postcard, and this time the sight of it gave me a strange, mystical feeling.

The following afternoon, I received a phone call. Upon my answering and saying hello, an Englishman's voice followed with "Hello, Elizabeth?" He did not wait for a response, but continued, "This is Peter Edgehill, your cousin, calling from England."

I closed my eyes while a combination of disbelief and relief came over me. I could not believe it. It had been eighteen years without any kind of correspondence from Peter. Eighteen years, I thought to myself! I glanced at the postcard of St. Mary's Church, now sitting on top of my dresser. It was an unbelievable coincidence.

The conversation was brief. "Would a visit be possible?" he asked.

I still could not believe I was talking with him, but I managed to say that a visit would be wonderful. He said he would immediately inquire about a ticket. I hung up the phone with an overwhelming sense of relief. I felt as though someone or something was looking out for me, but how, I wondered, could this logically be so?

On arriving, cousin Peter informed me that after our conversation, he had immediately made reservations for a flight arriving three days later. He then went to a local café, where he ordered a cup of coffee and also experienced what he called "an undeniable sense of relief"!

My family had been quite flabbergasted by the news of our upcoming visitor. The day after Peter's arrival, we visited with my parents, looked at family photo albums, discussed politics and the weather. This was Peter's first visit to Ohio, and so much had happened in all those years. It was not until the second evening that Peter and I became involved in a personal conversation.

I was skeptical when Peter brought out an astrology book. Was this something he always took with him when traveling? I wondered. I was curious to hear his explanation for his sudden call and visit to someone whom he really did not even know. I kept an open mind, but I was deliberately hesitant to say much. I was still completely amazed by this situation. I was bewildered as our conversation continued. Without any description of personality, character, or background, Peter informed me that my boyfriend was "not the one." He went on to say, "You would only be a token to him, nothing more than a token."

At first I took offense at these unsubstantiated comments. On what did he base this opinion? I asked myself. Yet, as the conversation continued, I became quite uneasy. He was describing my boyfriend with amazing detail and accuracy; he knew of his dominating and manipulating character. As strange as the words sounded coming off my lips, I asked Peter, "Are you psychic?"

"No, I am not," he replied. But as he continued his descriptions and predictions, I began to see clearly how life would really be with this person who claimed to care for me. Peter's observations were so different from those of my close circle of friends and my family, and yet so accurate. It was undeniable that Peter was aware not only of my inner doubts but of why they existed.

By then we were standing in my kitchen, and I could not help thinking that this was the most unusual experience I had ever had. Peter began pacing back and forth across the green and white tiled floor. In a loud voice he exclaimed, "You are sending up signals, Elizabeth, and I am the one receiving them! Someone rattled my cage, and the next thing I knew I was pulled out of London and was booking a flight to come to Ohio."

I stood shivering, with tears welling up in my eyes. I had told no one of my recent day of vigilant prayer. I had told no one of my complete mistrust of the man I was seeing. I had told no one of my uncanny fear of the future. I had told no one but God.

Peter began to feel a physical manifestation of His presence. I too could not deny this unbelievable feeling. A voice was speaking to me through this tall, thin Englishman whom I had known as a child. A voice was telling me that I had summoned help, and help had arrived.

Peter continued, "Think of who you were calling, Elizabeth. You are truly loved."

Still shaking, I acknowledged my prayers. I explained my fears, doubts, the uneasiness I had felt—my entire day of prayer. I saw Peter as a messenger of God. I had sent up a request and was blessed with a response: divine intervention!

That night marked a memorable turning point in my life, as well as in my cousin's life. It prevented me from making a terrible mistake. It also prepared me, and those near me, to continue on the path to love. My unexpected journey had just begun.

# Room with a View

## Anthony J. W. Benson

By the time I was twenty, my life had unraveled to the point of massive self-destruction. But through a series of miracles I was given back my life and had a powerful spiritual awakening that not only opened my eyes to the existence of God but also opened me to my own heart and to the infinite possibilities that my life still held.

Owning a house was part of my personal dream—a place to call my own that would be an environment that spoke to me and represented a part of who I am. Five years ago, I achieved that dream. My home is an important haven for me. It is a place to work, to nourish myself, to play, to rest, and to reflect. In my home, my bedroom serves as my little space to escape, when necessary, from the world around me and into the world within me. But never could I have predicted the series of events that were to unfold in my place of slumber and renewal.

On this particular night, I was reflecting on the words and thoughts of Jesus. I am not prone to do this, mostly because I am neither Christian nor particularly what one might call religious. Though open-minded, I was still a neophyte when it came to the teachings and life of Jesus. I have a lot to learn through my own studies and from the insights of those more knowledgeable than I.

I had recently befriended a man by the name of Nick Bunick, who is the subject of the best-selling book *The Messengers*. Nick claims to be have been, in a former life, Paul the Apostle. One of the main messages of Nick's work is the importance and value of angels, or guides, in our lives.

As I lay in my bed that night, not able to sleep and with thoughts of Jesus running through my head, a crystal-clear message coursed through my being. I was given clear understanding of the ultimate message of Jesus.

Eventually, around two a.m., I fell asleep with this new concept and understanding branded in my consciousness and psyche. But as I floated through dreamland, I was awakened by a gentle touch, a rocking, not unlike how a mother would wake her children so as not to startle them. As I awoke to this nudging, I saw that no one was there, which, given that I live alone, was a relief. I then remained quiet for a few moments to see if I had arisen to any danger or perhaps to something happening outside. Nothing.

I lay there in amazement and looked toward the bedroom door, not far from the foot of my bed. Though it had been shut, it was now open slightly, and a brilliant illumination of beautiful blue light emanated from its border. I felt no fear as I lay back, open to what was unfolding. I looked up at the ceiling, and in an instant, a flash of glorious, mesmerizing blue light streaked through my room, and then again, before it dissipated into the darkness.

I regained my breath and centered myself. What had just happened? It was a powerful and moving experience. The stillness was overwhelming as I listened to my heart and tried to catch one of the million thoughts whizzing through my mind. Chomping at the bit to tell my story to friends and colleagues the next day, I nevertheless endeavored to go to sleep.

In the morning, I immediately shared what had happened with my business partner, Cyndi, who is a gifted intuitive and healer. She said she thought I had been visited by Jesus or Archangel Michael. The same conclusion was reached by Doreen Virtue, a metaphysician and the author of the book *Angel Therapy*, who shared with me that the color blue was sometimes indeed indicative of Archangel Michael. Nick Bunick himself thought I had received a visit from Jesus. As I continued to share my story, the same feedback poured in, reinforcing my belief that I had indeed experienced a visitation of some kind. Hmmm. Why the undeniable visit? Why this intense, dramatic event? Why in my bedroom?

A couple of months later, I experienced yet another event in my bedroom that gave me great pause. I was preparing for a seminar called "What's Your Calling?" which Cyndi and I teach through our business, injoi Productions. I was extremely tired, overwhelmed, and scarcely feeling up to the effort of leading a daylong seminar. I was dreading the next morning and fell asleep with visions of a challenging day ahead. When I awoke, I stumbled into my bathroom in a fog. As I stared blankly into the mirror, I saw several prominent red marks blazoned across my chest. I quickly checked my whole body, looking to see if I had gotten a rash or an insect bite, hives, or whatever. But I hadn't. These weird red marks were only on my chest. They seemed to be simply random red splotches.

Then, as my eyes got a little clearer, I realized that there were five marks, with white spots, and that they were not random at all. These strange marks seemed to have a pattern, a familiar one. I placed my hand closer to my chest. One, two, three, four marks close together. And then one slightly farther away. A handprint! There was a huge handprint, bigger than my own, situated on my chest, with the center of the palm across my heart. I raced for my camera and took some photos at arm's length to document this unbelievable sight.

Upon this revelation, I hurried to meet Cyndi at the healing center where we were to present our seminar, and shared my news as I pulled up my shirt to show her my new cosmic tattoo. To my dismay, the handprint was no longer there. Gone. It had vanished as quickly as it had appeared. But as I spoke of the miraculous circumstances, she told me that she believed it was the hand of God. I eventually concurred with Cyndi, as I had struggled to no avail for another explanation.

It felt so amazing to have had these special moments—the blue light and the handprint—shared with me. I am not alone. I believe we all have our special moments of grace, lucidity, and knowingness. Sometimes the messages are quiet and understated; sometimes it takes a handprint on one's chest to get it. But however the messages are delivered, it is important to listen to the personal message available to each of us.

In my experience, I see these moments as personal conversations with God, reminders that when I go to those places of forgetfulness—and sometimes get lost amid the clutter and chaos of my life—there will always be a beacon of light to lead me back to a personal path of self. There are different lights for different people for different reasons. Maybe the light comes in the form of Jesus, or as a loved one, or maybe it's a blue light or a handprint, a voice or an image. It doesn't matter, so long as you pay attention. Sometimes the message is a gentle nudge, sometimes a loud bang. In my case, it was a handprint etched upon my chest. Hard to miss the point.

We must keep our literal and figurative eyes open. Sometimes the things that go bump in the night are meaningful messages catching us in a readied state, and it doesn't matter if they are real or imagined. What matters is what we can take away as the gift.

This visitation was a helpful reminder that the spiritual awakening I'd had eighteen years earlier, and the ensuing and continued recovery of self, were no fluke. It was a reminder that through the challenges of life and in the face of fear, I can reconnect with myself, God, and the universe. I must remember that in the sanctuary of my bedroom, in the quiet of my being, I have a remarkable place, a room with a view that reflects the best in me. It is a mystical room that has on occasion offered me gifts of love and gentle reminders to have continued faith and to remain true to myself. And on occasion, it has granted me a welcome night's sleep.

# 2
# ANGELS IN FUR COATS AND FLIPPERS

# Dancing with the Dolphins

## Allison Stillman

My life has been spent in the pursuit of the magical, the mystical, and the miraculous. Each of these luminous words could well be used to describe dolphins. So it is little wonder that life brought me to teach workshops in the tropics, where daily we took to the water and played with wild dolphins. It was there that the truly miraculous occurred.

On a paradisical island of Hawaii, I sat alone facing the bay in the early, dusky hours of morning. My journal and pen were in hand. My partner and I were hosting a group of women for a "Dancing with the Goddess" workshop at the Emerald Temple at the mouth of the bay known in legends as "the pathway to the gods." The temple lay quiet with the dreams of those still lingering inside. My sleepy eyes caught sight of the sun's golden rays inching their way across the Mother's azure waters.

Suddenly, I could feel the presence of the dolphins impulsing my consciousness. I was unable to locate them in the water, but I could feel their delightful laughter. As I silently beckoned them to show themselves, my excitement grew. On previous retreats I had been blessed to snorkel with them. There is no greater experience to accelerate an immersion into love and joy than to spend time in the water with the magical presence of dolphins. Dolphins carry a transcendent vibration that they are able to radiate into the fortunate people who are granted the privilege of swimming with them.

Suddenly, across the sea, the blue water broke and a lone dolphin leapt for my attention. Soon there were many dolphins dancing out of the water, performing for my grateful pleasure. It was as if the dolphins had acknowledged my prayers and were responding playfully. I began to hear voices whispering to me and realized that the dolphins were communicating telepathically. Astonished, I asked if there was something they wished me to know, or anything that we in the workshop needed to do in order to prepare ourselves before entering the water.

The dolphins were definitive in answering, and I entered their replies in my journal. They said: "If you wish to interact with our pod today, you will have to let down your walls, let go of your pain. We can feel your fear, but what is more important, we can feel your separation. Join together in a sacred union of oneness. Become a pod."

My pen could barely keep up with the words that began to scribe themselves across the pages of my journal, and my skepticism barely allowed me to believe that the dolphins were communicating with me. They continued: "Tomorrow marks the threshold of a new beginning for each of you. You are embarking on a journey home to your selves. You are all ready to take this journey, or you would not be here at this time."

The messages poured in from the dolphins, who continued to perform for my eyes' delight. "We will be here to initiate healing as you begin to acknowledge the deepest parts of yourselves. We bring love to you, and our sonar will move through you to help you heal. When you merge into oneness, you will understand that you lack nothing, because you are the all, we are the all, and therefore we are one. There is no separation other than the separation the mind creates."

I looked up incredulously from the pages of words I had just transcribed. How could the dolphins have communicated these messages? It seemed as if my imagination was working overtime. I decided to test the dolphins' powers of perception and ask for validation that it was indeed they who were inspiring my writing.

"Okay, here's the deal," I said out loud. "If this is really you sending me all this information, I want three of you to jump free of the water, spin around once, and then dive in unison back into the water." No sooner had the words left my mouth than three dolphins leapt clear of the water, did an acrobatic spin, and hit the water in unison. My eyes opened wide in disbelief.

Still not trusting our direct communication, I asked them to swim to the opposite side of the bay and perform another task. A moment later, at the other end of the bay, the dolphins performed impeccably, honoring my request. It was really true!

"We will be back to play when you have finished your work." With that, the dolphins turned and made their way to deeper waters for the remainder of the day.

I sat back in my chair for several minutes in utter amazement. Then I walked into the temple, retrieved the gong, and began to sound its deep resonant tones, awakening our group. As we gathered for our morning circle, I shared the message from the dolphins, and our healing and transformation began. It was a day of intense release and deep emotional clearing on many levels. By day's end we were all ready for the magic of sleep and drifted off early.

The dolphins had been very clear when they told me, "If you do the work, we will return to play with you, and to fill you with our love." The next morning, they were in the bay before the first light of day. They were lively and acrobatic, spinning and leaping in delight. I knew we were going to receive an extraordinary blessing in the water.

I awakened the slumbering pod. After coffee and doughnuts, we donned our snorkeling gear and spilled into the cool water. There were dolphins everywhere—someone counted sixty—and they were absolutely enchanting. They played with us for hours, and activated in us a childlike joy that radiated through the water.

Immersion into love is the only way to truly understand the

power of the radiant blessings that dolphins bestow. The dance of the dolphins changed each of us. It brought us into a place of unity and wholeness, filled us with love, joy, and the miracle of healing, and continues to evoke inspiration within our memories.

# Puppy Love

## Julie Zaslav

As I write this passage, his beautiful brown eyes are staring at me, eyes that have provided me with some of the most heart-warming and inspirational moments of the past three years. His name is Dino, and he is my mystical poodle. He came to me through sound vibrations carried through the air.

My memory is not one of my stronger assets, yet the day I met Dino is as clear to me as this moment. My partner, Allison, and I were on Long Island on a hot August day. We had gone to do some shopping and get out of Brooklyn for the afternoon. About one month prior, because of severe allergies I'd developed, I'd had to give away my three beloved cats, and I was secretly heartbroken. My days of owning cats were over, and my dreams of English sheepdogs would now never come true. I was told that my selection of dogs would be limited to a few breeds that didn't aggravate my condition. Poodles were on this short list because they have hair, not fur, but I laughed to myself, thinking, only a certain type of person owns a poodle, and I am definitely not that type!

On this particular day, I rather abruptly turned to Allison

and said, "We need to go to the animal shelter today. Now!" She looked at me curiously and reminded me that the only dog we could possibly have would be a poodle, and that the likelihood of a poodle being in the shelter was slim because they are so fancy. Besides, as I've said, I wasn't interested in a poodle anyway. And yet, I heard and felt a soul crying out to me to come to him.

I communicated the urgency to Allison, and she agreed to go with the flow. A voice inside me whispered exactly what I needed to do. We stopped at the nearest phone booth, got the number of the closest shelter, and headed east on the Long Island Expressway. The car ride took about thirty minutes.

The shelter was set up like a maze, with twists and blind turns leading us around. I remember feeling confused by the architecture. However, once again something pulled me. I found my way through the maze, in and out of rooms and around corners, past dozens of sweet animals, toward a beautiful little angel shivering and shaking. "Al," I cried, "this is the one who was calling me!" He touched our hearts immediately.

Right away, and in spite of strict rules against it, Allison opened the cage and picked him up. She cuddled him in her arms and started to cry. A worker came over to us and asked us to please put him back in the cage. He was flea-infested and bruised. Just days before, he'd been rescued by the shelter because he was being badly beaten and abused by his owners. We told the worker we wanted to adopt him. We had him bathed and dipped and took him home.

Dino has been our spirit guide ever since. He is teaching us about love and devotion, and he reminds us always to listen to the voices within, the voices that call us, for they are the answers.

# Animals on the Other Side

## *Kristin Kline*

When I was five years old, I had a beloved cat named Kidney-beans. He was solid black and my best playmate. My child-hood was not the happiest of times, yet Kidneybeans brought lots of joy to me. I would dress him up in doll clothes, put him in a Lego bag, and swing him round and round. At the time, I did not know that some of the things I did could hurt him. He loved me anyway, and would follow me around wherever I went. I loved him so much. When I was six, he developed pneumonia and was put to sleep without my knowledge. One day he just wasn't there anymore.

I vividly remember sitting in front of our old heat stove in the very, very early morning, before anyone else got up in our little house, praying to God to let me see the ghost of Kidney-beans just once. Every night for years I included Kidneybeans in my prayers. I begged God for one last good-bye.

Early one morning when I was thirteen years old, I was in my bedroom waiting for my turn in the shower. My younger brother Matt was lying on my bed waiting too. He dozed off to sleep. A cat came running—I saw it coming out of my closet—and jumped on my bed. It purred and purred, and balled up its legs, kneading them on the bed, and purred some more. "Oh, good kitty," I said, petting the cat. "Good kitty." It was dark in the room, and I thought it was our outside cat, Shermie.

As I stroked the warm cat, who purred so happily, thoughts came into my head. *Shermie, you're not supposed to be in the house! Dad will be so mad!* I kept on petting. Then like a bolt of lightning it hit me. *Shermie! The only other person up is my mother, and she would not allow you in the house. How can you be in the house?*

Right at that instant, while my hand was touching the warm cat flesh, I watched as the cat dissolved right before my eyes. I was not afraid at all. I was wide awake and listening to the shower. The indentation was still on my bed where that cat had been. I could still feel its warmth on my hands, and see its utter happiness to be with me.

What dimension it came from and who sent it . . . the thought is awe-inspiring. I felt, heard, and saw this cat. I was born without a sense of smell, so I do not know if I would have been able to smell it or not.

I think about this experience from time to time. I can still see the dark shape running out of the closet and jumping, purring, onto the bed. I think it was probably Kidneybeans coming to say good-bye to me, to show me that he loved me too. Why it took eight years I do not know. To this day, it is the most unexplainable event that has ever happened to me. As I write this, I almost have tears in my eyes. The bond between an unhappy, lonely child and a beloved pet is a very special, very pure unconditional bond of love.

# Bo

## *Elizabeth Russell*

It's every woman's biggest fear. The technician reenters that cold, gray room with the oh so flattering fluorescent lighting and simply states, "I have to take a couple of more views."

I felt like a crane as I sandwiched my breast uncomfortably between the two slabs of plastic and felt the pressure of that machine crunching my delicate tissue while my arm was holding an impossible position. I tried to think of other things that I had to accomplish. My schedule had been so overloaded that I had, for the first time in my adult life, put off getting my yearly mammogram. So of course the year had slipped by quickly, and then I was long overdue. And *that* will teach me!

I said to myself, "No problem, just a pain." As I was waiting in each position, I ran through my lists in my head. I had that whole stack of paperwork that was piling up on my desk, and so many items on my "to do" list that weren't checked off yet. I had to go to Federal Express, and I had to take my dog, Bo, to the vet.

I had found Bo when I was feeling horribly lost. I was going through the big heartbreak of my life, and it was as if God saw that I needed a big and fuzzy teddy bear of a dog to lie next to me on my bed at night and love me unconditionally. I first saw Bo outside a market. The store owner said he'd been hanging around a long time and kept running up to all the customers. I was shocked when I saw him because he looked exactly like my previous dog, Reno, whom I had had for thirteen years until a neck injury forced his passing. That had been a traumatic accident, and so unexpected. But that's what accidents are by nature: unexpected. I took Reno to the vet, who told me that Reno would have to be put to sleep. But the vet would not allow me to be with my dog, and the guilt of not having been present with Reno in his last moments haunted me for years.

But here was this adorable dog running up to me in the market parking lot, and honestly, he took my breath away. Seeing him seriously made me consider reincarnation. He looked just like Reno, and acted like him too! It had been five years since Reno's death, and I had not planned on getting another dog, but I found myself with this chocolate-nosed, brown-button-eyed, stinky-breathed dog on the way to a new vet to get him checked out. Snip snip here, scrub scrub there, and a couple of lah-dee-dahs. After being groomed and totally checked, my new buddy was on his way home with me.

I don't know how I picked the name Bo. It is a completely

unoriginal name, but it also seemed to fit Bo perfectly. The vet guessed that Bo was approximately five years old. I put signs up everywhere and posted pictures at the shelters and took out ads in the papers. Each day I found myself hoping that I wouldn't get that phone call, and I never did. Bo was home with me now. That was eight years ago.

Now I had to take Bo to the vet because he was getting up there in years and he was sore and stiff.

I heard the technician saying, "You can breathe," and I exhaled stressfully. "The radiologist is going to read these, and I'll be back."

Why are doctors like that always a bit short and balding? Why is he talking to me in that monotone voice? What do you mean, it looks like a tumor? Where do I go? What did you say? My hands are sweating, my mind is racing. Could you repeat that, please? Can you explain that once more, please?

I left the mammography appointment in a fog. Telling myself not to panic, and knowing that I had to make an appointment for a biopsy to determine if the tumor was cancerous, I headed home to pick up Bo for his vet's appointment.

We got to Dr. Steve's office, and he told me he was going to keep Bo for the night for some X rays and a minor surgical procedure. I fluffed Bo up, kissed him, told him to be a good boy and that Mom would be back tomorrow, and left for home. Lousy day for Bo to have to spend the night somewhere else, I thought. When he slept on my bed at night, the world felt very safe.

When I got home, I called the doctor I'd been referred to, and his office said they would get me in the next morning.

What is this, a conspiracy? This doctor is short and balding too! You have to stick a needle in my breast? A core biopsy? It *is* cancer? It's two types of cancer! Surgery in a few days? Well, if I have to. It shouldn't wait, and my life depends on it? Well, then, I guess we have a date. I can't breathe, my mind is racing. Could you repeat all that, please? I wonder who I can call? I wonder who I can talk to? I don't want to die. *I don't want to die!* I'm only forty-five, and I don't want to die.

After the intensity of the biopsy and the news of the cancer that was infiltrating my body, I couldn't wait to pick up Bo. I talked to Dr. Steve, who was so dear and concerned, and he proceeded to tell me that Bo had inoperable cancer and had only a few months left to live. This was all too much. I was totally overwhelmed. Driving home, I was crying and ran a yellow light.

Yup, you got it . . . there in the rearview mirror were the flashing reds. I pulled over and stepped out of my car. "Officer," I said through my tears, "I entered that intersection on a yellow light! I'm sorry I'm crying, but I just found out that my dog has cancer and I have cancer too!"

"I can't believe the stories people come up with to try to get out of a fine." He groaned as he handed me the ticket.

I made it through my surgery with the support of my cousin and my best friend, but the news kept getting worse at every stage. My odds of surviving were fifty-fifty, and I had to undergo intense doses of chemotherapy. And to top it off I was going to lose my leonine mane of hair in fourteen days. Damn vanity!

I decided to travel home to Minnesota and deliver the news to my dad in person. The doctor said it would be all right if I had my first dose of chemo before my trip. Then I could travel over the next twelve days to see my family before I lost my hair. (What is it with the bald thing, anyway?) My cousin, who was living at my house, promised to take good care of Bo while I was on my trip.

At home, after reassuring my dad that I had no intention of dying just yet, I woke up one day and felt beyond awful. I had a climbing fever and chills. I called my doctor's office back in Los Angeles, and they told me to go to the emergency room immediately.

That was the first of seven trips over the ensuing months to the intensive care unit. My body was having an unusually difficult time handling the chemo, and my white cell count was way too high. I was too sick to travel back to Los Angeles.

I kept having to get blood transfusions, and I would get

chemo every two weeks. For the next six months I lived with my family. As I fought to stay alive, I also healed many childhood wounds. I hadn't lived at home in twenty years, and this was turning out to be a major blessing in disguise. Who was writing this script, anyway?

I kept calling my cousin and checking in on Bo. She would hold the phone up to his ear and I would talk to him, asking him to hang on till I could get home and tell him in person that I loved him. All through the winter I felt my life shift into a completely different gear. There were no "to do" lists. I was serene and comforted by my faith. Even the branches on the trees outside my window looked intense and surreal to me. It was as if I could see the DNA of all the living things around me, and I don't think I ever felt so alive spiritually.

"Hang on, Bo, hang on. I will get home soon."

And you know something? I did make it back to L.A. It was finally time to return. I was well enough to fly home and to prepare for the upcoming regimen of radiation. And Bo, who'd hung on for me all those months, greeted me with big kisses when I got home. I made it through radiation, and Bo hung on. Bo hung on for the next year while my body repaired itself from the ravages of cancer and the treatment.

When I finally knew I was going to be fine, knew in my heart that my battle with the big C was over, Bo let go. One day he took a major turn for the worse, and I made an appointment for him to see Dr. Steve the next morning. That night I talked to a close friend all about her experience with her own dog's recent passing. She offered great advice to see me through what lay ahead. It was Bo's time.

I told Dr. Steve that I had to be with Bo until the end. Dr. Steve was so helpful and compassionate. He gave Bo a shot to relax him, and then I hugged Bo and stroked his shaggy coat. I told him how much I loved him, and I spoke softly into his ear and thanked him for holding on for me. I told him that he was going to meet a new friend named Reno in Heaven, and that he would be okay. Then Dr. Steve gave him the final shot. In a minute, his heart stopped beating.

I cried and held Bo and cried some more, and I stayed with him for a long time, knowing that his spirit was nearby.

When I got home, I lit a long-burning candle and put Bo's collar around it. I felt grief, but I was also grateful that my trusty old companion had lived a year and a half longer than expected and that I was able to be there with him as he left this world.

Sometimes, out of the corner of my eye, I swear I see him in the house. And I smile. I believe Bo felt that he had a mission to hang on for me until I was better. Now I believe I must discover the mission that I have survived to accomplish.

# A Conversation Under the Sea

## Bobbie Sandoz

I had been swimming for seven years with wild dolphins off the shores of my Hawaiian home, at a bay so beautifully marbled with turquoise and blue that Hawaiian royalty had chosen its cove and the valley overlooking it for their summer playground.

Initially, these encounters were centered on the joys of friendship and play between our species in a beautiful setting, and the dolphins appeared to enjoy our time together as much as I did. In fact, they seemed to take uncommon pleasure in engaging me and my friends in a variety of activities that not only revealed their exquisite sense of mischief, humor, and play but flooded us with endorphins that bubbled up from deep within like champagne distilled from joy.

Then, one day, something took place that completely altered my relationship with the dolphins. They began to send thoughts to me, much in the way they could send their sonar out ahead of themselves. Their ideas were *impressed* in my mind, and they were often followed by a variety of signs designed to verify that a communication had, indeed, taken place.

Yet in spite of the dolphins' efforts to assure me, I continued to struggle over whether or not I was actually talking to another species or was simply sharing the zany imaginings of a wannabe Dr. Doolittle. Even if I was truly communicating with the dolphins, I was too embarrassed to tell even my closest friends about it.

One of the ways the dolphins would convince me that I had understood their ideas was to send me bubbles—big bubbles, small bubbles, ringed bubbles, and cloud bubbles. The first of these brought me enormous delight, and I sensed instinctively that this bubble had not only served as a means to communicate but had been offered as a reward for my understanding a simple but profound thought the dolphins had just shared with me.

Following that day, I often asked for more bubbles. Not only did I long for more proof, but the bubbles anchored me in something tangible and real in the midst of this otherwise surreal experience of communicating with another species.

However, because a strong aspect of the nature of dolphins is that they are playfully "guru-like" and thus unpredictable, they prefer to tease and surprise us with the unexpected in order to evoke joy, rather than comply with our desire for predictability and control. Because of this quality, dolphins often resist surrendering to the requests people make of them, even when it means, for those in captivity, going without food rewards.

Thus, although the cherished bubbles came in many sizes and shapes, they always came on the dolphins' terms rather than mine. This unpredictable delivery of the bubbles added to their magic and my delight, and I came to view them as wonderfully precious gifts. Yet no matter how many bubbles the dolphins sent, my doubts about their role in confirming a communication between us persisted.

One day, I felt compelled to drive to our local dolphinarium in order to visit some captive dolphins. I had befriended them at a luxury hotel where they had lived in a spacious lagoon for years prior to being moved to the crowded park site. When I arrived at the park's central dolphin tank, looking for my hotel dolphin friends, a resident female named Laka swam over to greet me. As I asked the trainer where I might find the hotel dolphins, Laka engaged me in an eye-to-eye gaze, similar to ones I had experienced with free dolphins in the open ocean. I was enjoying this encounter and felt rather special and chosen as the trainer told me that Laka was the dominant dolphin in this tank. In fact, the trainer explained as Laka and I continued our unbroken gaze, the dolphinarium staff had recently discovered that when the other dolphins weren't cooperating, it wasn't necessarily because they were in a contrary mood, but because Laka had ordered them not to comply.

As I gazed back at Laka, I discerned a slight shift in her body position and a naughty twinkle light up her eye. Just as I was processing what was going on, she splashed me with a sizeable wall of water. I was shocked and looked down at my clothes to find that she had not held back one iota and had completely drenched me. I looked back at Laka in time to see her entire face light up as her eyes flashed gleefully. I couldn't help but burst out laughing. Laka then surprised me again with her imitation of my laugh, which made me laugh even harder. Next, Laukani, a dolphin from a nearby tank, joined in Laka's imitation, and I laughed even harder still, and so did both dolphins, until the three of us got downright hysterical.

After I recovered from this joyful, very dolphinlike encounter, the trainer took me downstairs to observe the dolphins from the underwater observation station. The moment we got to the curved surveillance window, Laka was there waiting for us. I put my hand on the window, and Laka nuzzled her cheek toward my hand from the other side and remained there gazing at me while the trainer and I talked. I returned Laka's steady gaze for the next ten minutes as I conversed with the trainer about the program.

When there was an opportunity for questions, I asked if the captive dolphins blew bubbles in their pool like the ones in the open ocean do. The moment my question was framed, Laka released an enormous bubble. Even the trainer, who did not believe in dolphin telepathy, was briefly startled by the gesture. But then she composed herself and continued with our conversation. I was thrilled by Laka's public demonstration of understanding between us, and I hoped to draw more of the trainer's attention to what had just happened. So I looked at Laka and said aloud, "You heard me ask about the bubbles, didn't you?"

Laka remained locked in our steady gaze, the same fixed stare that dolphins offer one another and that I had so often enjoyed with free dolphins in the open ocean. Realizing that the observation area was probably being videotaped, I decided to push the envelope and ask aloud if Laka would give me another bubble. She hesitated for a few moments, then with a mischievous glint in her eye produced a stream of the tiniest bubbles imaginable. I laughed again as this very funny dolphin found a way to achieve control under circumstances that afforded her very little opportunity to do so, while also responding to my request.

Later, as I prepared to leave the area to search for my hotel friends and was saying my good-byes to Laka, I silently asked for one more bubble, and she released one along with a soulful, less mischievous gaze. Tears spilled down my cheeks as I walked away, my heart filled with emotion. Not only had I enjoyed this delicious encounter with the funny Laka, but I *knew* once and for all that dolphins understood and communicated with me. Even more poignant was the fact that this proud and dominant dolphin had surrendered to my requests for bubbles in the presence of a third party. Although the trainer had been conditioned not to look for such communication or to attach too much importance to it, she had noticed. Even more important, I was finally convinced that the dolphins and I were holding a conversation under the sea.

As I left, I silently promised Laka that I would put aside my embarrassment about talking to dolphins and tell the story of the dolphins' sentient nature, their intelligence, and the special brand of wisdom, love, joy, and harmony they personify for humanity as they spin their beguiling dance across the horizon that bridges heaven and earth—enticing us to join them.

# Buddha and Angel

## *Carol Allen*

I'll never forget the day I knew that the white, sweet, shy stray cat with the faint black V on his forehead was mine. He'd been hanging around my apartment complex for weeks. He was really working the circuit: several people in the building were feeding him, and a few of us had named him. I called him Angel because of his coloring and tender temperament. I hadn't wanted another cat. I had Buddha, a gray tiger tabby who was the love of my life.

Buddha truly thought I was his woman. Daily he kissed me on the lips with his rough sandpaper tongue and stroked my cheeks with his soft paws, purring like a 747. He'd sleep right beside me each night, curled into a ball on my pillow. Buddha was definitely a one-person cat.

There had been times I'd thought I should get Buddha a companion cat. Months prior to Angel's arrival, I'd brought home a black-and-white homeless female. Buddha took one look at the poor, defenseless creature and decided she was his love slave! The unfortunate kitty and I were both mortified! She spent four days cowering behind my refrigerator, squished in about four inches of space between it and the wall, before I found her another home. I assumed Buddha was happy with only the two of us.

Suddenly, though, he was spending all his free time with Angel. I'd come home to find the two of them wrestling on the lawn or lying next to each other on the patio. When I called for Buddha, Angel was never far behind. One rainy day, I returned from Ralph's supermarket to discover them asleep on the porch, their arms wrapped around each other's necks, their faces buried in each other's fur. It absolutely melted my heart. That night I opened the door to call Buddha to dinner and there they were, side by side on my welcome mat, four pleading, hungry eyes looking up at me. They were two bookend kitties, twins except for their age and coloring: the same size, shape, and weight, the same perfect pink-eraser-tip noses. Buddha squeaked his high, tinkly meow as if to say, "Mom, can we keep him? Please?" And that was it. I knew these two had to stay together.

From that day forward, my four-legged family was complete. Shy Angel slowly but surely felt right at home. He started off sleeping on my wicker rocking chair beside the bed. I'd try to bring him onto the bed with Buddha and me, but he'd quickly return to the rocker. After a few weeks, he'd gingerly slip onto the foot of the bed in the middle of the night, still too shy to come up next to the pillow. Buddha would usually ease down the covers and join his new brother. I'd watch in wonder as they would eagerly lick each other's faces, grooming for several minutes until they'd settle in, again burying their faces in each other's fur.

They inspired me: true love does exist in this world! It brought me such joy to see them so happy together. I didn't mind for a minute how much less attention I received from Buddha once this truly angelic addition to the household arrived.

By night they were contented snuggle buddies. By day they were sportsmen, racing around my little apartment and wildly pouncing on each other, falling and rolling and howling as they played. When I came home at the end of the day, I'd call them both. On the few occasions when they came in separately, Angel would always race to Buddha's side the moment he walked through the door to sniff his face and kiss him hello. I could almost hear Buddha call out, "Honey, I'm home."

Upon seeing them together, my sister was so inspired by their closeness that she promptly adopted a dog for her dog, and then a cat for her cat. Soon I couldn't imagine having a solo pet, and could barely remember life before Angel and Buddha were a happy twosome. I would joke that Buddha was *my* cat while Angel was *Buddha's* cat.

It broke my heart for Buddha's sake to come home one day to find Angel's lifeless body on the floor. He'd been fine—no symptoms of anything wrong, no decline whatsoever. He was just old.

For months, Buddha looked out the window longingly as if waiting for his friend to come back. I wanted to get him another cat but felt he needed time to mourn. Besides, he'd picked Angel. They were soul mates. How could I hope to find him another partner of such epic proportions? How could lightning strike twice?

After a few months passed, I had the most beautiful dream. I was in a large park. There were rolling hills, tall, leafy trees, and lush green grasses so colorful they could have been in an Impressionistic painting. The park was filled with cats and kittens, hundreds of them—all shapes, sizes, and colors. It was a veritable feline sea. Suddenly I saw Angel. He sat perfectly still and serenely stared into my face. I remember thinking, Does he want me to take one of these home for Buddha?

I awoke and decided that this must be what the dream meant. Spring was coming. I'd get Buddha a kitten. Angel had come to say it was time. Buddha was young, and I owed it to him to find him a new companion.

To my shock and horror, Buddha was killed by a neighborhood dog shortly after I had the dream. And now I know what the dream meant. Angel was showing me that he was all right and in a good place—kitty heaven, to be exact!

Buddha and Angel are together again, I'm sure. It brings me such comfort to picture them there, reunited, catnapping in the long, lush grass under a large tree, or dashing after each other, pouncing and rolling down the soft hillsides. I imagine that every night they spend hours gently kissing each other's faces, then slowly wrap their arms around each other, bury their noses in each other's fur, and drift off into a perfect, peaceful sleep.

# The Illusion of Natural Differences

## Allen and Linda Anderson

Dogs and cats are supposed to be natural enemies. Certain groups of people are expected to be at odds with one another too. Race, politics, religion, and any number of other differences seem to be insurmountable barriers that separate us from one another.

Prana, our gentle golden retriever, whose name means "breath of life," is no longer with us. In her short life, she taught our family how to transcend differences in ways that constantly amazed us.

Prana befriended Feisty, a kitten we adopted from a local animal shelter. Their relationship demonstrated the power of love to crumble illusory walls that keep us from experiencing our deeper, spiritual connections with one another. These animals, who shared our home, inspired us with their selfless love and unstinting devotion. We'd look at one another and say, "Why can't everyone be more like them?"

Prana gently played with and mothered Feisty, raising him with unwavering patience, kindness, and consideration. For instance, Prana cherished the rawhide chew bones we'd give her in the evening. We began to look on these times she spent chewing on her bone as her way of meditating and communing with Spirit. We thought that she must surely be entering an alpha brain-wave state while chewing with such a look of pure ecstasy on her face. Yet Prana had learned the balance between prayer and service. When Feisty came over, Prana, without hesitation, would readily share her precious bone by holding it between her front paws for the kitten to lick.

As the kitten grew into a cat, the two friends became insep-arable, even sleeping next to each other. Prana often slept on her back with her mouth open. Feisty would stick his head in her mouth, waking up his playmate.

Allen had a special experience with Prana and Feisty that showed how their love enabled them to communicate with each other and with us when Prana needed a little divine intervention.

## Allen's Story

I had a job that required me to open and close a beautiful temple that was surrounded by a rolling prairie. This was a special place where people of many faiths came to pray and express their love for God. It was one of Prana's greatest joys to accompany me to visit the temple. She seemed to under-stand and respect that this was a sacred site. While I did my job, she ran through fields of flowers or snow, depending on the season. She chased the squirrels, birds, and deer on the temple grounds. Prana was so gentle that even though dogs of her breed are natural hunters, she would slow down if it looked like she'd actually catch another animal. She enjoyed the game but wasn't interested in capturing a fellow creature.

One day, I decided not to take Prana with me to the temple because she was shedding and I'd just vacuumed my car. Both Feisty and Prana sat side by side looking at me as I walked out the back door. Seeing the dejected look on Prana's face, I tried to explain to her why she couldn't go with me this time. Her ears and head drooped.

Feisty looked at his sad friend. Then he ran upstairs, where Linda was working in her office. Feisty meowed in a way that sounded more like he was yelling at the top of his lungs and immediately got Linda's attention. He continued to fuss as he ran back downstairs. Because of the alarm in his voice, Linda followed him, thinking that something dreadful must have happened. She found me in the garage. I told her that I'd have to leave Prana at home that day. My decision must have upset Feisty. He knew how much these trips meant to his pal.

I went back to the house and found Prana, her head still slumped down. Feisty stood next to her and glared at me.

He won.

Prana went to the temple that night, and after having almost lost one of her greatest treats, she played with even more gusto than usual. I vacuumed my car again, a small price to pay for placating Feisty and giving one of life's simple pleasures to such a golden-hearted creature as Prana. After we returned home, I found the two companions in the living room, lying next to each other. Feisty was carefully cleaning Prana, licking her hair and paws.

## Angel Animals

Prana and Feisty are examples of what we call "angel animals." These are creatures who walk, hop, crawl, fly, or swim. They share our homes or can be observed in the wild. Angel animals love, help, protect, and bring comfort.

Prana and Feisty, two animals who are supposed to be

naturally antagonistic toward each other, taught our family invaluable spiritual lessons in selfless giving, unconditional love, and the joy of friendship. How they communicated with and understood each other is a mystery—perhaps they were linked on a spiritual level?—but whatever their connection was, the bond was undeniable.

# My Miraculous Healing

## Montana Desiree Ford-Hilliard

It started in the spring. Every day I would barf up stringy hair balls, no matter how often my mom would brush my luxurious Persian coat. My mom took me to my vet, Dr. Morton, who prescribed some new laxative-like substance for me, but it didn't help.

Then a friend of Mom's told her about a specialist. The new vet was a nice guy, but I was still really scared. He poked and prodded and took blood and stuff, then I went home and took a long nap. He said that my problem was due to the fact that I am "a compulsive groomer." Well, I have never been so insulted in all of my life!

As the weeks passed, my problem grew worse. My mom was worried and called the specialist back and asked what we could do. The specialist suggested that they "scope" me. I am not really sure what that is, but it sounded awful. When Mom asked the specialist what he could expect to find with this fancy test, he told her things that made her very sad, and she cried.

Mom and I decided that the holistic route was what we

needed. She called her friend Dr. Gary Holz, of the Wellness Center in San Diego, who is a well-known hands-on healer. Dr. Holz said that his policy was to work on people only, but Mom persisted until he agreed to see me on his day off. Mom snuck me in hidden under a blanket.

Dr. Holz was very kind. He put me on his examination table and prayed with me while he held his hands around my abdomen. I could feel heat coming from his hands, and I just knew that his healing was working. After a few minutes, Dr. Holz told Mom that I was all better and could go home. I took a nap when we got there.

The next morning, I had one last small hair ball, and I'm happy to report I have been hair-ball free for more than a year now. I owe at least one of my nine lives to Dr. Holz—a cat's best friend.

# William Henry

## *James David Seddon*

William Henry—Willy, as he was known—was a friend of mine. He came to live with my wife and me at a time when we truly needed his kind of friendship. We were in our mid thirties and early forties and, like many people our age, suffered from overinflated egos and ambitions.

Willy was a golden retriever, and he spent his ten-year life with us. He was like most dogs, unquestionably loyal and loving, yet there was something much deeper. Although he submitted to his human environment and lived most of his life according to human rules, there was a part of him that he kept for himself—the wild part.

There was a switch in Willy's mind. He would follow all the human rules, he would tolerate being tied to a chain in the backyard, he would give up his seat on the couch, and if worse came to worst, he would ride in the back of the truck, but every so often something would click and he would have to escape for a while. Sometimes it was just for a few hours; other times it would be for a day or two.

The morning of the coldest day one winter, he slipped out of his collar and took off. My wife and I worried all day about him freezing to death. We got in the car several times and slowly drove down the streets looking for him, but he was too sly to be found. We didn't sleep much that night, worrying about Willy. At two or three in the morning, my wife jumped out of bed and said, "I hear him barking in the backyard." She ran downstairs and turned on the back porch light. Willy wasn't there.

The next morning, his tracks were all over the backyard, so we knew that the barking my wife had heard was not a figment of a hopeful imagination; he truly had been there sometime during the night. It was like he was just passing by and barked to say, "Hey, I'm all right. I'll be home after a while." True to his word, Willy showed up later that day. He ate a big meal and took a long nap.

Then there was the time Willy and I went to the woods to cut firewood. Ideally, cutting firewood is a pleasant time to enjoy Mother Nature, but usually it ends up being a task to be finished as soon as possible, in order to start another task.

As I tossed the last stick of wood into the back of my truck, I started calling, "Willy, let's go. Come on, Willy, let's go home." I repeated myself several times, but the woods were quiet. I hollered louder, "Willy, let's go!" but Willy never responded.

I started cursing under my breath as I walked in the direction I had last seen Willy running, his nose to the ground. I hadn't walked very far before I came to a clearing in the woods next to a pond. There in the middle of the clearing sat Willy, staring into the woods on the opposite side of the pond.

"Let's go!" I hollered.

Willy didn't move.

I got to thinking, maybe he's watching something, perhaps a deer or a turkey. So I walked down and sat beside him and looked in the direction he was staring. I didn't see anything. I studied Willy's eyes, hoping they would reveal what he was so intently watching; they gave no clue. It seemed as though he was watching everything.

After several minutes, Willy's attention turned from the woods, and for a few seconds he looked at me. Then he let out a deep sigh, rolled over against me, and closed his eyes. We sat there like that in the clearing for a long time. I don't remember when we finally got home. Somehow it doesn't seem important now.

That was the first time Willy and I shared such a moment. There were many others. In some strange way, Willy always seemed to know when I needed to be reminded of the important things.

It took several years before I began to understand what Willy was watching, but slowly I began to see through his eyes. He was watching the wisdom of the ages.

You see, God divided His wisdom and knowledge among all living things. The only way to find tranquillity and balance in life is to learn to love, understand, and respect the universe that He created. Willy showed me that humans are not the source of wisdom. They have but a slight understanding of their portion of it.

Willy and I had a favorite place where we used to go and share our lives. There was a little-used gravel road at the edge of town. On one side of the road were the remains of an old coal mine; on the other, a large open meadow. We would start walking down the road, but it wouldn't be too long before Willy put his nose to the ground and disappeared into the tall grass that covered the meadow. I could tell where Willy was by watching where the grass was moving. It looked as though there was a large, invisible snake crawling atop the grass.

Sooner or later, Willy would emerge from the tall grass and would sit in the road and wait for me. Most of the time he would be all wet and covered with weed seed, and his tongue would be hanging out of the side of his mouth, but in his eyes was a look of "Isn't the world a wonderful place?"

Willy died the day after Labor Day five years ago. I still miss him deeply. There is hardly a day when I don't live one of his lessons. I have no regrets about loving him. I buried Willy under an oak tree at the edge of our meadow. He liked that.

One summer morning, just before sunrise, I visited Willy's grave. I stood there beside him, looking out over the meadow. As the sun rose over the hill behind us, a slight breeze began to blow. Like an invisible snake, it moved the tops of the tall grass. And somewhere on that breeze came a silent question: "I wonder if that is Willy." And on that breeze came a silent answer: "Of course it is." The world is a wonderful place.

# 3

# VISITATIONS

# Opening the Lines of Communication

## Jenny Jobson

Life in the big city can be just as frightening as it is challenging and exciting for a young woman like me who grew up in a small midwestern town. People are busy and preoccupied in Manhattan. It's difficult to know whom you can trust, and at the same time, it just doesn't seem easy to get to know anyone at all. So yes, I'll admit it, at the age of thirty-two, I still needed my mommy. We talked on the phone for an hour every night. She was my entire support system. I knew that whatever I said to her would never be repeated or used against me in the future.

I honestly couldn't imagine life without her. When her doctor said that Mom needed a liver transplant, I just knew that she would be okay. But I was wrong.

We could see the hospital's helicopter landing pad from Mom's room. Each time a copter would touch down, Mom would say, "Maybe that's my new liver."

Six weeks had passed since Mom had checked into the hospital, and the doctor said that she would be receiving a transplant any day.

During her last three days of life on this earth, I saw her lose strength, something I'd never seen before. She hadn't been given any pain medication, as it might have further reduced her liver's ability to function, so up until her last breath, her mind was as clear as ever, which was both a blessing and a curse. Mom had been a jaundiced baby and had struggled with poor health off and on throughout her life. I kept thinking that God must be allowing her to live until technology could extend her life even further.

The hours and days melted into one another. Mom began speaking of her final wishes. She told me things that she'd always wanted to say. Fatigue and weakness increased the strength of death's grip. Then our dialogue shifted to my personal monologue. I knew that this was my last chance to apologize for everything horrible and thoughtless that I'd done. Even though her eyes were closed, I knew by the appropriate smiles that touched her lips and the times that she would summon enough energy to whisper "I love you" that Mom was listening and understood.

I found myself repeating to her over and over again, "Please, Mom, let's not lose touch. I'll listen for you. If you can, please communicate with me when you reach the other side. I'll listen for you."

My father and I had never spoken very much. Mom had been his support system just as she had been mine. Throughout her life she had made repeated attempts to get Dad and me to spend more time talking to each other, but still, conversations between the two of us were stilted at best. Now here we were, after Mom's death, Dad, my brother, and I—all strangers. We each felt the horrendous impact of her loss and weren't in an emotional state that allowed building new communication.

It all started with a knock on the door in the middle of the night, a knock to which no physical being seemed to be a party. Seconds later, my father heard a tremendous amount of noise coming from my childhood bedroom. There was a lamp in that room that my mother treasured, and now Dad said that it was virtually exploding with electrical snapping. There was a series of pops that sounded almost like lightbulbs breaking. Dad set mousetraps for days. Each night there was so much noise coming from my old bedroom that it would wake him up, but each morning, when he checked the mousetraps, there was nothing in them.

Determined to find out what was causing the nightly ruckus, he waited one night until the popping and snapping had swung into full tilt. He quietly snuck in the door and switched on the lights. But now the pops, skipping only a second's beat, were no longer in front of him where they had been. He now heard the same intensity of sound coming from the bathroom across the hall.

He crept quietly to the bathroom door, quickly switching on the bathroom light to surprise whatever it was that was causing this unusual disturbance. But once again, the snapping and popping shifted, only now the sound was coming from the room that my mother and father had shared.

Dad was calling me every other night now, telling me about all the noise that had now taken up residence in the master bedroom. I was glad that we were spending so much time talking to each other, but I was really growing concerned for my father's mental health. I thought that perhaps he'd gone crazy with grief.

It was the first Thanksgiving without Mom, the first time I'd be cooking the holiday dinner by myself. I drove the sixteen hours from New York City into mid Michigan. I was exhausted by the time I arrived, so tired that I didn't think I could make it even as far as my old bedroom. Instead, I collapsed on the family room floor. But I couldn't sleep, rest, or even relax. I was surrounded by electrical snapping. It was excitement in the air, in the fullest sense. But there was something that Dad hadn't described. This wasn't just sound as I'd ever experienced it before; it seemed to split the atmosphere, almost like a bolt of lightning would. The best I can do is describe it as three-dimensional sound.

When I returned to New York, she came with me—the electricity that I believe is my mother. It was four o'clock in the morning. I was asleep. The television was off. Only a nightlight was on to illuminate the room.

To turn on my television, you must first turn on the cable box, then the television itself. Well, suddenly, somehow, the

television turned itself on at the same time that a wall orna-
ment (which had been hanging securely for eight years) flew
into the middle of the room. Simultaneously, all the power in
the apartment blew out.

The next morning, when I asked the super to fix the power,
he said, "What were you doing up there last night? You would
have needed fifteen television sets plugged in to blow out both
of those fuses."

I told him that only the night-light had been on.

"Well, you must have a ghost up there," he said.

I asked him if it couldn't have just been a power surge.

"No," he answered, "or everyone else on your line would
have blown out too."

By this time I was convinced that my father and I were both
crazy from grief. I was hearing electrical snapping in the air
on a regular basis now. If I overslept, an enormous pop right
beside my ear would wake me up in the nick of time. Or if I
happened to be speaking of a subject about which my mother
had held a strong opinion, the air would explode with expressive electricity. Dad had agreed to call me on certain evenings,
and if he forgot, a giant pop would remind him at the appropriate time.

I enjoyed all of this and didn't want to tell anyone. I felt that
no one would believe it. Why should they? I hadn't believed it
when my own father had told me.

But then, one afternoon, I was conversing on the telephone
with my best friend and the matter was taken out of my hands.
Suddenly there was so much noise in the air that Elizabeth
said, "What's going on over there?"

I didn't know what to say, so in desperation I decide to take
a chance and tell the truth. Her response shocked me. "I know
what you're talking about," she said. "When my brother died,
I experienced the same thing."

I started wondering how many people have experienced
this sort of thing and just disregarded it, thinking that they
were imagining things. One thing that I do know for sure: all

this has opened the lines of communication between my father and me as nothing else could have. And that is something my mother always wanted.

# The Sign

## *Jim Wright*

After reading both of Rosemary Altea's best-selling books, *The Eagle and the Rose* and *Proud Spirit*, in which she wrote about her abilities as a medium, I went to see her at a presentation in Vancouver, British Columbia. I wanted her to contact my brother Stephen, who had died in 1976 at age twenty-one from a brain aneurysm. It had been a particularly horrible scene, since he died in just three hours after being perfectly healthy all of his life. Our parents were both there, along with me, my wife, our minister, Stephen's fiancée, and her mother. He was supposed to get married the following month. We literally watched him die right in front of us.

This traumatic event began my studies into near-death experiences. I had an insatiable desire to contact him again in spirit because I had never been able to say good-bye. I missed him terribly. So as I sat in the audience and watched Rosemary Altea do her thing, I was extremely impressed. I knew that she was contacting the spirits of loved ones who had come to help in the grieving process. The love that flowed from the families upon hearing that their deceased loved ones were all right and had messages to pass on to them was incredible.

I remember one grieving family that had lost a daughter.

The father asked why his daughter couldn't just give him a sign that she was okay. Through Rosemary, the daughter said that she had been doing that very thing. She had been moving a specific picture in her bedroom that the father would constantly come in and straighten. The father verified the description and location of the picture and admitted that he always fixed it. Moving that picture was the daughter's way of giving a sign to the family that she was with them and doing fine. But not all signs are that obvious, Rosemary said, and many can be very subtle.

I sat there wondering why Rosemary had not called on me. Where was Stephen? I wanted my sign, too, and I was growing impatient; this continued for almost three hours. Finally, Rosemary stood next to me and said, "There is a brother named Stephen here." She asked me to step up to the front along with a few other people.

As I stood up front with four other people, Rosemary told each of us who the spirits were that wanted to make themselves known and what they had to say. Everything she said was accurate. I was excited beyond words, because she had described Stephen and his death perfectly. I knew he was there. I had waited so long for this moment. But I wanted my sign, and it was the end of the program. Rosemary was giving her closing remarks as all of us up front had our arms around one another.

Suddenly, I felt the floor move under my feet as if we were having an earthquake. Now keep in mind, this presentation was taking place in the oldest church in Vancouver. Made out of huge stones, it looked like it could survive a nuclear attack. The floor was solid stone. I was instantly startled out of my contemplation, but I heard Rosemary continue on in the background. I looked to my right to see how other people were reacting to these strong vibrations. Yet in spite of the fact that we were all holding on to one another, there was no reaction.

Rosemary continued to talk as if nothing were happening. But I knew that it would have been impossible for her and the others not to feel it. Earthquakes don't happen directly under one person. No one in the audience in front of me moved, and no one and nothing there had been capable of causing this effect. That is when my rational mind quit working and the true realization finally hit me. I had asked for a sign, and Stephen had given it to me: dramatic, clear, and irrefutable proof. For the spot I was standing on was solid stone, unmovable by man. But Stephen had different ideas.

After twenty-one years, I said good-bye. I know he heard me.

# I'll Always Be Nearby

## Carol Willette Bachofner

I am the eldest of four children. Daddy always expected a lot more from me than from the others. "I'm counting on you," he'd say. Whatever it was he wanted me to do, I could not resist his confidence in me.

When he was diagnosed with lung cancer in 1993, I braced myself for the eventuality of losing him, and tried to fight off the sadness by imagining the list of things he'd expect me to handle. Then in my late forties, I was certain that he would having something monumental for me to take care of: his burial arrangements, his will.

The family gathered in Miami at Veterans Hospital. Daddy was undergoing chemo and radiation and myriad tests. My brothers were not handling things well. One was angry at God, the other was feeling guilty for smoking around our father. My sister was running around like a decapitated fowl, one minute crying her eyes out, the next collapsing in silence. Mom was being Mom, calm, unmoving, *there* at Daddy's bedside.

I arrived from California in the middle of the night and went straight to the hospital. I was nervous as I waited for him to reveal the plan he'd laid out for his number one daughter. Nothing. All he wanted to do was talk about the cancer and what I knew of it from my own bout with leukemia a few years earlier. "You're the only one who understands," he said. His voice already seemed far away. We talked for an hour or so; then he suggested that I go get some sleep.

The day before I was to return to California, the whole family assembled at the hospital. Dad wanted to see us all together before I left. We all fussed at him, assuring him that surely we'd all be together again soon. He insisted, and we obeyed. There was a fair amount of distracting chatter, some posed pictures, and words of encouragement to him about toughing it out through the chemo and radiation.

Toward the end of the visiting hours, Daddy suggested to Mom that he'd like to see each of us alone. The boys went in, Mike first, then Barry. My sister was next. I wondered what Daddy had said to each of them. I waited and pondered.

My turn came, and I slipped uncomfortably onto the bed next to him, sitting carefully as if I might break him if I got too close. "What do you want me to do?" I ventured. "I can handle anything." Inside, I felt as if I couldn't handle my next breath, but I had to convince him that I was the tough girl he'd raised. "What can I do for you?"

He explained that he had told the others to take care of Mom. That was his biggest concern. Of course, I had grown up seeing firsthand that Mom was always his first and last thought. Mom was his number one, just slightly behind God Himself.

"But what do you want from me?" I asked.

"Nothing, little girl. Just knowing you are safe and strong and happy is enough. I feel relieved that you have a good husband, fine children, and have been restored to health. That's enough."

"But, Daddy," I pleaded. "I feel useless. I will feel so alone without you. Let me help you in some way."

"Well, promise me that you won't fall apart. The rest of them aren't handling this very well. Be my strong girl. Don't worry. You'll never be alone. I will always be nearby."

After that, I did exactly what he'd asked. Strong. That was me, never giving in to despair or open worry. Not to him and not to the rest of my family. Only in the dark, to my husband, did I give in to my fear of losing my anchor, my sunlight.

The news came to me by telephone from my brother. Five months, almost to the day, from when they had told us Daddy had five months left. July 8, 1993. The day my heart broke into a million pieces.

I hurried to Florida for the funeral, arriving just in time for the wake. I was unprepared for the sight of my dear father lying in a coffin. All the chemo had stripped him of his hair. My sister was hysterical, my brothers oddly quiet. Mom was stoically bearing up in front of their friends and neighbors. I went alone to talk with him one last time. I decided to sing him away with a song he had sung to me as a child when I couldn't sleep. I must have looked silly, standing there at the coffin, singing a baby song.

It had always been my father's desire to be cremated and buried at Arlington National Cemetery. Charlie Willette was a soldier, a former P.O.W., and a Purple Heart veteran. He had earned his place there among all the others. In October, I flew east once again, to honor him one last time and say good-bye.

I had great difficulty with the pomp and circumstance of a military burial. Each crack of the guns shot right through my soul. I cried as I had never cried before. When it came time to place the urn into the niche, the funeral director asked if one of the family wanted to do it. As the eldest, I once again stepped forward to be strong. I slipped the urn into place, along with a hawk feather to help him soar into the next life. I had brought some little red glitter hearts with me. I sprinkled them into the vault and all over the area. I wanted people to see how much this man meant to all of us.

It was finally done. All the formalities were completed. Now it was time to heal, time to get used to being without him for the rest of my life. His words to me kept echoing: "I will always be nearby."

Things started happening to show me that he was not that far away. Two weeks after the burial at Arlington, my husband and I were driving down the road from our house at about ten o'clock at night. Suddenly something white bounced down the middle of the road ahead and hit our windshield. It was a golf ball. This road was not near the golf course at all. But there was the golf ball, bouncing out of the darkness onto our car. Dad and my husband had loved to golf together. Golf was Daddy's big relaxation. I began to laugh and said, "So, his golf game hasn't improved even now!" We both saw it. We both knew that he was saying hello. I was numb enough still that it didn't bother me.

As time went on, I grew more sensitive to the loss. I zig-zagged back and forth between being strong and falling apart in a puddle of tears. Certain things would crumple me. Any singing of "How Great Thou Art" in church would ruin me for hours. This was the song he had sung all the way to the hospital the day he died. His faith was strong, and now I couldn't seem to be. I felt increasingly alone.

Nearly three years had passed since I'd put the urn into the niche at Arlington, and I was still not doing very well. Oh sure, most days I maintained my outward strength. But I was not fooling myself. The father who had been a source of life and light for me was gone. I felt stunningly empty and alone.

That was about to change. Help was on the way.

One Sunday I was in the shower, preparing to go to church. The water was hot, and I was crying as hard and fast as the water was pouring down over me. I was wailing out loud. "Daddy, where are you? You said you'd always be nearby. Why won't you come?" Just at that moment, I caught a glimpse of something falling next to me. I saw a bright flicker of something as it passed my left shoulder. I turned the shower off and looked down. To my amazement, there on the shower floor was a tiny red glitter heart.

Yes, indeed! Charlie Willette was a man of his word. And I would be a woman of my word, too. I knew now that he was nearby, and I knew that I could be strong, as I had promised. I was not alone, and he was not really gone.

I don't cry anymore. Thinking of him every day is my joy. I can hardly wait to see him again and ask him just how he did that heart thing, though. What a guy!

# A Silent Candle Burning

## *Jeremiah Abrams*

My father died suddenly, without notice. I was twenty-two years old and a graduate student in Boston. One day he was here, the next day he was gone. I remember the day clearly. In the early morning of a wet and wintry day, January 6, 1970, I received a call from one of our plant managers, telling me that I had better come home right away, that my dad was real sick. (My father was a manufacturer, and our family employed many of the people in the small Pennsylvania mountain town of Freeland, where I grew up.)

Within hours I was at his bedside in a northeastern Pennsylvania hospital. My father was unconscious, being kept barely alive on a respirator. I sat there and watched, teary-eyed, as his body expanded and contracted like a balloon. He turned gray, then light blue, as his soul slowly slipped away. In less than an hour he had left his body. He was fifty-nine years old. I never did get to say good-bye, or thank you, or I love you.

That morning, the world became a much smaller place for me. After the funeral, I returned to Boston and spent the better part of the next few years languishing, pickling in a depression, defended against grief. I suppose this was self-preservation. Only years later did I see the truth of just how lost I was.

I did know at the time, however, that I was being initiated, sent off to find myself on a night-sea journey. Given the circumstances, I was functioning surprisingly well. I taught college for three semesters and finished my graduate work. My plan was to buy a Volkswagen camper and set out on the road in my new red land-schooner. For nine months I journeyed from coast to coast across Canada, down to California, then back again across the States. I built log cabins on a British Columbian commune, set up household for two months in a driftwood-and-plastic shantytown on the outer banks of Vancouver Island, fell in and out of love several times, then came roaring back to civilization, culminating the journey in the ferment of the San Francisco Bay Area of the early 1970s.

In the fall of 1972, I returned to Boston to embark on my professional life. Still haunted by saturnine moods, I had come back to my life with new resolve. I began a Jungian analysis, which helped open me to the truth of my predicament and my possibilities. I was slowly learning to trust my inner voice.

Almost two years after my father's death, another New England winter morning brought news, this time a package with a note from my mother. She and I had had very little contact in the intervening time, and so her package came as a surprise.

I didn't know what to expect, and I felt a rush of sadness as I opened the box. The package contained two twenty-four-hour candles, simple white candles in thick glasses that felt like jars. Each one had a plain white label with blue Hebrew letters and a Star of David. These were traditional Jewish Yahrzeit candles—I recognized them—meant to be lit to commemorate the anniversary of the death of an immediate family member. In the note, my mother asked me to burn one of the

candles on the anniversary of my father's passing—on the exact
day it occurred in the Jewish lunar calendar. She gave me the
date. I guess she sent two candles as an added incentive.

Now, my mother was not a religious woman in any sense of
the word, but she had kept her patriarchal bargain with my
father and maintained the Sabbath and the High Holy Days
like a faithful wife, even though she never practiced the ob-
servances on her own. My father, on the other hand, had been
quite religious, increasingly so as he grew older. He had what I
call the charisma of faith, something his parents had possessed
as well. He practiced traditional Judaism with a spiritual clarity
that I envied. I was always the questioning, challenging son,
hampered by the need to understand before I could believe.
I knew my father had gone to God—long before he left his
body—but I couldn't comprehend where that was or what re-
gards now existed between us.

I dutifully filed the candles away and forgot about them for
several weeks. One evening, while I was cozied up studying,
my gaze fixed upon the Yahrzeit candles on the desk in front of
me. I searched the desk for the note with the Jewish date in it,
to no avail. I got it in my mind to light the candle anyway.

That night, I set it on the desk in the study just as I went to
bed. I was living in a rambling New England country house
where my bedroom had a generous little study attached. From
my bed, I could look directly through a doorway into the study
and see that silent candle burning. With the door open, candlelight poured into the dark bedroom. The scene was dramatic.

I fell immediately into a deep sleep, dropping into a dreaming state of momentous feelings, a big dream:

*I'm not sure where I am. It's a gentle outdoor elevation, a hillside
near the ocean. There is a long tiered structure built into the side
of the mountain, a massive building camouflaged with sod roofs
and lots of glass and views. I am prowling around. I walk through
a side door and begin exploring the interior. There are long hallways with doors on either side. I notice a figure approaching down*

*the hallway. It's a man. He's got green skin! As he gets closer, I recognize him. It's my father!*

*He's somewhat younger than at our last encounter, and looks healthy, except that he has green skin. He hugs me and says how glad he is that I could come, how happy he is to see me. As we walk together, he gives me a tour of the building. I am squeezing his hand as we walk. Apparently there are many others living here, but we don't see another soul. It seems an endless series of hallways. I am incredulous. When I come to my senses, the first thing I want to ask is why he is green.*

*He doesn't answer me directly, but says to follow him. He leads me to a room that feels like a spa. There's a very large porcelain tub there, filled with green liquid. He demonstrates how he has to submerge in the spa water regularly, go completely under, head and all. This gives him vigor and strength. I can see the effects immediately, in his renewed energy, in his bearing. We look at each other and I am overwhelmed with happiness and relief.*

I woke up with a start. It was the middle of the night. The room was bathed in the magic glow of candlelight. I sat up and stared at that Yahrzeit candle, electrified, grinning.

Over the next few weeks, my depression lifted. I was back from the underworld. I had a lot to think about . . . about dreams, about green, about Jewish mourning rituals, about life after life, about my life spreading out before me.

# Dying to Know

## *Eddie Conner*

When I saw my first ghost, I was nine years old, visiting my grandmother in North Carolina. I was playing on the front porch when an old man appeared. He was sitting at the opposite end of the porch, fast asleep and snoring loudly. At first, he startled me, because he hadn't been there a minute before. But I couldn't take my eyes off him. I was riveted by his every move, and an eerie feeling enveloped my body. Suddenly, he woke up from his nap, grabbed his chest, and fell right off the porch and onto Grandma's flower bed. I rushed over to help him, but when I looked into the flower bed he had vanished!

Covered with goose bumps and with my hair standing straight up on my head, I looked over at my brothers. Before I could ask them if they'd seen the old man, I already knew they hadn't. So I did what I was good at: I kept my mouth shut and didn't tell anyone. Months later, I overheard Grandma telling a friend about the former tenant who had died before she'd moved in. In a matter-of-fact voice she said, "Yes sir, he died of a heart attack right there on the front porch."

Raised in a strict family where the motto was "Young 'uns are to be seen and not heard," my brothers and I knew better than to go against the grain, or else a hard backhand was sure to follow. Grandma baby-sat my three brothers and me during the summer while Mama worked two jobs. My brothers and I were afraid of our grandmother. Staying with Grandma meant living in a world of emotional, verbal, and physical abuse. I vowed that as soon as I was old enough to leave, I'd never go back to her hellhole of a house. Ever!

I met Tim in the early 1980s, when I was twenty years old. Immediately, we were best friends. I confided in Tim about

seeing dead people and angels as a little boy. Tim was fascinated, and he also believed that something great happened
to us when we died. "It can't all just stop when we're six feet
under," he would say.

Later, after years of sharing Grandma horror stories with
Tim, he said I should make peace with her before she died. I
strongly disagreed, but Tim was persistent. He promised he'd
come back to my old stomping ground and be supportive.
Two weeks later, Tim and I were sitting in Grandma's darkened living room. Grandma and I had little to say, but we managed to keep a conversation going despite our discomfort. She
sat there in her rocking chair with a stack of Bibles on the floor
beside her, a glass of bittersweet tea in one hand, fanning herself with her trusty butter-bean hat with the other hand. When
it was time to go, I hugged her good-bye and kissed her on the
cheek like I had done a hundred times as a kid.

A year later, Grandma died. I thought the only reason for
being at her funeral was to support my mom. Less than a
month later, Tim was hospitalized with chronic pneumonia.
Within forty-eight hours of his admittance into Duke University Medical Center, he was diagnosed with AIDS. We were
devastated.

For the next three and a half years, Tim was in and out of
the hospital more times than I care to count. We talked openly
about what happens when you die. I did everything possible
to empower Tim before he transitioned from the physical realm
to the nonphysical realm.

During one of Tim's numerous hospital stays, I recall bouncing into his room with his favorite family pictures to cheer him
up. He was sitting in his bed, as white as a ghost. I asked if
he wanted me to call a nurse, and he just held his palm to me,
gesturing no. When he regained his composure, he told me
what had happened.

"A hospital volunteer came into my room and stood beside
the bed. She was an old lady who smiled at me and straight-
ened the bed sheets. She never said a word to me. Then I began

to recognize her, but I wasn't certain how I remembered her. She made me feel like everything was going to be all right.

"The weird thing was that she was fanning herself with a funny-looking straw hat, sort of like a garden hat. When I asked her about it, she just smiled at me. Then a nurse knocked on the door to check my vitals, and the volunteer beside my bed vanished right in front of me! That's when it hit me who she was!

"Eddie, it was your grandmother, and she was holding that damn butter-bean hat that you used to always make fun of!"

I was excited for Tim about his communication with the other side. However, Tim was not as enthusiastic about Grandma coming to check on him. But we did agree on one thing: this was a clear sign to us that the spirit world was alive and well and on our side.

I left Tim's hospital room late that night. Getting into my car, I said a prayer to Grandma, thanking her for assisting me with Tim. Before I could finish my thoughts of appreciation, I felt her essence respond with a sincere "You're welcome, honey!"

As Tim grew closer to leaving his physical body, we talked extensively about our friendship and love for each other. I made a promise to walk him across to the other side when his time came. "Hand in hand, we'll walk across," I gently told my best friend of eleven years. "You're not going to have to do this alone."

Two months before Tim transitioned, he began to experience tremendous bouts of dementia. His parents decided it would be best if he lived with them until he died. His mom orchestrated her work schedule and took a leave of absence to be with her son. The day his parents came for him, Tim seemed better, almost coherent. We were both sad he was leaving, but we knew it was for the best. It was an emotional moment for us, and I was grateful that Tim was aware of his surroundings. I was nervous that he wouldn't know me when his time came to transition. I was scared that his conscious thinking mind wouldn't remember me, and that as the result of his dementia he might be too afraid or confused to cross over.

We hugged each other tightly and quietly cried in each other's arms. In that moment I realized this was probably the last hug we would share. We felt helpless and oddly invincible as our love for each other reached a new level.

"If you help me get over there safe and sound, I'll see that your dreams come true," he said, laughing and crying at the same time. "And I'll give you lots of signs so you'll know it's really me helping you out from the other side." We laughed and made jokes back and forth until his parents arrived and took him home.

A few weeks later, surrounded by his family and friends, Tim lay practically lifeless in another hospital bed. His room was filled with many people who loved him. Each person took a turn holding Tim's hand, saying a final good-bye. I patiently waited for everyone else to say farewell so that I could take my time getting Tim across to the other side without his family realizing what we had agreed to do.

Holding Tim's hand and rubbing his arm, I monitored his breath closely. His exhalations grew weaker by the moment. I closed my eyes, said a prayer, and began sending telepathic messages and feelings to Tim. I could feel and sense his essence in the room and all around his loved ones. He was inside and outside of us at the same time. I held his physical hand tightly while waiting to feel the spirit hand touch mine.

Suddenly a glorious light emerged from everywhere and nowhere at the same time, as if I were floating in the core of the sun. I felt my best friend's warm spiritual hand holding mine. His smiling face filled my mind's eye. His pure positive essence caught me a little off guard. Tim's soul self looked and felt radiant and healthy. He was whole and complete. Without words, we moved deeper into the light. Hand in hand we became light bodies, as the angelic essence of the nonphysical realm welcomed Tim with an open and unconditional heart.

I felt like a little boy again, the same little boy who saw angels and spiritual bodies in his bedroom, the kid who saw ghosts around him. This feeling, which I was experiencing on a cellular level, was the identical energy I had experienced as a child, yet it was a timeless, ageless stream of consciousness that words cannot describe. Tim and I floated inside it for what seemed like one second of eternity on the faceless clock of the universe. From inside the veil of light emerged images and beings moving toward Tim.

We realized this was farewell. Energetically we hugged each other and said our good-byes. I thanked him for being my best friend in the whole world and vowed that we would, somehow, be together again soon. In my mind's eye, the image of Tim and me hugging transformed itself to the picture of me hugging Grandma good-bye the year before she died. In that same moment, Grandma was standing beside Tim and me. More people from the other side, people I didn't recognize, came forward through the invisible veil to assist Tim on his journey home.

With his radiant smile and unconditional heart, Tim lovingly gave me the signal that he was okay. He motioned for me to return to the hospital room to be with his family. Upon opening my eyes and adjusting my energy back to the hospital room, I realized that Tim's physical hand was still in mine. Looking at his worn-out shell of a body, I knew he was no longer inside it. His family and friends stood by his bed as Tim released the final breath that held him bound to a physical body in pain and suffering. Seconds later, my best friend was *free*!

# Mother Turned Angel

## *Linda Tisch Sivertsen*

My mother and I frequently discussed life after death. A few mystical things happened during my growing years to warrant such discussions.

The first time the topic came up was after I had decided that our house was haunted. It wasn't a scary thing; in fact, I liked this ghost. I could see her in my mind and decided that the reason our lights or stereo would turn off and back on again (when I jokingly ordered them to do so) was that a benevolent elderly woman with white hair was at the center of the unexplainable happening. I always felt her loving presence, and used to tell my mother that this woman was our protector. My mother concurred; she knew that an elderly woman had died in our home nearly forty years before.

Mom and I talked about this situation as if it was as natural as anything else. I was grateful that she was so cool, and that she never laughed at what some other mothers might have dismissed as an imagination run amuck.

The second time the topic came up was when our German shepherd, Leo, died, an extremely traumatic event for our family. Leo had lived a vibrant life until he was eight, when he contracted kidney disease. When I say vibrant, that's a bit of an understatement. Leo was as hyper as they come. He was a very big dog and had a habit of thrusting his huge frame up on the sliding glass door of our dining room when he wanted to come inside. He would stand on his hind legs and rock the glass back and forth with his front paws, throwing his entire weight into the effort. It was a loud, bad habit, but my family didn't mind his intense display of energy. We'd laugh and talk to him while we ate at the dining room table in front of the glass door. It was amazing that the whole thing didn't come crashing down.

Mom and I didn't handle Leo's death well. We were a spiritual family; we knew that it must have been his time; we knew that he was in a better place; we even knew that we would see him again one day. But our hearts and intellects were not in sync. Nothing seemed to help our grief. In other words, we weren't letting him go.

One afternoon, I was by myself in the house, standing at the dining room table, when suddenly the sliding glass door began to rock wildly back and forth. Living in California, I assumed we were having an earthquake and started to run outside. But I noticed on my way out that nothing else was moving. Something whispered to me that it was Leo, that he was trying to get my attention. I slowly walked over to the shaking glass and stared in amazement. Leo had my attention and I knew what he wanted. He wanted my mother and me to let him rest in peace. He wanted us to move on. When my mother came home, I told her what had happened, and she knew without a doubt that we had to stop mourning him once and for all.

So when I found out that my mother was dying of cancer at the young age of fifty-nine, I was certain that one day, somewhere, she would contact me from beyond. As she lay dying in her bed, she repeatedly told my sister and me that she would always be with us. She told us that she would always watch over us and help when needed. A few days after she died, I was walking in her garden, crying and praying to God, when I heard footsteps behind me in the gravel. They were fast and purposeful steps, just as Mom's had been, but when I turned around, no one was there. I knew it was her, just as I'd known it was her when her favorite rosebush went into full bloom the day of her funeral. I could go on and on, because over time she left many telltale signs of her loving presence.

That said, I was still surprised when she came to me during a crisis in my life. I had had to call an ambulance for my husband, Mark, because I was sure his appendix had just burst.

My usual strong-as-an-ox ex-stuntman husband was doubled over crying in our bed, and he couldn't move. He was rushed to a hospital, where, because of atypical symptoms, he was misdiagnosed as having a severe case of food poisoning. For days he appeared to be in crisis, and I started the process of canceling the most important business trip of my life.

For years I had worked on a project that was to culminate that week. Mark knew that a lot of money and dreams were wrapped up in my traveling to Florida, and he forbade me from canceling my travel plans on his behalf. The morning I was scheduled to leave, Mark looked fantastic. He sat up in the hospital bed, something he hadn't been able to do, and said that he would be home before I would. Relieved to see him so much better, and believing that the "poison" was leaving his system, I rushed to the airport.

Once in Florida, I called home to find out that Mark had taken a major turn for the worse. The nurses explained to me that his appendix *had* burst days before, but that because it had moved up behind his stomach they hadn't been able to tell. His organs had begun to shut down from the internal toxins; when they opened him up, he was minutes from death. The operation that had just taken place appeared to be a success, but it would be a week or so before we could know if he would live. I was told to bring a friend with me when I went to the ICU because what I would see—my husband attached to many machines and tubes—would be too much to experience alone.

I hung up the phone and began to sob uncontrollably. Here I was in a distant city, in a lonely hotel room, away from the most important person in my life, who might be dying. All for business. I was desperate, but because Orlando was experiencing tornado warnings, I couldn't get on a plane for another twenty-four hours. As I lay on the floor bawling, a feeling made me open my purse.

In my rush to get to the airport two days earlier, I had noticed that my dress had a hole in it, so I had stuffed a small box containing a needle and thread into my handbag. I had picked up this little box, filled with old buttons, at my parents' home and had had it for a year, carrying it with me from time to time. But it wasn't until that moment that I noticed what was written on the bottom of the box. In my father's distinctive handwriting it said, "To my gal Joanne, from your not-too-secret admirer. xxoo."

My father had given this box to my mother, and instantly I knew that she was trying to get my attention. I could feel her in the room and suddenly heard her voice for the first time since she had died: "He's going to be okay." That's all she said, but it was so clear that I knew she was right. I knew that she had that magical knowledge, and I knew she wouldn't have given it to me unless it was true.

I had a fantastic business meeting that afternoon in Florida, the best meeting of my life. In fact, the trip was the culmination of all the dreams that I had worked so long and hard for, and I knew I had made the right decision after all. The next morning, though, when I called the hospital, the news was grim. As I cried and cried in the hotel shower, I heard my mother's strong, loving voice once more: "He's going to be okay."

I wish I could say that my mother and I spent the next hour laughing and catching up. Alas, I didn't hear her voice again. But those words soothed my aching heart and let me know that all would be well. And she was right. My husband went through a very hard time, but he made it through.

I hope Mom never has to come to me during a crisis again, but I know that if she's needed, she'll be right there, guiding me from that place of ultimate knowledge. Few things bring comfort like a heavenly vantage point.

# Final Gifts

## Susan Stroud Long

My mother was living with me and my husband in Colorado. We had moved her from California to live out the rest of her life after we'd been told by doctors that she had had several small strokes. As it turned out, we soon discovered that she actually had a brain tumor and had only a couple of months to live.

My mother was not on any drugs and she was not in pain. Only during the last two weeks of her life was she given morphine. I was happy to care for Mother, but it was not always easy for either of us, because she had lost control of her bodily functions and was soon confined to a bed and a wheelchair. I considered it the final act of dignity for her to die at home with family.

I often read books to her on life after death, and at times I thought I was perhaps getting her to believe that she would continue to live, that her death was just a passage into something far better than we could imagine. "Mom," I said, "do you believe now in an afterlife?"

"No, Susie, I don't."

My sister came to town to say her good-byes about three weeks before Mom died. We were happy that Mom was coherent and able to talk and share time with us. One morning, we brought her breakfast and she said, "I am so tired from all that dancing."

I said, "What dancing?"

She said, "Oh, I was with your father and Anne and Bill." Anne and Bill were my parents' best friends, and they, like my father, were deceased. "We were having the best time."

My sister said, "What a wonderful dream."

"No, it wasn't a dream! Your father hugged me and said he loved me, and that I should go with him, but I said I couldn't."

"Why not?" we asked.

Mom replied, "Because I wasn't ready to go, and I told him I was sorry, but that I just couldn't go yet."

I asked, "Did they say they would see you again?"

Mom said, "Yes, but they really wanted me to go with them then. Your father said he would see me soon."

I asked, "Do you really think you will see Daddy again?"

Mom answered, "Oh yes, before I die."

"But, Mom, Dad is dead," my sister said.

"That doesn't mean he's not coming. Really, darling, he'll be here. I'm certain he'll come for me when I die. It's something I know deep in my heart: he will come." Then she looked us straight in the eyes and said, "Your father has been watching over you both and all of us, and he said to tell you that he loves you and is with you always."

My sister and I looked at each other in awe, and I was so thankful that I grabbed a piece of paper and a pen and wrote down everything that Mom had told us.

The day my mother died, I sat with her, never leaving her side. I knew that she could hear me when I said, "I love you, Mom," because her lips would mouth, "I love you, too." But soon I could tell she was someplace far away. While I sat there and just stared at her, I wondered if she was seeing my father or Anne or Bill or her deceased mother or father, or maybe her brother. I was praying that she would not be alone when she left this earth, that she would soar away and fly high with my father.

Just as I was thinking all of this, I noticed my mother's hand reach up and out as if she were shaking someone's hand, but then I realized she was *holding* someone's hand—although I could see only hers. She held her hand that way for a minute or so and then brought her arm down slowly. Whom did she see? Who was there for her? She continued to do this every couple of hours until that night, when her time finally ran out.

My husband had been out of town for two days, so Mother

and I were alone together to share her final moments. When her breathing went from fast and heavy to slow and faint, I knew she was going to die. I held her hand and said, "Go with God, Mom, go with God," and with that her heart stopped beating. I sat there not believing this was real, and at that moment the front door opened and my husband said, "Honey, I'm home." It was just like my mother to wait for my husband to get home so that I wouldn't be alone when she died. Perhaps that was her final gift to me. . . .

When I was going through my mother's things, I found a piece of paper stuck in my father's Bible. It was a list of relatives who had died, with the causes and the dates. My father died on October 16, 1985. My mother had just died on October 25, 1996. But my mom had made a mistake and listed my father's date of death as hers: October 25. I have no idea why she did that, but I will always wonder why.


# A Change of Heart

*Rich Clark*


I was lying in the fetal position on the floor in my bedroom, crying and asking for insight into my crumbling relationship. Hoping for understanding and wishing to feel more comfortable, I prayed to God for help. I was looking for something greater than myself in God's white light of protection. The tears that I shed were from my own remorse and self-pity. I had to gather strength and courage in order to leave Larry, to find a place of my own.

Years of trying to do more than my fair share had led me to believe that there would be no possibility to repair this relationship. The pain I attributed to a broken heart was always around me, growing stronger instead of weaker. I had hoped at one time to mend this union, and I sought a better way, but now it was clear to me that the end was near.

As I continued to pray for an answer, I heard a loving voice say, "It's okay, my dear, I am here. I will comfort and love you . . . and show you the way."

Much to my surprise, this female voice sounded very familiar. It was extremely soothing. Only the day before I had heard it for the first time. In the beginning it was soft and faint; now it was more affirming.

My first encounter with this voice came during my visit to a historical site, the Franklin Delano Roosevelt Home in Hyde Park, New York. As Larry, and I approached the mansion, nestled among lush rolling hills and with a breathtaking view of the Hudson River, I got caught up in a romantic notion and impulsively asked for a tour from one of the residents. I wondered what it had been like for the Roosevelts to have occupied such an estate. I silently made a short request in my mind: *How wonderful it would be to have Eleanor Roosevelt with us as we make our way through this remarkable home.* This was a private request; by now I had been working psychically for more than six months, and Larry had made it abundantly clear that he was disgruntled by these activities. It was a real point of contention between us.

We entered the foyer of the house, and I noticed the grand staircase on the right-hand side. Instantly, like a thought of love and inspiration, it came to me that Eleanor Roosevelt must be upstairs. So I said in my mind, telepathically, *Eleanor, are you here?* I don't recall a response, but I knew intuitively that upstairs was where I needed to go.

I climbed the stairs and felt myself being pulled toward her bedroom. I walked down a long corridor, past many rooms. Finally, I came to a simple room marked with a very simple plaque saying that this was Eleanor's room. I stood there in front of it. It seemed out of place amid the elegance of the mansion. There was just an ordinary twin bed, an end table, a dressing table, and a side chair beside the window; a connecting door led to another room. Once again I asked, *Are you here, Eleanor?* And again there was no response.

Then, as I stood transfixed, sadness overwhelmed me. I began to cry tears that I could not hold back. My body trembled as if the flood gates of a river had been opened and there was nothing to hold back the raging waters. Some tourists were behind me, so I tried quickly to mask my emotions. One of the other visitors, frustrated by my inaction, said, "It's just one room. Can't you please move on?"

I turned and ran back down the stairs toward the exit. Larry followed right behind me and commented tersely, "I'm never taking you anywhere ever again."

At the bottom of the stairs, much to his surprise—as well as mine—my reply to him came in a woman's voice, trembling with emotion: "Yes, my dear, but get me out of here. Please, please, let me leave here now!"

Larry wanted to get me away from the tourists. It was clear that I was causing him pain and humiliation. It must have been about one hundred degrees that August day, and I thought I had been overcome by heat exhaustion. Larry went to get me some water. However, once we left the building, I discovered that every five minutes or so this same female voice would overtake me. I continued to cry uncontrollably. The voice begged, "Please, get me away from here."

The tears I was crying weren't my own, although they originated from my tear ducts. My body was consumed by a powerful sense of loss, of things forgotten. I sat down near the edge of the park, on a curb, and prayed for someone to take away this sadness. I had no idea what was happening to me.

By this point, Larry had left me and gone to wander alone. He'd said, "I'll be in the library when you've calmed down." He could no longer tolerate what was happening, and I don't blame him—it was very strange indeed. In hindsight, I'm sure he must have mistakenly thought that I was responsible for what was unveiling, or that I could control it. Regardless, it was time for me to understand what I had encountered.

"It's just me, my dear—Eleanor Roosevelt," she said in a whisper. "You're going to be fine, but I have tried to forget about this home for quite some time. I don't like it here. This is not my home; this was my mother-in-law's home." I knew that Franklin's mother, Sara, had dominated that household. There was a moment's quiet, and I turned my gaze to the sky.

Eleanor was there to protect me, but I didn't know it at the time. I began to sob again, this time letting my tears flow in a catharsis and allowing her to comfort me. Her voice said, "Nothing can hurt you now. In the strength of these emotions you will find a change of heart and peace of mind." I felt the truth of her words all around me, with me, and through me. My life was changing and I welcomed the transformation, but I was having growing pains. Now her emotions were caressing and nurturing me instead of overwhelming me, and I could sense the boundlessness of her love and understanding. It was as if the tour I had asked for was only just beginning.

The next day in my room, when I was upset and praying for guidance, Eleanor's voice was with me again. I felt uncertain and afraid of the unknown life that lay ahead of me. Through a harmonious message, as from a mother to a son, the ending of one relationship was blossoming into the beginning of a new one. These were her words to me: "I'll help you learn love, my dear Richard. Trust me, I'm Eleanor Roosevelt and I will be strong for you and teach you. Today, I will hold you until you feel comfortable. . . . I love you, my dear."

As I lay there, my tears slowly subsided, and a wonderful glow of warmth traveled through my body. I felt more connected to God and spirit than I ever had before. It was something new: love.

This was just the beginning. Since then, Eleanor and I have spoken on a daily basis. I have become a medium, filled with God's white light and Eleanor's insight. Eleanor is just one loving soul in my life today who nourishes my self-esteem and harmony so that I can encourage others in need of support.

In essence, you could say that in one day God closed one door and opened another. I will never regret my change of heart.

Three years have passed since that day, and I have forgiven my former partner. We have grown into a new, more compassionate relationship. We are on paths of our own now, and growing in enlightenment. We have found common ground, a new kind of love, friendship.

# Stock Tip

## *Corinne Edwards*

He's been gone for over a year, but I can feel that Jules—we called him Julie—is still in this house. He even talks to me.

The other morning, for example, I heard him when I was in a sweat, doing my aerobics. You know how it gets when you're overextending your capacity? It's like being in an altered state of consciousness. There I was, exercising away, and all of a sudden I heard a voice in my head—so clearly—that said, "If you want to play, put in a buy order for IBM at 120. It will probably go through that to 118, but don't be a pig. As soon as you get it, put a sell in at 130. You'll pick up a little fast, safe money."

The voice added, "Buy five hundred shares of Standard Oil of Indiana at the market. Hold it. I'll let you know when to sell."

It was Julie!

Julie had been our stockbroker and had handled our finances. He was a great broker, but he never talked about his business. If I'd ask what the market did on any given day, he'd tell me, "Read the paper!"

So since he'd died, I'd been reading a lot of books on investing. I needed to find out what to do with money, so I'd been studying.

Intrigued with my stock tip from "the other side," I looked in the paper. IBM was at 152. I could not find Standard Oil of Indiana anywhere, so I called my new broker, Alice. (Though she had worked with Julie for thirty years, when I'd asked him which stockbroker to use in the unlikely event of his not being around, he'd told me, "No one. They'll all churn your money." But after he died, I remembered Alice. Julie had always disapproved of women in business, but he used to admit begrudgingly that Alice was pretty smart.)

I told Alice the story, and explained that I could not find Standard Oil of Indiana in the paper. She laughed weakly—I think the whole thing spooked her—and said that all the older brokers still referred to Amoco by its former name: Standard Oil of Indiana. We agreed that if anyone could communicate from the grave, it would be Julie.

I bought Amoco. Alice put in the order for IBM too, rather reluctantly. It seemed like a waste of time—120 was so far below the market. The rest is history. IBM did hit 118, and I did sell at 130. I made more than five thousand dollars!

It's funny, but having Julie around doesn't scare me at all. As a matter of fact, it's comforting to feel he's still taking care of me.

I just hope he comes back to tell me when to sell Amoco.

# A Gift from God

## Pamela McGee

My father's illness was lengthy and filled with a full range of emotions and lessons. Despite the deep love I had for my father, feelings of anger and resentment surfaced when it was apparent to me that he was slowly and methodically killing himself by overeating. How could he do this to himself? How could he do this to me? My pleas and suggestions of programs that would help him handle this disease fell on deaf ears as he became heavier. Health problems arose. My initial thought was that Dad was getting back at my mother for transitioning sixteen years earlier. Her final words to him were "Take care of yourself, and be there for the kids."

Dad lived in Salt Lake City, Utah, and I had established a wonderful life in Southern California with my husband and son. In the year prior to Dad's transition, he often asked me to be his caretaker. I lovingly declined, as I had no qualifications to offer in caring for a bedridden man weighing well over four hundred pounds and experiencing other medical problems. It was obvious that in-home professional care was the only reasonable course to take. Besides, a part of me did not want to remember him in this grotesque physical condition. Although I remained loving and compassionate and visited as often as possible, my feelings of anger were still alive and well.

Christmas that year was most difficult for me and my family. My son, then seven, experienced great pain at seeing his grandfather, whom he loved so dearly, deteriorate before his eyes. I sensed that this would be the last time we were to see Dad physically, and it was extremely tough to say good-bye.

On the evening of January twenty-fourth, during sleep, I experienced an unusually vivid dream. In the middle of a non-descript white room filled with light, I sat side by side with my father at a small café table. He looked twenty years younger. He was without pain. His mood was happy, loving, and jovial as we drank coffee together. We shared many happy memories and laughed heartily on several occasions.

As he finished his coffee, Dad turned to me and said, "I love you, and you know it is time for me to go."

"I know," I said. "Be sure to say hi to Mom for me." Peacefully he stood, turned, and slowly walked away, vanishing into the bright light. Harmony and ease overcame me, and I knew all was well and as it should be.

As I awoke, fear and panic overtook my entire body. My spiritual confidence was not as strong as it is today, and I didn't believe dreams held much significance. Even so, I wondered why the dream was there and what it meant. At that moment, the phone rang. It was my brother calling to inform me that Dad had taken his last breath and passed on. I told my brother about the wonderful visit with Dad in the dream, and that when the phone rang I knew it would be news of his passing.

In retrospect, the dream was a gift from God to fill my heart with love, forgiveness, and understanding. It was an opportunity to understand that we are always connected to the ones we love, and that their presence can be felt and seen on so many levels of reality; an opportunity to have compassion for a man in great pain; an opportunity to step aside from my selfish desires to keep him locked to the physical world when it was transition he truly needed; an opportunity to remember a beloved father in a way that reflected his true being.

On occasion, my father and I will get together in my dream state, and we have continued our loving, insightful, and positive visits. Thank you, God.

# An Angel Gets Her Wings

## *Barbara Horner*

A gentle tap on my shoulder awakened me from a deep sleep on the night my sister joined God's Army of Angels. I gently rose to greet whoever was there, but I couldn't see anyone or anything. I had the urge to write and turned on the lamp. After writing for a few moments, I asked myself: Could this really be her?

I didn't review what I'd written until the following day, when I was traveling to join the rest of our family to reminisce and celebrate my sister's life. Cruising along at thirty-four thousand feet, I looked out the window of the aircraft, again sensed her presence, and remembered the paper I had tucked into my handbag. Then I realized that my sister had dictated to me how she wanted her family and friends to remember her.

At the family residence, I could see her presence everywhere and decided to wait to share her remembrance. Soon I found myself at her computer, inputting the words. One of my sisters came into the room as I printed them out. One by one, family and friends joined me in that room to share this beautiful remembrance.

Later that night, my older sister and I lay awake, visiting, as we'd done so many times when we were younger. We finally drifted off to sleep. I was suddenly awakened by the chime of a single bell at the foot of my bed. I rose, looked around, saw no one, and snuggled back into my pillow. Then another chime . . . Could this again be her? And then a third chime. I raised myself on my pillow and said, "You must have gotten your wings." With those words and a very peaceful feeling, I went to sleep. I learned the next morning that my niece and a friend had had the same experience of bells ringing at the foot of their beds.

# Sign of Nature

## *Gerri Magee*

*We do not remember days*
*We remember moments*

The phone kept ringing. I was leaving to go to my mom's house and was calling to let them know I was coming. Finally, my youngest sister, Rene, answered.

"How's Mom?" I asked.

"She's gone" was the reply.

For a moment I thought she had been rushed to the hospital again, as she had been so many times this last year. "What do you mean, Rene?"

The reply was very emphatic. "She's *gone*, Gerri." I knew then that my mother had just passed away. I froze. Time stood still, my body and mind became numb, but somehow I was able to call my twin sister, Gloria, and let her know. I picked her up and we sat in silence, each of us deep in thought, as we drove to our mom's house in the pouring rain. Our sisters Dannie and Rene were phoning friends and relatives; otherwise the house was quiet.

Mom had been ill for over a year, and we had all spent many hours at the hospital and her bedside, caring for her and just being with her. We were told on two different occasions that she wouldn't make it through the night, yet her strength of character carried her through.

Two days before she passed, I had a strong urge to spend the night and be with her. I had not spent the night in her house since I'd left to get married several years before. She was in a hospital bed in the living room, and I spent most of the night lying awake on the couch, holding her hand and listening to her breathing. My sister Rene and I were the only ones at home at the time. The next morning, as I came downstairs, I noticed the priest and a woman from the church standing near my mother. I joined them, and we all held hands and prayed. Then the priest anointed Mom and asked Rene and me if we would like to give her the last rites. He told us that he didn't often make that offer, but he thought he'd present the opportunity to us. We both felt very honored to be allowed this special privilege, and it felt very sacred.

The priest was getting ready to leave when we heard a knock on the door. It was Aunt Sophia, my mother's last living sibling, her older sister. Aunt Sophia was also offered the privilege of giving my mother her last sacrament, and she did. I realized as this was happening that there are no accidents in the universe. This event had been divinely orchestrated. The oldest daughter, the youngest daughter, and the last living sibling were all there to share in this blessed, sacred ritual. I don't believe in coincidences; I believe we are all at the right place at the right time when things work out perfectly.

I returned again that same evening and saw that Mom was weaker and that her vital signs were slowing down.

The next day, I went into the office and tried to keep my mind on my work. All day long, the Frank Sinatra song "My Way" kept running through my head. The song stayed with me throughout the day, and I wondered if it was a sign. Was I being told something? Later that afternoon, my cohost and I did a live interview for our radio show with Linda Georgian, who had just written a book called *Communicating with the Dead*. She told us that she communicated with her deceased mother who had encouraged her to write the book. Again, this was by divine plan. The lyrics of "My Way" were a sign of events to come, and another sign was Linda Georgian speaking about her mother and how they communicated more since she had passed on. The messages were coming to me loud and clear. That evening, Mom made her transition.

My daughter, Theresa, and my son, Gary, flew in from Atlanta to be with me and to pay their respects. We all went through the motions for the next few days at the funeral home. We had brought a large photo album that included pictures of us as we were growing up and that contained pictures of Mom and all of us at different times during the past few years. Flowers arrived; friends and acquaintances came by, held our hands, and shared their stories of our mom. My brother, Billy, and his wife, Marion, came from Charlevoix. I was surprised to see so many people come who didn't even know my mom. They came to support me and the family. That's when I realized that the funeral was for the living, for those who were left behind, as well as to celebrate my mother's life.

The priest conducted a short service in the evening in which he wanted people to relate their stories about Mom. We each spoke of her and commented on things we remembered. We laughed and shed tears as we celebrated the rich life she had lived and what she had given to each of us.

The first day at the funeral home, I had mentally asked my mother to give me a sign that she was still with me. I peered in corners and looked around, but nothing appeared.

After the service, people broke into little groups to talk, and I found myself wandering over to be with my mother, to share a last bit of time together. I was appreciating her as I recalled memories through the years. I remembered how I had talked to her many months before, and how we had made our peace with each other and done a lot of healing. We had talked on a heart-to-heart, soul-to-soul level. I was so glad we had had that time before she became really sick and unable to communicate or understand anymore. We had had quality time together, and I was glad.

As I was appreciating Mom, I held her hand and caressed

her shoulder. My eyes welled up with tears of joy as I remembered how she liked to have her fingernails painted. I recalled that when I was a little girl, she would hold my hand in church as she prayed the rosary and as we would take walks. Her hands had strength. She worked in the earth and could grow anything. Everyone always commented on her green thumb.

After I finished reflecting on these special times, I turned around to see my sister Rene walking toward me with both arms outstretched. She held a huge maple leaf in her hands, and as she gave it to me, she said, "This is from Mom to you."

"What do you mean?" I asked. Then she told me that she'd been walking outside and noticed leaves all over the ground. One particular leaf had stood straight up on its end as she'd walked past. She'd thought how strange it was and had felt it calling to her to come back. So she'd gone back to this leaf and it had spoken to her, saying, "Take me to Gerri. This is from Mom." Rene then took that leaf and brought it to me and knew my mother had sent it as my sign. She was really around us. She had given me a gift, one that I will always treasure.

It's true that when we die, we shed our bodies, but our spirit lives on.

A year before, I had stopped by Mom's house with my camera to take pictures of the beautiful autumn leaves on her street. My mother and I had gathered leaves together in the front yard and enjoyed our time together. That's why she'd come back with that sign, that leaf. It proved to me beyond a shadow of a doubt that we do not die and that we can still be in touch with our loved ones. The spirit lives on!

By the way, Rene had never had communication with a leaf, a tree, or anything nonphysical before. Yet she was not shocked that this had happened to her. She believed, as I do, that my mother really communicated through this leaf.

I know my mom is only a heartbeat away.

# A Vision of Jesus

## Shawne Mitchell

It was April 1988. I was eight months pregnant with my second son. My baby was due to be born on or about May tenth, when Nostradamus had predicted a massive earthquake in Southern California. I was nervous that we would be in the hospital if and when the earthquake struck.

A few people I knew actually left Los Angeles and moved east. I felt that if the earthquake was actually going to happen, God would give me some kind of a sign to move away. In my thoughts and prayers, I often asked God to give me a sign. "What should I do?" I waited and waited . . . but no sign.

I was scheduled to go into Santa Monica Hospital for a C-section on May ninth. The days drifted by. My husband, J.D., and I had named our baby son-to-be Austin. I could feel him moving around in my belly and could hardly wait for him to be born.

Normally I don't pay attention to predictions of this sort, but I admit that I was pretty anxious at the thought of being trapped with my new baby in a high-rise hospital during an earthquake, cut off from J.D. and my other little boy, Travis.

As May drew near, I became more involved in the excitement of the impending birth. I could hardly wait! Yet deep in my heart, a tinge of anxiety continued to mar my sense of the joy surrounding the miracle of Austin's arrival.

Then, one night, I had the most extraordinary and glorious dream of my life.

I was standing in the first pew of Our Lady of the Snows Church in Sun Valley, Idaho. Standing next to me were my husband and Travis. To my right was Linda, a friend from my grade-school days who had died during our college years. The dream was so lucid that I remember wondering how she could be there.

We were the only ones in the church except for the transcendental being standing in front of the altar facing us. Jesus stood there, glowing, beaming at us, His arms open as if to enfold us in His light and love. Emanating and flowing from His entire body, head to toe, were brilliant colored streams of light. I was transfixed and in awe. I could feel Jesus' love and compassion like an invisible energy. It was as if we could tangibly touch and feel His loving energy enveloping us. I was breathless. As I looked upon His radiant face, He smiled at me and I could feel His grace flow into me.

That moment has been, and always will be, the most extraordinary and blessed moment of my life. I instantaneously knew that I didn't need to worry about anything, that I was doing okay. I was completely loved, and Jesus would always be that near to me. I would always be cared for . . . like the lilies of the field.

Weeping with joy and trembling from the energy and light and love that filled me, I awoke.

I went into labor on April twenty-eighth, and my beautiful son Austin came into the world. Today, Austin is ten years old. He is a constant reminder to me of Jesus' presence in my life and that whenever I want to, I can see Jesus in my mind's eye, radiantly smiling at me.

# 4

# OTHER DIMENSIONS AND MYSTICAL PHENOMENA

# The Ice Yogi

## Nancy Cooke de Herrera

MARCH 1962, INDIA

It was a sunny, springlike day as our old taxi rattled into the sacred Valley of the Saints. Our turbaned Sikh driver ignored all the rules of safe driving as he wheeled around ruts in the curving road that led through the forest.

I implored Tom to make him slow down. "It will be a miracle if we arrive in one piece," I cried.

"Isn't that what we're looking for?" was his laughing reply. I had joined two parapsychologists for a month in the Himalayas while they searched for physical and psychic phenomena that could be repeated under scientifically controlled conditions. Tom Slick, a wealthy oil man, had created and owned The Mind Science Foundation in San Antonio, Texas. Ranjit Ganguli was his assistant on this trip.

"I doubt it's your karma to be killed in Hardwar, the second holiest place in India," Tom said.

"What if it's the driver's karma to die in such a holy place?"

We'd been told about a yogi with extraordinary abilities who lived on top of a temple in Hardwar. Our mission on that particular day was to find him. I was skeptical; we had such vague notions as to his whereabouts.

Finally we arrived at the top of the stairs that led down to the Ganges, the spiritual river of India. Faded white stone temples of various sizes and shapes lined the ghats, where bodies wrapped in cloth were often laid out for burning. Hindus never bury their dead; they believe that fire purifies and releases the soul for its next trip through eternity. Therefore, the only cemeteries in India are for Moslems, Christians, and people of other religions.

After making numerous inquiries, Ranjit eventually led us to the abode of the yogi. After a scary climb, up crumbling, uneven stairs to the temple roof, we found a leathery, shriveled-up man wearing only a loincloth around his emaciated frame. There was no roof or canopy to shield him from the unrelenting sun. I was thankful for my wide-brimmed hat, which covered my blond hair and shaded my face.

The yogi looked at Tom and me, two pale-complexioned strangers, with disdain. Ranjit explained, "My reference to science has angered him. He says that scientists will destroy the world, that man has to learn control over himself before he can control the universe."

But Ranjit kept talking, and finally the yogi turned and studied Tom's mystical-looking gray eyes. Evidently he approved of what he saw, for he abruptly told Ranjit to bring him a glass of water from the river. He would demonstrate man's ability to control nature. In order to obtain the title "Yogi," one had to exhibit this power.

Ranjit soon returned, breathing heavily after climbing the temple steps. He gave the glass to the yogi, who then requested, through Ranjit's interpreting, that we each put a finger inside to verify that the glass was indeed filled with water. This we did, as he signaled Tom to put away his camera.

While we watched in silence, the yogi held the glass and chanted in Sanskrit. Then he moved the glass in our direction and invited us to put our fingers inside again. *The water had turned to ice!* We couldn't believe it. We were thunderstruck. The man was practically naked, he had no props, it was a hot day, and we were sure we had not been hypnotized.

The yogi told Ranjit, "Water is made up of so many molecules of hydrogen and oxygen. Ice is the same; all I have done is to change the characteristic of the water by altering the rate of vibration of the molecules. Now leave this place and learn union with God."

Later, in the noisy taxi, we debated what we had seen. We concluded that there was no scientific explanation for what we had just observed with our own eyes. Tom was a trained scientist, and I had majored in chemistry and other sciences while at Stanford University. We were scientifically oriented.

"That old boy certainly earned his title if he could pull off a feat like that!" Tom commented. "What a shame I couldn't use my movie camera."

"Someone would insist you'd faked it," I consoled him. But at the same time, I knew that we had just witnessed the impossible. We were slowly learning not to expect the usual in India.

# Let Nature Take Its Course

## *Anne Ford*

It was an auspicious beginning to a new life. The day my son was born, November 16, 1995, my day began before the sun rose. I was restless and couldn't sleep. I thought maybe my water had broken, but my husband, Michael, told me, "When your water breaks, you'll know it!"

I tried to fall back to sleep, but I couldn't. Even though my due date was still five weeks away, my instincts told me to get to the hospital. So after a large helping of blueberry pancakes, we took a leisurely drive to Presbyterian Hospital, where my doctor maintains his office. On the way, Michael picked out a place for us to have lunch on the way home. But there would be no lunch and no going home that day.

I had packed a few toiletries, some leggings, and a big shirt (just in case). We arrived at the hospital at about eleven a.m., and after a quick exam it was determined that my amniotic sac had indeed broken, but not in the usual way—I was experiencing a stalled labor, so my water was trickling slowly, not the standard gush. They told me I was not going home; Logan was on his way!

I spent the morning walking around, trying to speed up the pace of my labor. I visited my doctor's office and saw all the staff I had come to know during my pregnancy. I was about to be blessed with the most incredible labor experience, and I didn't have a clue. All I knew was that I felt as though I were in a state of grace, a feeling that I will never forget and that overwhelms me with the presence of God every time I remember that mystical day.

I sat on my bed in a nice birthing room, the lights dimmed, contemplating how I would ever get through labor. You see, that evening I was supposed to be learning about breathing in my Lamaze class! I called my instructor, Glenda, to tell her I would not be in class that evening, and I asked her to give me a crash course over the phone, like right *now*! I really felt as if I might be in a little bit of trouble on this one, but fortunately my nurse, Elizabeth, was thirty-five weeks pregnant and had been through this before. She led me through the whole thing beautifully. It was a case of monkey see, monkey do, and it worked! But I'm getting a little ahead of myself here.

By two p.m. I was still just having a few cramps, so the doctor on duty (wouldn't you know it, it was my doctor's day off) told the nurse, in my presence, that they were going to put me on pitocin at three o'clock. I had done my reading and knew that pitocin was an inducing agent. It was at that moment that I recalled a day nearly five months earlier. . . .

It was a Sunday in July, and my fourteen-year-old step-daughter, Ashley, had asked me to take her to a psychic fair in Dallas. We checked out all the booths and laughed and joked over some of the strange things we saw. Ashley wanted to get her tarot read, so first we hung out and listened as other people had their readings done. We were both attracted to one particular reader, a woman named Suzann Osborne, who had an Australian accent and wonderful energy. There was something very special about her. Before Ashley's reading, we asked Suzann about the unusual-looking tarot cards she was using. She explained to us that they were aboriginal tarot cards, which encompassed the biomolecular level. The cards were so beautiful and complex that we could not take our eyes off them. Suzann further told us how, as a child, she'd been taught this wonderful art by the shamans of her country.

What she revealed was astounding. First she read Ashley's cards, and the things she revealed were both personal and verifiable! Before Ashley's reading I had been somewhat hesitant, but now I decided I would like to participate as well. What came up first in my reading were unusual circumstances and powerful emotions that I had experienced long ago, in childhood. Then she spoke of a male child who would soon be born. Suzann said that this would be his first visit to earth, but that he and I had been together before. She also said that in this life he would be instrumental in the convergence of spirituality with the financial world, and that he was a very evolved soul with a lot to teach the universe. Then she told me that he would be delivered quite early and that under no circumstances should his birth be induced. "This child will not be pushed."

I thought this odd, because inducement is usually considered only when a baby is late, and she had said he would be early. Although I was confused, I sensed she had offered important information. Little did I know at the time how I would remember and heed her advice. . . .

When the doctor and nurse had gone, I looked at Michael in disbelief. I told him that I wasn't taking the pitocin. He knew there was no changing my mind. Fearing that they would move me from the maternity ward to the psychiatric ward, Michael suggested that I not reveal my reason for rejecting the doctor's advice. I stood my ground, vowed not to use pitocin, and called my girlfriends between slight contractions.

Soon after, the nurse came in to give me the pitocin. I told her I was not taking the drug—that I was forty-one years old and had gotten pregnant naturally, that I'd had an uneventful and wonderful pregnancy, and that when my baby was ready he would make his move. I had had amniocentesis, so I knew he was normal and healthy (the test had also confirmed that the baby was male). The nurse was a little disconcerted and said that she would have to speak with the doctor. The doctor came in and put great pressure on me to change my mind. Finally, she agreed to wait until six o'clock before using the pitocin.

Hey, it just didn't make sense to me: I wasn't dilated, the baby hadn't dropped yet, and Suzann Osborne, my new mystical friend, had told me, "This child will not be pushed."

I decided to meditate, so I went into level and talked to my son. I said, "Look, sweetie, you've got to help me out here. We have to do this thing together. You've got to drop down into position, and I've got to get these contractions going, or they are going to put a firecracker up your butt and all hell is going to break loose!"

I immediately felt him start to drop . . . it was the most amazing sensation to feel him lowering, getting ready for his birth. I was still deep in meditation, so I spoke to my body. I imagined the birth canal expanding and flowering, beckoning Logan to follow his path out into the world. I felt the power of nature within me.

Thirty minutes later, at six p.m., I was in labor. The monitor showed definite contractions, and when they checked for dilation I was at three centimeters. The doctor stopped harping on pitocin, and I continued to dilate . . . *fast*. I went from three to eight centimeters in twenty minutes. I guess my body had taken the instruction well. I still had not taken anything for pain; I think I was so high from the experience that I was producing my own painkiller. At eight p.m., I had an epidural to take the edge off and was given a little oxygen for a pick-me-up. (The oxygen was great, because while I was pushing I could make all the goofy faces I wanted under the face mask.) Even though Logan weighed only five pounds and was five weeks early, his heartbeat never wavered for a minute during the entire labor. During the final push, he literally flew out, and the doctor almost didn't catch him.

Logan was put in intensive care for observation. After two days he was released, and a day later he came home. Every day he has been on earth has been a blessing for those who have been in his presence.

# A Small Miracle

## Barbara Tse Tyler

My parents came to this country as immigrants in 1961, my father from China and my mother from Germany. They had met in England and were married on my mother's arrival in America. Both of them had struggled through the wars of the first half of the twentieth century, and the struggle had affected them in many ways, even thousands of miles away from their own lands. They came here with the same dreams as other young people. They wanted to start over, and when they'd left home they'd also left their religions behind. I think my parents hoped their children would find their own way to God, but somehow my brothers and I never did. Religion was not an issue in our household while we were growing up.

After spending three years in the Marines, marrying very young, having four children, and struggling for years to find happiness in myself, I finally came to inner peace. But I always felt curiosity and confusion about what might be out there in the universe, be it God or some other kind of higher force. Deep down, I had always believed that we are alone on this planet, that bad things happen randomly, destroying people's lives. I believed that we all had to do our best to be good, honest people and to keep a positive attitude. I've always relied heavily on my own strength, and it has kept me going even through the most difficult times, but I've always been deeply saddened by loneliness.

I had been blessed with a wonderful family and the best friends a person could want, but I felt insecure without a faith of some kind. I didn't think I had a right to pray, because I was moved to pray only when something really horrible was happening. But new light has been shed on my thoughts. Recently, while thinking out loud to my husband, Ron, I told him about my desire to pray, how it seemed unnatural for me, and how I felt it was wrong to pray just because I had a problem.

Ron was raised as a Catholic, but over the years he'd distanced himself from the Church. He told me that he believed God is out there everywhere. "He's in your heart and thoughts," he said to me, adding that he believed you didn't have to pray at all to be heard. Ron thought I should pray whenever and however I chose.

I didn't really give the conversation much thought afterward—at least, not until I went to my friend Judy's house one night for dinner. Judy, my friend Cathy, and I had a strange conversation with Judy's mother, Marietta. Marietta spoke about receiving gifts from the universe. The way she talked of things happening to people when they were ready and open to them, I honestly thought she was a little nutty. She told us some of the occurrences over the years that had secured her belief that she wasn't alone on this earth. I did not take what she said seriously.

But the next day, something strange, profound, and powerful happened to me. My three-year-old daughter, Kayla, and I were sitting in the kitchen after the older children had gone off to school, just like we do every morning. I was reading the paper, and she was happily playing with her magnetic alphabet letters on the refrigerator. After working for a while, she put a few letters together on the fridge. Suddenly she asked me, "What that say?"

I looked up from my paper, not expecting to read letters that spelled anything that even resembled a word. To my surprise she had formed the word *pray*.

I was shocked and in disbelief. At first, I tried to dismiss it as a coincidence or a fluke, but the more I tried to disregard it, the more it occupied me. How could a child who cannot spell or read just randomly throw together those four letters, and in the correct order? Wouldn't she have a better chance of winning the lottery? Could it have been a gift from God? Could it be His way of letting me know that He wants me to pray and feel close to him?

My whole view on life has changed. I truly accept the idea that my family and I are not alone in this world. It's a gift that I will now be able to give to my children, a gift of faith. Over the years I'd labored over how to raise my children, and I knew that not having a belief in something greater watching over me meant that I was missing something crucial, but I could not teach my children what I didn't believe to be true. I'd struggled with the issue, but then I found an answer.

I tried to let go of the refrigerator incident, but I found myself going back again and again in my mind to the ordinary magnets that spelled that simple word. Today I feel God's presence. I have chosen to embrace Him and the idea that a greater being is in me and all around me. I've made the decision to share this belief with my children. And I am filled with thanks. I am grateful for the miracle that happened to me and my little girl in our kitchen, on just an ordinary day.

# The Question of the Faery Realm

*Cyndi Dale*

Now, don't let me mislead you. During several years of my impressionable youth, I had devoured my share of fairy stories, inhaling the Red, Pink Olive, and every other color of Fairy Book in the local library. I had since relegated such tales to some semiliterary division of "secular humanism," a division of "the occult." And so, I was quite unprepared for my first journey to Wales.

Having saved pocket change and scrimped on groceries for well over a year, I had stowed away enough money to maneuver a trip to the British Isles. I was eager. I was scared. After researching ancient and contemporary myths about various "sacred sites" in England and Wales, my friend Cat and I set off.

If any of you have chanced driving on the left side of the road, you might say that our first encounter with the realm of the miraculous was surviving my driving. Losing only a hubcap—and that pulling out of the rental place—our car became a magic carpet. Salisbury Cathedral, Stonehenge, Glastonbury Abbey, Land's End, the Men-an-tol, Merlin's Cave . . . ancient places of mystery, we flew to them all. Oh, we read the legends . . . fairies, sprites, earth beings and druids. The stories were interesting, sometimes amusing. But, one might say, we laughed in the face of destiny.

The first crack in the siding occurred at dusk outside of Bettws y Coed, a resort town in Wales. According to our map, and directions we'd received in the last town, we were about five minutes away. We needed only to go straight through to the next stop sign. In jest, I suggested that if the faery folk were going to show themselves, this would be the time.

We spotted the stop sign. It had a funny black cloverleaf

mark on it. Even English schoolchildren pull pranks, I mused. Briefly noting that the intersecting street was a farm road, stretching in infinite lines away from us, we proceeded—and were immediately smothered in the thickest blanket of pea-soup fog imaginable.

We drove for what seemed hours—and found ourselves staring at the same stop sign. We laughed. We must have taken a wrong turn. Hard to imagine, as the road leading into town was *this* road, but then again . . .

Now there was no fog, and so we searched for housing on either side. There wasn't any. There were no turns in the road, no side roads, and there was no town. Again, we pulled up to the same stop sign.

This cycle continued for two hours. Cat finally said, "In the name of the blessed Lord, we'd like a reprieve!"

Within five minutes, we'd arrived at Bettws y Coed. Upon relating our story to the innkeeper, we were assured that we must have just been imagining our troubles; there were no converging, intersecting, or "doubling-back" roads.

Despite our confusion, we slept well, awakening to a soft, ever-lifting cloud of fog, which evaporated as we headed out of Bettws y Coed at noon. Our goal that day was a six-hour drive to Holyhead, after visiting other sites. Holyhead was said to be the home of the druids, the ancient priesthood killed by marauders and Christians. After a couple of hours, we began to look for the bridge, the only way onto the island from the road we'd taken. I began to spot water and small houses dotting the landscape. The smell of salt pervaded the car. I spotted a town marker.

"Cat," I said, my stomach beginning to flip over. "Where is . . . ?" and I mumbled the consonant-only name on the sign.

She looked at the map, then looked at me. "You're not going to believe this," she began. "But it's on the end of Holyhead— the *other* end." Sure enough, within a few minutes, we were at the far end of Holyhead. Hours ahead of schedule. Having traversed no bridge.

We both agreed to just get out of there. So we drove in the

opposite direction—four hours—to find ourselves facing a long, giant wooden bridge.

By early evening, shaken and confused, we were safe within Castletown, a city built within castle walls. "Let's walk around," I suggested, and Cat agreed. Before we left our car in a parking ramp, she rather nervously but jokingly spoke aloud: "Whatever spirits are making fools of us, we would like a sign of your presence."

One hour later, we returned to the car, having immensely enjoyed a full glass of a different sort of spirits. As I fired up the car, we shrieked. The lights began blinking on and off; the windshield wipers frantically waved; and the radio was emitting inhuman voices in punctuated verses. We could make out the words "Always here."

Now, I would like to say that it all ended there, but that night, as I slept, I heard a voice: "You will be inflicted with a sign of your doubt, that will clear only upon belief."

I awoke to find that during the night I had grown a three-inch cyst on my arm. I cried. I didn't understand any of this. Yet there seemed to be nothing to do about it, so we kept going, this time to a coastal town.

In that town there was a castle, at the center of which was a small chapel containing a wooden cross. As Cat wandered, I sat down and prayed. I felt a flush of warmth and found, to my surprise, that the cyst had completely disappeared. I called Cat over and showed her. Then, together, we asked to be released from the learning we were on. When we emerged from the chapel, we stared up into the arc of an overwhelming Crayola-colored rainbow.

The rest of our journey continued as planned. For years, we didn't talk about our days with the fairies, although we both kept on our desks a photo of that rainbow.

# Flying

## *Scott F. Chesney*

On December 28, 1985, my life in physical form changed, and as a result, my spiritual journey began. At the age of fifteen, a very rare arterial-venus malfunction (AVM) left me paralyzed from the waist down. Like all fifteen-year-olds, I was just getting acquainted with my body, observing its changes, judging its quality, and hoping for the best as I entered into early stages of manhood. And then, when I awoke one morning, three days after Christmas, I was greeted by a numb left toe. It was a similar feeling to the experience you have when your foot falls asleep, like pins and needles. Within forty-eight hours, that numbness had climbed up both legs and paralyzed me, detaching me from the lower half of my body.

As a teenager, I never could understand the philosophy that we are "much more than our physical bodies." Though my heart and mind were still functioning, communication with my legs had been disrupted. My dreams of playing college basketball, running along the shoreline, and possibly fathering my own children were no longer within my grasp. All because I had the belief that I was just my physical body. Wow, was I wrong!

In March 1997, I began a journey around the world to research alternative forms of medicine as they relate to paralysis. My journey took me to sixteen different countries, and I met with incredible teachers like Deepak Chopra, Tony Robbins, Stuart Wilde, Wayne Dyer, and Leonard Laskow. Each of these individuals, along with many other angels, helped me come to the conclusion that I am so much more than just my physical body. Tony Robbins assisted me in walking on my hands across a forty-foot path of burning hot coals during one of his firewalks. That was certainly an example of mind over matter! It was the first experience in which I truly became one with fear and embraced its uncertainty. But I knew at the time that it was only one of many more magical experiences to come.

One year after I had officially begun my journey, I found myself back in Goa, a beautiful getaway on the west coast of India, where Deepak Chopra was conducting his "Seduction of Spirit" seminar. I had already participated in it the year before but felt I needed to take part again. The first time around, I had needed to have the experience of being "in a fight with myself." Now I was anxious to reap the benefits by revisiting the course, and it made all the difference.

During this particular seminar, about four hours a day were dedicated to primordial sound meditation. A number of us who had attended the seminar the year before, so Deepak thought it would be appropriate to divide us from the rest of the attendees and teach some advanced meditation techniques. These would enhance our chances of levitating. Yes, levitating!

On March 6, 1998, the second-to-last day of the eight-day seminar, I was sitting on the ground, Indian-style, meditating with the rest of the group, silently repeating my mantra and sutras, when the magic began. In the first fifteen minutes of the hourlong meditation, I began to be filled with an overwhelming sadness. Tears soaked my eyes and drenched my entire face. Ten minutes later, the tears of sadness turned into tears of joy, and a resurgence of energy began to fill my body. Rather than question what all those emotions meant, I simply surrendered and embraced the uncertainty, and knew that all was well. Suddenly, I felt my body begin to tremble. Now, not only had I surrendered control, but the most intense feeling of helplessness that I had ever experienced evolved.

At the height of surrender, a jolt, which appeared to come up from the ground into my tailbone, lifted me off the ground about five inches and landed me in exactly the same spot. Deepak, who was observing, told me what had happened. Minutes later, the urge to hop overcame me once again, and I landed about a foot away from where I had originally been positioned. Never before had I felt that Spirit was so present. As intense a moment as this was, a very peaceful and soothing state had settled in my physical and emotional bodies.

At the conclusion of the meditation, Deepak asked me to share my experience with the rest of the group, who were somewhat stunned by this phenomenon. He also told us that there are three stages of levitation: hopping, which I experienced, hovering, and flying. Many who approached me afterward thanked me for sharing because they had been thinking that the call to levitate would be felt in their legs.

Today I am a true believer, convinced beyond a shadow of a doubt that we are much more than our physical bodies, and I know anything is possible. For I am paralyzed, yet I levitated! Now I have every intention of reaching each of the stages of levitation, and when Spirit calls, I plan on walking again very soon!

# Can You See the Light of God— Even If You're Blind?

## *Eric Troup*

I heard about Eckankar from my fiancée, Michelle. One day she decided to try a spiritual exercise. I felt strange singing the ancient name for God, HU, out loud. So I just sat listening. Then she went into silent contemplation.

One part of the ECK teachings I puzzled over was how to see the Light of God. I have been blind all my life, with no concept of light.

If I saw the inner Light, I probably wouldn't even realize it. If you've never seen a thing, you don't know what to look for.

Some very light American Indian music played softly in the background. Having nothing better to do, I tried to imagine something in my Spiritual Eye that matched the music.

I feel things in my imagination more than see them. The music felt like a wolf running. I had some idea what this might feel like, because I'm friendly with the part-wolf dog that lives next door to me. So in my imagination, I ran with my dog friend.

All of a sudden I thought I could jump, as Soul, into a wolf's body. I don't know where the notion came from. But the next thing I knew, I was a wolf, running and running.

And I could see!

It was a complete shock. I was running through the forest, a maze of branches and undergrowth. Then I spied a cave and ran inside. A round, light-reflecting crystal hung from the ceiling. I leapt up to grab the crystal and put it in my mouth. After a few tries, I was successful.

Instinctively, I ran outside to a tree in the forest, where I saw Wah Z (the spiritual name for the leader of Eckankar, Harold Klemp).

I dropped the crystal and said telepathically, "I think this is yours."

He replied, "No, it's yours. It is your awareness of God. What are you going to do with it?"

The crystal was about the size of a fist. It was blue. I had never seen the color blue before, but somehow I knew that this was blue! The crystal was a solid form of light—the Light of God. So, as the wolf, I swallowed it. Then I had my own inner light!

Wah Z said, "You have always had your own light, and you have HU. The howl of the wolf is like the HU."

I came out of my vision and was dumbfounded. I've always been a dog lover, so what Wah Z had said made singing HU even more interesting and special for me.

After Michelle finished her silent contemplation, I asked if we could sing HU together. As soon as we began, the most amazing thing happened! The dog next door—who is always silent unless sirens are blaring—gave a long howl.

Soul to Soul, he and Divine Spirit were telling me: Your experience is real. The Light and Sound are a part of you always.

# "Who Did?"

## Sam Crespi

We'd just finished dinner and adjourned to the high-ceilinged salon of an old palace in the center of Rome. Our host, an Italian prince whose heritage included high church dignitaries and senators and more than one castle, was giving us a guided tour of his collection of paintings and *objets* from the Far East. He had spent six months of each of the last twenty years in Laos or Thailand or Cambodia, and his treasures were beautiful; some, I thought, were surely priceless.

Along one wall was a large built-in glass case that was softly lit. He took a key from a desk drawer and unlocked the doors so that we could see more closely what was inside. I heard him talking to my husband, but as I was fixated on a small clear glass vial on the shelf in front of me, I was unaware of what he was saying. The vial contained a colorless liquid in which sat two tiny carved figures, one bright orange and female, the other black and male. They were in a traditional tantric position of lovemaking.

Just as I reached to pick up the vial, our host yelled, "No!

Don't do that! The last woman who touched that bottle became pregnant almost immediately!"

Stunned, I listened as he explained that the vial came from
Thailand. "The monks there pray and meditate while they carve
the figures, fill the bottle with oil, and tamp it with a cork. If a
woman wishes to become pregnant, she gives the temple an
offering in exchange for the bottle. When she makes love, she
rubs the oil on herself. It rarely fails."

My husband and I had recently decided that we were ready
to have a child, and with our friend's permission, I took the
bottle home with me that night. To my great surprise, however, my mate told me he didn't want to use it. Unable to tell
me why, he remained adamant. And so, with a sigh, I left the
vial standing upright next to the bed, still tightly corked.

We made love that night, but without the oil.

The next morning, when I awakened, the bottle was still
standing upright next to the bed, but the liquid was gone and
the cork was still in place!

Two weeks later, we left for South America on a cargo ship.
While at sea, the Italian sailors began to tease me, saying I had
that pregnant look in my eyes. It turned out that they were right,
and we called to tell my husband's parents the good news.

A few days later, my mother-in-law was at a gathering
where she ran into the friend who'd given us the vial. After
she told him the news, he leaped up and yelled, "I did it! It's
all my fault!"

It was a stunning experience for her, and the story has remained legendary in the family. I've always felt it was a most
appropriate beginning for the very special daughter we had
nine months later

# A Question Answered

*Celeste Huttes*

We are not always aware of the impact we have on the lives of others. One February night a couple of years ago, I witnessed a serious car accident. As I drove toward the scene of the crash, my attention was drawn to a young girl who bolted from the truck that had been hit and ran to the side of the road. I was concerned about her, thinking she was in shock and could be injured, so I pulled my car off the road and went to her.

The girl was extremely upset and in some pain, although she was able to move. As it turned out, she was also five months pregnant. I did my best to comfort her, but there was frustratingly little I could do to help. I stayed until the ambulance came, gave my statement to the police, and went home in a daze.

I had recently finished reading *The Celestine Prophecy*, which teaches us that there are no coincidences in life and that everything happens for a reason. I found this hard to believe. On my way to work the next morning, I spoke to God: "Okay. If it's true that everything happens for a reason, then please tell me for what conceivable reason I was there when that horrible accident took place?"

I received a clear—and prompt—answer to my prayer that very evening, when I received an unexpected phone call. It was the mother of the young girl I had assisted. She thanked me and said that it was as if I had been a mother for her daughter when she couldn't be. "God bless you!" she said. I felt a sense of unity with this unknown woman.

Later, I received a thank-you card from the daughter, who wrote, in part, "You will never know what it meant for you to be with me."

I thank God for answering my question in such a beautiful, comforting, and—for me—unmistakable way. In this way I learned that even simple gestures made from the heart can make more of a difference than one ever knows.

# My Magical New Name

## *Arielle Ford*

For as long as I could remember, I had always wanted a different name. My given name was Linda, and it seemed that every other little girl of my generation was also a Linda. In truth, I just didn't feel like a Linda. I always felt I deserved a much more exotic name. For a time in junior high school I tried out the name Morgana, but it never stuck. When I attended a special six-month college program in London, my classmates nicknamed me Sri Hata, after my favorite Indian restaurant, and called me Miss Sri. But by the time I returned home to the University of Florida, I was Linda Ford again. In fact, I was one of *eleven* Linda Fords at U of F!

When I was born, my name was Linda Barbara Fishbein. When I was six months old, my parents, for a variety of reasons, changed our last name to Ford. Linda Barbara Ford was my name for close to forty years. Then, on September 12, 1994, I had an epiphany. I was sitting in an auditorium listening to Marlo Morgan discuss her best-selling book *Mutant Message Down Under*. She described how the Australian aborigines give babies a name at birth, but that when children reach the age of four, they can choose a new name. And if that isn't good enough, they can rename themselves at will throughout their lives, so that they always have a name appropriate for who they feel themselves to be. At that moment, sitting there, I just *knew* it was time for me to find a new name.

As I thought about all of the possible names I could choose, I found myself drawn to the name Sydney. It sounded very sophisticated and sexy to me. I called my sister to see what she thought, and all she could say was "Ugh! I'll never be able to call you Sydney. It makes me think of that awful boy named Sidney in kindergarten who always tortured me!"

My next choice was Zoe—so unique and exotic, I thought. My sister didn't like Zoe much better than Sydney. Then she suggested that we involve our entire family in selecting my new name. She reasoned that they would be much more likely to adapt to a new name if they were part of the selection process.

As it turned out, our entire family was planning to gather in San Diego the following week. They would be arriving from Florida, New York, and Texas. Finally, when we were all in the same room, I announced my plan to change my name and asked for their assistance. I tried out Sydney, and everyone had the same reaction my sister had had. Then I tried out Zoe. My father said that there was no possible way he could ever have a daughter named Zoe. Finally, my stepmother said, "How about Ariel, like the Little Mermaid? You love swimming with dolphins and playing underwater!"

Well, we spent the next hour discussing the pros and cons of my becoming Ariel. I did like the name, but I wasn't sure I wanted a name that was so closely associated with a cartoon character. After a while I grew tired of being the center of attention and wanted to end the debate about my new name. I had an idea. Sitting in my lap was a book called *20,001 Baby Names*. I announced to my family that I was going to close my eyes, open the book, and randomly point to a name. Whatever name I pointed to, even if it was Ralph, would be my new name.

I closed my eyes, flipped open the book, and quickly pointed to a name. An instant later I opened my eyes. Before I could even register what had happened, my sister shrieked, "I can't believe it! Out of twenty thousand names, she's pointing to Ariel!"

Sure enough, the index finger of my right hand was smack in the middle of a description of the meaning of the name Ariel. Well, that settled it for everyone. My new name was to be Ariel.

A few days later, when the excitement died down, I decided to call a friend who studied numerology. I told her that I wanted my new name to be a "six," and that in order to be a "six" I would be willing to create a new middle name. Years before I had seen a professional numerologist who had told me that the name Linda Barbara Ford was very powerful numerologically, and that I had some of the most powerful combinations of numbers he had ever seen. I now wanted to be a "six," because that is the number of love and intimacy. I was not interested in having an overabundance of power. All that power was great for my career, but it wasn't doing much for my love life.

We played around with the spelling of my new name, and when we spelled it Arielle instead of Ariel and added Ford to it, I was then a "six." How perfectly easy! I would finally have a name that fit me and would have a numerological vibration that felt right. A few days later, I found out something more: the name Linda Barbara Fishbein was also a "six." Without realizing, I had returned to the vibration of my original name.

People often ask me what changes happened after I legally changed my name. I just tell them that *everything* changed. My sister claims that soon after I changed my name I began pulling practical jokes on her and showing a sense of humor that Linda had never had. My income just about tripled within months. I finally met my soul mate, and we were married last summer. By the way, I didn't take his last name. I've been through enough name changes for one lifetime!

# Receiving Is Believing

*Rik Cooke*

BOMBAY, INDIA, 1970

What a luxury for my mother, Nancy Cooke de Herrera, and me to be the guests of Sir Homi Mody and his wife, Lady Jeroo, in their beautiful home on Carmichael Road. It was the most posh address in Bombay. As the first governor of the state of Maharashtra, Sir Homi was one of the few Indian citizens knighted by the British. We were old friends of their middle son, Piloo, who was a much admired member of parliament.

The Modys are Parsees, whose ancestors were descendants of the Persians who originally settled in India. As Zoroastrians, they worship the god Ahura Mazda. Many Parsee families live in Bombay, where they have been highly successful. There is an old saying: "There is no such thing as a poor Parsee."

It was early afternoon, and we were sitting on the terrace, where I was having my fortune told by a woman who read and analyzed shadows. This was the scene that Kali, the Modys' youngest son, walked in on. "Oh, I see Mother has her favorite seer telling you all about your future," he said. "If you are interested, I'll invite an incredible woman to come to the house tomorrow night when you bring your friends for dinner. She is from a nearby village and has extraordinary abilities."

We indicated that our friends would be thrilled, so Kali immediately went into action. With his long, sloping, upturned nose, he was known as the Indian Bob Hope, and he had the same outgoing personality.

We were a group of about fifteen friends traveling around India for a month. For a special treat, Kali and Nina, his American wife, had invited us for a typical Parsee dinner, a meal impossible to experience in a restaurant. After stuffing ourselves with one exotic dish after another, including red-hot Goa curry, we joined our hosts on their penthouse terrace. It was there that we were introduced to the village woman, Lakshmi, who sat quietly in the balmy night awaiting us. She must have been about fifty, and had partly grayed hair and a small frame. She offered the traditional *"Namaste"* with her palms held together, as she gently nodded.

Kali encouraged us to ask questions, which we did while he translated. Nothing very interesting came from this. One person even asked if the Dodgers or the Giants would win the Pennant! Then Kali announced that Lakshmi wanted to give each of us a personal blessing. "As she comes to you, hold your hands together to receive the *vibuthi* she manifests. This is a holy powder that reportedly has healing qualities."

I was the first to extend my hands. Lakshmi smiled at me, chanted a few words in Sanskrit, and then held one hand about six inches above mine. From her outstretched palm, fine red powder flowed into mine! We all gasped in wonderment.

One friend wanted to touch the powder, but Nina handed me a paper and said, "Each of you will receive your own *vibuthi*. Put it in the envelope and save it for when you might need it. It's the same powder that saints touch to your forehead when they bless you."

Slowly, Lakshmi repeated this process with each of our group. We tried to detect anything hidden on her body, but we could see nothing. One of her shoulders was covered by her sari, but the slim brown arm she held out was bare from her short-sleeved *choli* down to her wrist. There was no way she could have hid a container of any kind. Observing our amazement, Kali stated, "I've seen her do this with a hundred people. She refuses to take any money for this demonstration. She considers this ability a gift from Brahma, and would never commercialize it."

Later, as we departed, expressing profuse thanks, each of us clutched a precious envelope. It was an evening that none of us would ever forget.

# Bearing the Wounds

## *LaJeanne Doucet*

My grandmother always said that one of her grandchildren was spiritual. I tell my own children that we were touched by an angel. I've always had something unusual happening in my life. I thought everyone did—and in truth, everyone does, if they only open their hearts to realize it. When I recognize a blessing in my life, I try to use it to help others. But when the stigmata started, I didn't know that they were a blessing.

When I first had these stigmata experiences, I wasn't sure what was happening. In early April 1996, I woke up one morning, turned on the bedside lamp, looked at my left hand, and saw a small hole in the center of my palm with a slow stream of blood trickling out of it. The pain was negligible, nothing more than a tingle. Three days later, the hole was gone, with no trace that it had ever been there—no scarring, no bruise, no scab.

The next year, three days after Easter, I felt light tingling pains in both my palms. I was more prepared for the experience this time. The pain was more intense than the previous year, but without blood this time. My left palm hurt more severely than my right. It felt as if someone were drilling a sharp metal object into my hand. I stayed in my bedroom for several hours after the pain began. I meditated and rubbed my hand, and fell into a trancelike state in which my mind reached a tranquil condition. During this episode, I realized that the pain always occurred during the Easter season. My husband said that I was feeling the stigmata, the wounds of Christ, and that this was a more common experience than most people realize.

At the time, I didn't even know what stigmata were. Shortly after this episode, Spirit led me to watch a program on television about stigmatics through the centuries, people with much more severe cases than mine. This program was an eye-opener for me; I no longer felt alone in the experience.

In 1998, I was waiting for the day to come. As in the previous years, the pains arrived during the Easter season. As Holy Week approached, I began experiencing light-headedness, and would slip very easily into trances. During one of these trances, Spirit revealed to me that I should wear white during Holy Week, so I dressed in white cotton dresses from Palm Sunday until after Easter. The pain in my hands returned, but I felt it most acutely in my feet, especially my left foot. I'm not sure why my left side attracts the pain, but there must be some significance to it. For the first time, I also felt a dull ache in the left side of my torso, but again, there was no bleeding this year. My husband rubbed my feet to help me through the pain.

Although my case of stigmata has not been especially severe, the pain has become more acute each year, and the symptoms are spreading to the different parts of my body corresponding to the parts of the Nazarene's body that were pierced. Now I know enough just to feel the pain, listen to the silence, and pray. Through study of the phenomenon, I have learned that the touch of stigmatics can be healing and a blessing to the recipients of the touch. Now I try to touch those around me as much as possible in order to pass on the blessing. However, I don't reveal why I'm laying on hands. I don't tell, because what I'm doing is a secret blessing for those who receive my touch, a secret between the Universe and me.

# The Immortals

## Michael Peter Langevin

In my youth, I had a mystical encounter that changed my view of reality forever. My friend Rick knew a guy named Samuel, who was very spiritual. He lived alone and prayed, doing yoga and meditation all day, most days, and we visited him on occasion to catch up on the latest spiritual news and ask about shortcuts to enlightenment.

On one such visit, we found Samuel waiting for us, overflowing with excitement. He told us he had met an amazing person, and believed that she was one of a group of immortals who live quietly, almost in hiding, on Earth and control humanity's destiny. This woman had first appeared in Samuel's dreams and given him clear instructions to perform specific yoga practices. When he did the instructed moves with vocal tones, he entered an altered state of consciousness in which he saw the woman again in astral form.

After a few days of astral instruction, Samuel had radically changed his diet and stopped getting tired or feeling any need to sleep. The woman told Samuel that when Rick and I visited that Friday, we were to drive to an address thirty-five miles away.

Rick and I were skeptical but curious, so off we went. After getting lost and driving in circles, we were surprised when we actually found the address, a cottage on a dirt road. We knocked on the door, and a beautiful elderly woman answered. She greeted us by name and said, "I am Ravenwood. You shall share the night with me and then not see me again until you are an elder. Each of you has an important role to play in the unfolding of a specific future for the planet Earth. You agreed to this before you were born into this life. I have been instructed to ensure that you are prepared to perform the right actions at the exact right times, or a glorious destiny for Earth will be missed."

I was very doubtful. I wanted to believe her, yet I was young, still in college, and the situation was too much like a weird movie. I was afraid of falling for a scam, being brain-washed, or arriving at some other negative outcome, but as she talked I felt something like a refreshing spiritual mist fall over me. And as that happened, I felt my fears transform. A heightened awareness entered my mind, as if I were more and better than I had ever been. My fears gave way to optimism and the joy of being chosen. I was inspired by the idea that I was a person born to change the future of the whole planet.

Ravenwood then made a tea that she said would raise our vision to include many levels of perception. Upon drinking the strange-tasting brew, I felt as if I had been given the elixir of life. My body tingled, my spirit soared, my mind raced. At first the feeling was just wonderful, then it intensified until it was nearly overwhelming.

Ravenwood spoke to us about a small group of physical be-ings who have achieved a heightened spiritual awareness, of how they find one another and share knowledge and spiritual insights. Together they plan the best actions to help shepherd the Earth and all who live on it through the best possible evo-lutionary course.

Soon I lost my ability to focus, as if I had taken a powerful hallucinogenic. What was in that tea? I wondered. Raven-wood's words took on shapes and beautiful scents. I began to watch them dance, and smelled their meanings. I was in-trigued by her exotic way of using words as tools. I felt that she was using her words and thoughts to clean our auras, re-align our chakras, and raise our energies, while opening up never-used parts of our brains. I was no longer thinking logi-cally. I was dissolving into an invisible connection with the other three people in the room. I smiled as best I could, and said too loudly, "What does any of this truly mean?"

Ravenwood replied, "Since you were moved to ask, I should

let you experience it." Then she touched my forehead. I felt a gentle, warm, shifting sensation that was rather disorienting but pleasant. I closed my eyes to focus. When I opened them, I was looking at myself though different eyes. Actually, my consciousness was in a different body. I was in Ravenwood's mind and body, looking at my body. It was astonishing. I watched with another's eyes and listened with another's ears as my mouth spoke Ravenwood's special words. She said, "You can feel many aspects unique to my essence while I have shifted our consciousness."

Her body was erotically female, rather lustful and limber, yet old—no, ancient—and I felt the wisdom of her brain. It contained a seemingly endless tumble of memories of love and changes, failures and victories, friendships and a burning mission. Her body was a comic-book superhero body, and my consciousness was inside that body and mind. While I was working to comprehend this state of affairs, my usual body's hands reached out and touched my forehead again.

In that moment, I think I glimpsed enlightenment. I felt like a god. It was as if I had died and been reborn. I was overwhelmed by bits and pieces of Ravenwood's memories. Her connection with the creation force was too amazing to perceive fully. She had been offered many opportunities to shed her body and grow spiritually as a member of the cosmic all, and I experienced her succession of growth-filled lives—in a Christian-like heaven, as a fourth-dimensional angel, as a sorcerer, as an adventurer, and as innumerable other selves. Somewhere, by miracle or coincidence, Ravenwood had learned the secret of immortality and had refused to give up her mortal frame. She unselfishly sacrificed her own evolution to become a hidden avatar.

Ravenwood had chosen to live eternally as an unthanked, unknown, often unsure guide and catalyst, so that Earth, humanity, and all that lives in nature—all that exists on Earth in our three-dimensional plane—might evolve in ways never before achieved in the universe. While we touched, a story unfolded before my soul.

The Earth is a unique creation. It is a cosmic library set up to hold and share special cosmic knowledge. But the storage place was taken over long ago by twisted angels, demigods, and beings from other planets, who felt that they could pervert Earth to feed their own deadened spiritual evolution and lack of fulfillment. They wanted to use Earth for strange purposes, and to feed off the emotions of those who live and incarnate here, to generate emotions and ambitions rare in the universe: greed, hate, fear, stupidity, and the desire to exploit and hurt. But eventually the rebels of light—the immortals—had arisen as champions in opposition.

Ravenwood had won many victories as a priestess in ancient Africa. She had met other immortals, and their combined purpose had grown until it became a reality. Their cause was to bring Earth back to its original path as a library of all the cosmic wonders and free choice. Earth, she had learned, exists simultaneously as billions of individual wills and as one entity.

After what seemed an eternity, Ravenwood reached out with her other hand and touched Samuel's forehead. My consciousness now flowed into his body. I was Samuel. Then I touched Rick's forehead, and he began to sing. I was in Rick's mind and body. I had never guessed how differently he thought, almost entirely in music.

We were four separate beings, yet our existence was, for that moment in time, as a single being. It remains a memory beyond description. I was each of them, and we were a united entity sharing love and the spirit of wishing the best for one another. I could have stayed in that night for all eternity. It was almost as wonderful as when your child says, "I love you," or when your wife tells you that your love gives her life meaning.

The next day, at sunset, I awoke from a deep sleep. I was at home, alone. I had no memory of how the night had ended, or even of leaving and driving home. I called Rick. He didn't know what I was talking about. He said he was certain he hadn't seen me the day before. He'd been extremely tired and gone to bed early.

Then I called Samuel, and he said, "Yes, it happened. First Rick, then you, passed your threshold of ability to register the experiences. The other-dimensional interactions blocked your mind's limited ability to stretch." And he added, "Don't ever tell Rick that this was more than a dream. I'm surprised you retained any memory. You must be more evolved than I realized. I'm leaving tonight to begin a new life. I know what I must do now. We will not meet again. May the unconditional love we shared always inspire you, and the memory of last night spur you on to take important risks."

"Yes, but what actions am I to take?" I asked. "Ravenwood never told me! When will I see Ravenwood again?"

Samuel said sadly, "I am not allowed to tell you any of what I know. Your actions will be clear to you when they are to be taken. Good-bye."

Then I awoke again, and it was Sunday morning. I felt great, but I was confused. When had I hung up the phone? When had I changed into pajamas and gotten into bed? I tried to call Samuel, but he didn't answer his phone, so I called Rick. He told me that Samuel had just stopped by, acting blissed-out and secretive. Samuel had said he'd decided to move to Florida, and had said good-bye in a way that seemed very final.

I tried to tell Rick my memories. He knew that I always had wildly detailed dreams, so he was quite sure I was confusing dreams with reality. Did I think I could find the cottage and the immortal again? He would love for me to prove my story. We did drive the thirty-five miles, but once there we couldn't find a dirt road, never mind a cottage.

Now, years later, I find myself writing about this experience that I long ago convinced myself was only a very special dream. I never did see Samuel again, though Rick and I stayed close friends for years. If anyone reading this knows anything about an underground society of immortals that exists to shepherd Earth and humanity's evolution, I invite you to contact me. I would love to hear from you.

# Mystical Child

*Julie Hill*

Most parents notice their babies staring off into space, seemingly mesmerized by something the parent can't see. "What is she/he staring at?" can often be heard when a baby is present. When my third son, Sutton, was born, I learned what it was that he was seeing that I could not. And more.

As a baby, Sutton was completely typical in every way. He blended in with family easily and congenially. No surprises for me, now the experienced and confident mother. Then he learned to talk. Sutton was no longer an assembly-line toddler. He followed me around the house, telling me what color my "light" was. He even told me the meanings of the colors, and what I could do if mine was not as balanced or peaceful as he thought I wanted it to be.

My father died when Sutton was three. Then things *really* got interesting. Sutton became the bearer of messages from my departed father, relaying things that no one could have known, and things he didn't always understand. But he delivered the messages anyway, dutifully. He also began giving me, unsolicited, news and messages from and about all my dead relatives. My father was the only one he had known. How could he know that my grandmother loved the beach? How could he have known that my mother always made pie crust and wanted me to make more pie for my boys? Did people in the hereafter really concern themselves with such things?

The messages—sometimes mundane, sometimes absolutely inspired—didn't stop for some years. One day, Sutton started speaking German to me and was surprised I didn't understand. "Don't you remember, Mommy," he explained, "when I was the doctor and you were the nurse, and we were taking care of the soldiers? That time I didn't listen to them, but this time I'm going to." Some German soldiers had been telling him then about their transcendent experiences near the time of death, which he had ignored in an earlier life.

He told me of a life we'd had together in which he'd brought me jewelry, and described the earrings that he thought had made me the prettiest lady in our midst. He told me how we'd had an arranged marriage, that my mother in this life had been his mother in that one, and had chosen me for him. He recounted this story in front of a neighbor, who was, well, awestruck.

When he told me these stories, they weren't just the prattle of a preschooler. He told them as if he were an adult, and experiencing everything as an adult, but his vocabulary would be only partly adult, and he would get a look in his eyes as if he weren't really using them just then. They had that faraway look.

I tried to get information about how to raise a special child, but no one knew about such children. A haunting question remained: was I doing everything I could for this special being in my house? I'd have to do whatever my heart said was right.

One day, when Sutton was about eight, I was driving him to school and asked why he didn't talk much anymore about the "lights" around people and plants. He replied, "Mother, it's time for me to be an earth person." His tone was so authoritative, so sure. He hasn't mentioned anything paranormal since, and he's nineteen.

Those were magical and mystical years he and I had. I still miss those far-out conversations about angels and our past lives together, dead people, God, where babies come from, and which of his friends could see the dead or go out of body at will.

I hope I did the right thing by encouraging his spontaneous and natural self. I guess I'll never know, but it felt right then and it feels right now. He's in college, plays a few instruments, and is majoring in Mass Communication. Seems appropriate.

# The Miracle of the Second Bucket

## *Dharma Singh Khalsa, M.D.*

*humbly dedicated to my spiritual teacher, Yogi Bhajan*

I awoke precisely at the appointed time of eleven-thirty p.m. Outside my quarters in the concrete guesthouse on the campus of the Golden Temple, the air was clear, cool, and still. I was in the holy city of Amritsar, India: *the city of immortality.* My soul had been awakened. It felt special to be alive.

The cleaning of the floors of the Golden Temple is no simple matter; one has to have permission. Earlier that morning, Ajit Singh, the chief of staff of the guesthouse, ushered me into the office of the head of security for the whole Golden Temple compound, and I was granted the blessing of this midnight *seva*, or selfless service. When one performs midnight *seva* at the Golden Temple, one wonders who is serving whom, because the blessing received is immeasurably more than any one person could ever give. Guru Nanak, the founder of the Sikh religion, said it best when he wrote in Japji, the morning prayer of the Sikhs: "I cannot once be a sacrifice to You." He was referring to God; he could never give God anything.

Thinking of this, I arose and took a cold shower in my primitive bathroom. Barefoot, I walked down the three flights of stairs leading to the narrow, dusty street. I then crossed to the white marble walkway surrounding the healing body of water upon which the Golden Temple seems to float in a pool of nectar.

This pool was originally no more than a pond that lay amid thick forests. But the tradition of centuries has sanctified it, and legend and mythology made it a holy place long before the Golden Temple stood serenely in its center. The Puranas, the Reservoir of Nectar, is said to have lain between the rivers

Ravi and Beas. One legend says that an Iksuaku king performed many religious rites here. Its deepest early associations, however, are with the Hindu epic the *Ramayana*, and one story recounts that this was the scene of the battle between the Hindu deity Rama and his two sons, Lav and Kush. During the course of the battle, Rama was mortally wounded. When his sons realized his identity as their father, they took the healing Amrit and restored him to health. The liquid left over was poured into the pond, rendering it sacred for all time.

Lord Buddha is said to have passed by this place with his monks and remarked on its being an excellent site for meditation. Centuries later, Guru Nanak himself is said to have foretold that one day there would be a great temple here and a flourishing city in its environs. The city sprang up around the temple that was built, and I was on my way to being one of only a handful of Westerners ever to wash its floors.

The air was thick with spiritual energy as I approached the line of Indian men sitting by the front entrance to the causeway leading out to the Golden Temple. I sat down next to a large, well-built man. He could play for the Green Bay Packers, I thought. Gradually, about a dozen men of various sizes arrived. Dressed in Indian garb, including colorful turbans, they all carried the distinguishing *kirpan*, or dagger, worn by Sikhs to symbolize their willingness to defend another in time of need.

We sat peacefully together and began softly repeating Japji to ourselves. "There is just one Creator of the creation. The true essence of God. The doer of everything. Without anger, without fear, and free from the cycle of births and deaths. He is self-enlightened and realized through His grace. Meditate. He was true in the beginning. He is true now, He will be true in the future, He shall forever be true."

Just after midnight, a solitary figure approached and came to the front of the line. He brought his hands to the center of his chest in prayer pose, and we all echoed the traditional Sikh greeting: *"Wha he gutu ji ka khalsa, wha he guru ji ke fateh."* "The pure ones belong to God. All victory is His." We were then led up the causeway to the back entrance of the temple. Once inside, we got on our hands and knees. In the quiet cool of the night, we began to spread water buffalo's milk, poured from large urns, onto the floor. We then mixed it with the water from the Tank of Nectar.

After a few minutes, we stood and began the real work of cleaning the Golden Temple. It reminded me of a session of aerobics mixed with weight training. I grabbed a steel bucket and quickly walked over to the side of the temple, where I handed the bucket to a man leaning over the outside of the railing. He powerfully scooped the bucket into the holy water with a *woomph*, and handed it back to me in an instant. I again proceeded into the temple, where I handed my bucket to another man, who poured its contents onto the wet surface.

This bucket brigade continued in a well-synchronized procession inside and outside of the temple. I began to perspire—not heavily, but enough to know I was involved in physical labor. This is hard work, I thought. Yes, I continued. Good, hard, meditative work: walking, handing the bucket, receiving it, carrying it, and walking. As we worked, we all softly chanted a beautiful mantra: "*Wha he guru*: From darkness to light. Ecstasy is in the infinity of consciousness."

My eyes soon fell on a short, wiry, gray-bearded gentleman wearing a flat, light blue turban. He was carrying two buckets. I wonder what it would be like to have a second bucket, I thought. Please understand, there was no desire, no attachment, nor any intentionality associated with this thought. It lasted less time than it has taken me to write it down.

I went back to work. The cleaner returned my empty bucket, and I walked over to the side of the temple, where another was waiting to receive it. Yet something was different. There was a clear, mystical presence in the air. And yes, there was no one else around. How unusual, I thought. Normally, when having our buckets filled, we had to jockey for position, elbow to elbow, like the big boys in the National Basketball Association waiting for a rebound. But now I was alone, and the water filler wasn't paying attention to me. He was staring off into the space of a deep, dark night.

And then I saw it. On the floor about three feet from the man and equally distant from me was a bright, brand-new-looking steel bucket. I stopped and glanced around. It didn't seem to belong to anyone. I felt suspended in time.

The slow motion stopped, and I heard again the clanging of the buckets touching one another, and the water splashing. I picked up the second bucket and handed each in succession to the man who filled and returned them to me. Another four or five turns, and it was finished. The temple had been purified.

I was so exhilarated, and at the same time so spaced out, that all I could do was go back to my room. I couldn't even stay for the morning prayers. Soon it was clear to me why. In a deep meditative state, I went through the incredibly intense episode of personal and spiritual growth.

If our intention is pure, and free from the grasping nature of attachment, we can effortlessly manifest anything we want or truly need in our lives, be it health, wealth, or happiness.

Imagine I was in your home and asked for a glass of water. Surely you would give it to me. In this case, I was in the house of Guru Ram Das, the founder of the Golden Temple. I simply wondered about a second bucket, and it appeared. Clearly, I had been blessed.

May you always be guided in your life, and may the one God bless this world with peace. *Sat nam.*

# Someone to Watch over Me

## Jeanne Smearsoll

My husband of thirty years died suddenly at the age of fifty-one. We buried him and mourned. And for a week I was unable to sleep.

On the seventh sleepless night, I was lying in bed, distraught, when I sensed a kind presence, and felt—and saw—myself moving into an iridescent bubble that floated above me. As the bubble encased me, I felt warmth and comfort. Everything was going to be okay, and I would be able to go on alone. Then I fell asleep, reassured that I was being watched over and that the iridescent bubble would protect me.

Almost a year from the day of my husband's death, in a dream, I saw my bubble being punctured, and heard air hissing out, while the comforting presence said that I didn't need the bubble anymore. I would be all right.

# Meeting the Dalai Lama

## *Bruce Fields*

Sometimes the spiritual arrives totally uninvited and unexpected, leaving you with a sense of timelessness in the joy you feel.

In August 1993, I was in Chicago at the Parliament of the World's Religions, a pan-religious gathering that had last occurred exactly one hundred years before. As a photographer with a press card, I was privy to certain events, such as the pre-conference press meeting with the Dalai Lama.

The pressroom was filled with excited energy as more than a hundred of us jockeyed for position before the arrival of the great man. Suddenly a phalanx of orange-robed monks, seeming more like body guards than clerics, entered the chamber and effectively surrounded the dais in front of the crowd. The Dalai Lama entered behind them to a round of enthusiastic applause. He spoke to us and answered a few questions, then bid us thanks and gave his blessing.

The Dalai Lama's departure seemed like a choreographed performance. His entourage of monks created a gauntlet around him, like a huge V, protecting him from contact with the crowd of reporters, photographers, and organizers who were all buzzing with the excitement of schoolchildren on a special class trip. I'd found a place by the exit door and awaited his passing with the other crowding participants, many of whom were continuing to take pictures, shout questions, or just grin broadly.

There was great commotion from every direction as the Dalai Lama, insulated from us by his protective horde, slowly moved out. Lights flashed, arms waved, and I found myself unable to take a single picture. Instead, I just stared at him, and I was smiling as much as anyone else.

At that moment I realized that he was staring at me also, and smiling. I felt my arm rise up. He approached slowly, and as he neared me his arm rose as well and our hands clasped together, fingers entwining, for one brief moment. And then he was gone.

I felt a surge of great joy. And I felt blessed. It was a moment of universal unity. The glow of the Dalai Lama's warmth and of our mutual recognition has stayed with me to this very day.

# Malaria Pills

## *Sri Harold Klemp*

A group of ECKists—members of Eckankar, the religion of light and sound—were traveling with me to the ECK African Seminar in Nigeria. As a precaution, we all had to take malaria pills. Nobody wanted to, but it was important. We each took a pill a week before we got there, the day we got there, and then once each week for four weeks.

The night before we left for Africa, our group was staying together in a hotel in the Netherlands. We were there for the ECK European Seminar. A few of us were going out to eat, and I asked the others, "By the way, did you take your malaria pill?" Everyone had except one man, who said he had forgotten. "Don't worry," he told the group. "If you remind me, I'll do it when I get back to my room." But when we got back to the hotel, we all forgot.

In the middle of the night, I woke up. "We forgot to tell him to take his malaria pill," I said to my wife.

"We can tell him in the morning," she said, and we settled back down to sleep.

Then I remembered something else. "He has to take the pill with food," I said.

"We'll tell him in the morning," my wife said again.

The next morning we met the man for breakfast. He looked at me strangely. "About five a.m. I woke up suddenly and clearly heard you say, 'You have to take your malaria pill,' " he said. "So I got out of bed and got the pill. I was just crawling back under the covers for a little more sleep when I heard your voice say, 'But you've got to take it with food.' So I ate some cookies."

# A Mother-Daughter Connection

## *Judith Ford*

In 1934, my mother, Gertrude, was newly married and living in Brooklyn. One evening, when she was on her way to a bridge game, she tripped over a rope extending from a truck in the street across the sidewalk and into a basement. She fell on her side on the pavement, where some concerned passersby helped her up, then she went home and to bed. The next morning, she couldn't get out of bed and was in great pain. Apparently, a severe infection was developing in her ovary as a result of the fall. She continued to be in great pain all day.

At the time, her mother and father—my grandmother and grandfather—lived in Newark, New Jersey, with no telephone. Late that evening, my grandmother made my grandfather dress and drive her to my mother's place, saying, "Goldilah needs us." (Golda was my mother's Yiddish name.) My grand-mother had apparently never made a late-night demand of that sort prior to that night, and never did again. But sensing the seriousness and urgency of my grandmother's entreaty, my grandfather did what he was told.

They arrived at Mom's house and found her in terrible pain. My father was very relieved that they had come. They took my mother back to Newark, to Beth Israel Hospital, where a noted Ob-Gyn performed an emergency operation on her and removed her ruptured ovary.

If my grandmother hadn't trusted her intuition, my mother might have died. It still gives me chills that my grandmother knew my mother was in trouble.

# Beads of Light

## *Peggy Carter*

In 1972, my husband and I visited Sathya Sai Baba's ashram in Bangalore, India.

One day, Baba looked at some long earrings I was wearing and said, "So heavy." I took one off and handed it to him. He pretended to be surprises and said, "Not heavy—light."

A few days later, I was sitting beside him and he reached over and touched a ring I was wearing and asked, "What is it?"

I said, "An Australian agate."

He proceeded to materialize some pieces of jewelry for two others in the room. I thought they were ugly. That night I said to my husband, "I hope he doesn't give me anything, because I would have to wear it and like it if he gave it to me."

Our visit was coming to a close, and Baba asked us to attend a private interview with six other people. I sat on the floor. He spoke to each of us, and when he got to me his eyes sparkled. He asked, "What do you want?"

I said something I had never even thought of until then: "I want my two other boys to come to you." My son Landon had been with him for eight months. Baba knew that I meant I wanted them all to find their way to God.

Baba put out his hand and wiggled it a little, and lo and behold there appeared a beautiful necklace made of nine colors of agate. Five colors represented the five chakras, and four represented the elements. He put it on me, and I never took it off. I believe the beads are blessed and carry blessings to whoever possesses them.

Two years passed, and one night the necklace broke when I turned over in bed. I picked up the beads, checking the floor to be sure I had them all, but when they were restrung the necklace was shorter. I wondered about it but went on with life, again never taking off the necklace.

Another year passed, and the necklace broke in my car when I leaned from the front seat to the backseat. Again I picked up all the beads and had the necklace restrung, and this time it was even shorter. I thought, If it breaks another time, it will be so short that it will choke me.

The third time it broke, I was riding my horse and forgot to tuck my shirt into my breeches. When I got home, I discovered six beads in my bra. That night I thought I would cry, but I didn't. At about five a.m. I woke up and received a message from Baba: *It is time to shine forth your own light; the beads were doing it for you.* As I lay there, I thought of all the people who had been helped by the beads.

Once I was at a large garden party on Lake Minnetonka, and a woman zeroed in on my beads from across the lawn. She came up and didn't even introduce herself or look at me. She just stared at the beads and said, "Tell me about them." I was taken by surprise, but we walked away from the party and sat in another part of the garden and talked. She was sad and needed my help, which I gave her. The beads had led her to me.

Another woman led to me by the beads was a dressmaker whom I had never met before. She told me about a near-death experience she had not even told her husband about, for fear he would think her crazy. I was a good listener for her.

Now there were six beads left. But not for long.

During a peace-pipe ceremony given by my hairdresser–turned–Baba devotee, Laverne, Baba came through with another message: *Give the white bead to Laverne for her medicine bag.* Laverne was grateful for the significant addition.

Soon after, I gave the gray bead to the chief of the Mohawk tribe, because I believe that we will have world peace when white people learn the ways of the Indians.

As I flew to Sedona, Arizona, Baba told me in a vision that a bead should go to the Hopis, to bring the East and the West together. I went to the reservation there to deliver it, but it must not have been the right time, as I was not directed what to do with it. I still have that bead.

My school roommate had cancer, and the green bead went to her for healing. She lived four years without medication. I believe the energy of the bead helped maintain her strength.

Next I was swimming with the dolphins off Hawaii Island, the Big Island, and was instructed to drop the black bead into the ocean at a place where there's a vortex. The dolphins are known to come there. I did this, and on the way home I read a book that informed me obsidian (black) is the crystal for the Big Island. Coincidence? No. Baba knows everything.

So I have two beads left. One is for the Hopis, and the other— who knows? All I can report is that the others have been blessings to those whose lives have been touched by them.

# 5

# MAGICAL LOVE

# Finding My Soul Mate

## Arielle Ford

"Amma," I whispered into the Divine Mother's ear, "please heal my heart of everything that is stopping me from finding my soul mate."

I felt her arms hug me even tighter as she laughed out loud at my request and said, "Oh, darling, darling, darling." I felt her lightly press something into the palm of my right hand as I backed away and let the next person in line receive her blessing. As I walked away, blissed out from Ammachi's embrace, I looked to see what she had given me. In my hand was a Hershey's Kiss and some beautiful flower petals.

Since it was already past midnight, I ate my chocolate, put the flower petals in a special pouch, and went to bed. During the night, one dream stood out. There were many people singing to me: "Arielle is the woman who comes after Beth."

When I woke up, I had a feeling that the dream meant that my soul mate was on the way, and that he was currently in a relationship with a woman named Beth.

I had first read about Ammachi years before that she was an enlightened being whose touch could heal. One magazine reported that they had witnessed her kissing the open wounds of a child with leprosy and watched them heal instantly. Nearly every day of the year, Ammachi gives *darshan*, or blessing, to thousands of people. She hugs everyone as if they are the most special person in the world, and for the few moments they are in her presence, they are.

I had signed up for a weekend with Ammachi. The two days consisted of receiving *darshan*, which meant sitting in line for up to five hours at a time, singing devotional songs and listening to special lectures by her swami. My friend Michael had lived on her ashram in India for three years, and told me that special prayers could be whispered in Ammachi's ear while she was hugging you. Before arriving at the weekend, I had mapped out exactly what I wanted to ask.

That Saturday, June twenty-second, I spent many hours in the *darshan* line, waiting my turn to be embraced by Ammachi. When I was in her arms, I whispered in her ear, asking her to send my soul mate to me. I asked that he be happy, healthy, spiritual, tall, good-looking, fun to be with, and *looking for me*. Again she laughed when I whispered in her ear, but she squeezed me so tight that I just knew she had understood my request.

A few weeks after my visit with Ammachi, I was sent to Portland by one of my clients to supervise a television shoot for an author. I called the author's office to make arrangements with his partner, Brian. He agreed to pick me up at the airport, gave me careful instructions as to where to meet him, and told me what he looked like.

At the Portland airport, I exited and headed for my meeting place with Brian. I heard my name being called. In front of me was a man who did not fit Brian's description at all. He explained that he had come from the author's office to meet me. I felt an overwhelming sense of disappointment. I quietly wondered where this feeling had come from. I had spoken to Brian on the phone many times during the past months, but our calls were always business-related. We had never met in person, and I'd never given him a second thought. Now I felt terribly disappointed that the plans had changed.

I followed the man, Gary, through the airport, and he led me to the exact spot where Brian was to meet me. As soon as I realized that Brian was standing in front of me, I felt incredibly happy. He was tall and very handsome and seemed excited to meet me. I had a feeling that something special was happening.

The next morning, we all gathered for the TV shoot. The crew set up lights in the author's house, and Brian and I sat on a bench in the back of the room. The room was dark except for the bright lights fixed on the author, who was discussing his book. I felt an overwhelming urge to touch Brian. I thought I was going crazy. The urge continued, so I decided to sit on my hands before I embarrassed myself. Then a voice in my head said, "This is the one. This is who you are going to spend the rest of your life with." I thought I was losing it. I barely knew this man. He could have been married, for all I knew. But the voice was insistent. "Nope," it said. "This is how it happens."

When the interview was over, we all stood up and went into the hallway. Brian walked up to me and said, "You know, I've been dreaming about you." I didn't have the presence of mind to ask him what kind of dreams he'd been having. At that point, all I wanted to do was either kiss him or ask him who Beth was. I didn't dare do either.

A little while later, the author walked over to Brian and said, "Let's take Arielle out to dinner tonight before she has to catch her plane. Why don't you call Elizabeth and see if she would like to join us?"

Even though Brian wasn't wearing a wedding band, I figured Elizabeth must be his wife. Still, I thought, Elizabeth sure is close to Beth. . . . Maybe, just maybe . . .

The TV shoot was taking all day, but I didn't care. I was having a great time observing this beautiful man. I felt an electricity between us, and I wondered if he felt it too. At the end of the day, Elizabeth arrived. I saw them standing together, and my first thought was: They are like brother and sister. Even though I had no proof, somehow I knew that they were no longer romantically connected.

A bunch of us went to the restaurant for an early dinner. Brian was planning to drive me back to the airport for my seven o'clock flight. At six-fifteen, our dinner still hadn't been served, and it was clear that if we didn't leave for the airport, I would miss my flight. Brian arranged to have my dinner put in a "to go" box, and we jumped in the car. As he sped down the freeway, I fed my trout dinner to both of us.

I felt so comfortable with him, and some of the things that came out of my mouth were just amazing. At one point I told him that I was searching for my soul mate–tantra partner. He nearly drove off the road. When we got to the airport, we hugged good-bye.

Brian and the author were scheduled to be in San Diego, my hometown, on the book tour in five days. I was scheduled to take a special course at Stanford on those dates, but when I called to double-check on the course, it turned out that they had never received my registration and the course was sold out! I guess the angels of romance were hard at work to assure that Brian and I would meet again.

During the next several days, we spoke on the phone for hours. It felt as if we had to catch up on lifetimes of knowing each other. Late one night, he told me about the dreams he had been having before we met. They were very detailed and intimate. He said he could see me clearly in his dreams, even though we had never met. At the Portland airport, he had been absolutely stunned to find that I was the woman in his dreams.

Brian and the author arrived in San Diego for a fast twenty-four hours. We all went to lunch and then drove around the city visiting various bookstores.

That night, the author had a speaking engagement. Brian and I sat in the back of the room. Instead of quietly listening to the speech, we were very busy passing each other notes, just like in junior high school. These notes, however, were profoundly different. Brian had tapped into an ancient river of knowledge and was writing an amazing tale of our past lives together, the reasons why we had chosen to come back together in this life, and some of the things we would be doing. In these notes he told me that we were here to nurture and heal each other and to share a magnificent love that had been divinely orchestrated. Needless to say, I was nearly overwhelmed.

After seventeen pages of notes, the author's speech was over and it was time to leave. Brian and I made plans to see each other in a few weeks and to spend a lot of time talking on the phone, getting caught up on everything we had each done in this lifetime.

I don't even remember when we first spoke about getting married. We just knew immediately that getting married was inevitable. Finally we told everyone that we would be getting married the next summer. Just before Thanksgiving, we went to see Ammachi while she was visiting her ashram in San Ramon, California. When it was our turn for *darshan*, we passed her a note telling her that she had brought us together and that we were engaged. She was overjoyed. She blessed us and laughed and hugged us.

We made plans with our friends and family to go to Bali in June to be married there by the high priest of the island. Soon it was clear that due to civil unrest in Indonesia, we would have to cancel. Brian was confident that the Universe had other, more magnificent plans for our wedding.

Luckily for us, Ammachi had plans to stop at her ashram in June. We knew that she performed wedding ceremonies and would grant a special blessing. So we went to San Ramon to ask her to marry us, and to our delight she enthusiastically said yes!

Her weddings are performed at the end of Devi Bhava, a very special ceremony in which she goes into the highest states of consciousness. Thousands of people congregate to receive her blessing on this night, and the atmosphere is festive and spiritually charged with singing. The next Devi Bhava was scheduled for the following Sunday.

On June twenty-second, at five-fifty in the morning, exactly one year to the day after I first asked Amma to send me my soul mate, she married us in a beautiful and fascinating ceremony. More than a thousand people were there, including my parents and sister; they showered us with flower petals and blessings as Amma performed the rites of the sacred union.

We knew that it was Amma's grace that had united us, and as we gazed into each other's eyes during the ceremony, we knew that we were meant to be together forever.

# It Had to Be You

## *Brent BecVar*

There are times in our lives when we really have to stop and wonder: Who is pulling the strings, anyway? Who really is writing this play we're living in? Whenever I remember the events of the story you're about to read, I find myself still wondering.

In the summer of 1972, I was living in Northern California but had returned to visit the city where I had grown up in Kentucky. I was twenty-two and staying at my parents' home for a week. I had spent a restless few years traveling in California, Colorado, and Hawaii, so this brief stay in the old familiar landscape of my hometown had been wonderfully restful and refreshing. With only one day left there, I stopped at a pay phone to make a few farewell calls to friends.

Short of coins, I went into the ice cream shop next door for change. There I discovered a cheerfully friendly and very attractive young female employee in a flatteringly tight white uniform. Her familiarity was immediate and completely natural. I became totally absorbed in her as we began to talk. Gradually the conversation touched on details of our lives, and we discovered some coincidental similarities between our families. Time seemed not to exist as we exchanged bits of information about ourselves, until suddenly I realized that forty-five minutes had passed almost without my noticing. I felt a little embarrassed that I had been keeping her from her work, and although the conversation had been enjoyable, I felt I had better say good-bye.

As I drove away, forgetting all about my phone calls, I found myself thinking, I'm going to miss that girl. She was only sixteen, six years younger than I, yet she seemed to be completely my contemporary. We shared so many interests that we could have gone on talking for hours. When I remembered I was leaving the next day to return to the West Coast, I felt a deep longing for this "most familiar girl."

Eight years passed. After finishing graduate school, I began working as a university administrator in a college on the Gulf Coast of Alabama. On my thirtieth birthday, two of my close married friends convinced me, with great difficulty, to go with them to an Irish dance workshop in Fairhope. Since I had been a bit lonely at the time, and maybe a little too shy to have met many girls, my friends thought it might be good for me to cut loose a little, especially on this big day.

In spite of my reticence, when I entered the dance hall I became transfixed at the sight of a girl's long braided hair. And in what was for me an uncharacteristically bold move, even before I saw her face I approached her and asked her to dance.

I found this young woman captivatingly attractive, and something about her made me sense that she was not from around there. When we got a chance to speak at the break and I asked her where she came from, I was surprised to hear her say, "From Kentucky." I told her I was also from there, and I asked where in particular she had lived. When she answered, "Outside of Louisville, near Prospect," for some reason I pictured a large, somewhat ostentatious Colonial house on a hill that I remembered from my childhood. It was in the area that she had mentioned.

I asked her if she knew a neighborhood called Hills and Dales, which is where that Colonial house was, and she said that yes, she had lived in that neighborhood. When I asked if she knew of the Hollenbach family there—I remembered that they had lived in that big Colonial house—she looked at me in total amazement. She said, "My parents bought the Hollenbachs' house. That's the house where I grew up!"

For a moment, neither of us could speak. The coincidence of this discovery seemed so incredible and bizarre. My heart was beating excitedly. Not only did I find this mysterious girl completely engaging, but I seemed to have known where she had lived growing up. I couldn't explain it. So for this and other reasons, not the least of which was our strong chemical attraction, Leanne and I began dating soon after, and eventually we began living together.

A year and many interesting experiences later, I was offered a job in Austin, Texas, which I accepted. Leanne and I decided to live apart for a time while I got settled in the new city. After a month, she came to visit me there. I picked her up at the Dallas airport, and then we began driving along the highway to Austin under a big, starry Texas night sky. Conversation turned to some of the old jobs we had had, and Leanne started talking about the time she had worked at an ice cream ship in Louisville called Don's. Suddenly, in a flood of memory, emotion, and astonishment, I pulled the car off the road and looked at her. "You were that girl!" I said. "The girl in the ice cream shop when I came in to get change all those years ago! Now I remember. It was you!"

Somehow the memory of that scene nine years before came to her also then, and she said, "I remember. . . . You were that really attractive older man who came in. I remember thinking I really liked that guy." We sat for a long time, wondering how this could have happened and how it had taken us all this time to remember.

Though I have experienced many amazing and unexplainable coincidences in my life, this one really left me speechless. After that, I never doubted that there are people in our lives we are destined to meet, or that we will encounter these very special souls again and again, in life after life, at just the right moment. It finds a way to happen—in spite of everything.

# Love and Power

## *Kenny and Julia Loggins*

Our final morning in Hana, Hawaii, we awoke in time to watch a pink-violet sun rising over the ocean. The night before was the second time I'd had a dream of Julia and me at sea in an ancient wooden sailboat. The dream was so real, I couldn't help but think it was a kind of vision. By this time in our journey, I was so surrendered to magic, I decided to call around Maui until I found a ship that fit the description of the one in the dream. My task was made considerably easier by the fact that there was only one wooden ship in harbor anywhere on the island. She was moored on the Lahaina side and her name was the *Paramour*. A 1920s twin-masted schooner, the *Paramour* was usually chartered for parties—say thirty people or so—but yes, coincidentally there had been a cancellation. She *was* available later that day. I booked her. Julia and I packed up, paid up, left the hotel, and headed west.

On the way out of town we took a short detour to bid adieu to a favorite beach of ours. We hadn't traveled very far when I impetuously turned to the right, up a thin, red dirt road. Julia was getting used to my sudden intuitive changes of plan by then, and she gave me an excited smile, like a kid on a new adventure. Up we rode through lush vegetation, passing a flower farm, turning left at the rusted-out auto carcasses and coming to an abrupt stop at the end of the road.

When I saw the white shutters, corrugated tin roof, and clay-potted flowers hanging from the eaves of the simple front porch framed by magenta bougainvillea, I knew that this was what had called to me on the highway: this quintessential Hawaiian house. We sat there together silently taking it in, overwhelmed by a sense of homecoming, as if recognizing an old dear friend quietly saying hello and good-bye, and we began to cry.

For an instant, Julia and I saw ourselves living in a little house like this, making soup, writing poetry, and rocking babies. This little house in the forest felt like a distant memory of a time past, or perhaps a vision of peace yet to be fulfilled. But we knew it would be many years, if ever, before we could have such a simple, peaceful life. The sadness in my chest said it all. "Perhaps someday," answered my inner voice, "when your work in the world is done." We sat there staring at that cottage for I don't know how long before reality set in and we felt ready to move on.

A few hours later, we arrived at the harbor and boarded the *Paramour*.

"Good afternoon," said the captain. "How soon can we expect the rest of your party?"

"The rest?" I said. "I guess I forgot to tell you. It's only the two of us."

Julia and I were the smallest party that had ever set sail on the *Paramour*. The crew of six was already on board, and I smiled to myself as I watched them exchange quizzical looks with one another, which I took to mean: Crazy rock 'n' roller!

"Two?" The captain smiled. "Okay, then. The ship is yours. Let's cast off."

Julia and I got out of the way while the crew scurried all around us, preparing sails, untying ropes, and getting under way. The afternoon was unusually perfect for a sail. "We haven't seen a great day like this all month," said one hand. "You guys are really lucky."

"Yeah, I guess we are," I said, half smiling to Julia. From somewhere deep inside me, the anxiety had been rising, reaching up, and pulling me in. I was retreating, overwhelmed by the reality of love. Perhaps I'd hit my personal quota of joy, or maybe I just wanted to see if I was still in some kind of control. Why the heart opens and closes is a mystery to me; I simply know that it is as inevitable as the tides.

After pretending for as long as I could stand it that I was

fine and that nothing was the least bit different about me, I finally let out a sigh and confessed, "Julia, I'm sorry, but I feel a little shut down today. I guess my heart's closed. I don't know why."

"I've been feeling that," she replied. "I can almost see the clouds around it." Julia touched my chest. "The sun will come out when it's ready. It's always there, you know, clouds and all."

"Maybe it's just too early for the sun today," I said. Picking up my guitar, I quietly sang a new idea, just then forming:

> *Never believed that I could*
> *love somebody*
> *Someone like you*

"I think this goes with the melody I played for you this morning," I told her. Music had once again become a part of my life; I constantly reaffirmed and celebrated our love with it. Every song that came to me was connecting Julia's heart to mine. No longer seen as a rival lover, my music was free to underscore our lives, our love. And today, on this ship, in this moment, it began to sing to me like a maniac on a street corner in New York City. An ode to madness, to magic. Everything was becoming a song, even my fear.

> *I've never been so afraid*
> *That love is just a dream*
> *And darlin'*
> *I'll awake*
> *And you'll be gone*

Then it came to me: "Any club that would have me as a member isn't good enough for me!" I said to the sky.

Thank you, Groucho. So *this* was my story, my hidden belief about myself and love: If I loved someone too openly, that person must be crazy, stupid, blind, thickheaded, conniving, ulterior-motivated, not good enough for me, below my standards, defective, insane, self-deluded. I, therefore, needn't bother returning the love of so obviously sick a mind! This woman was just a stupid child, a dumb good review! Of course, only the bad reviews are real, intelligent, and worth believing. Talk about a catch-22!

Julia was laughing. I started laughing too. This was all very funny. I was funny. It was my drama turned into comedy, with me cast as the central clown. It was all a big cosmic joke, hilarious, simplistic, transparent. I laughed and I cried. Without noticing it, I had also started to shake. . . .

I'm laughing, crying, shaking, I thought. I've gone mad, out of my mind at last.

And at that, the interior clouds moved, my heart opened, the sun was out. I was in love again.

"Coming about," shouted the captain at the helm.

"Yes," I agreed. "But what *are* we about?"

"Looks to me," he said, "it's about L-O-V-E."

We smiled. Everyone on the ship was stoned on it, big-time. In love, of love. And Julia was a part of my heart again. But this time it kept getting deeper and stronger. As we walked toward the bow, I had the mental image of Julia with flowers in her hair, hoop earrings, and a golden bracelet around her upper arm. I suddenly understood everything about the ship, what each crew member was doing.

"The ship's yours," the captain had said. Perhaps, in some mystical way that none of us understood, he was right. Now, standing on the bow beside Julia, I was filled with another foreign feeling: my power! Love *and* power, together in me for the first time. What an amazing sensation! It was all clear: I knew who I was, I knew who Julia was, I knew who we were together and where we were going. Our love was as vast as the sky, sun setting on one side, moons and stars rising on the other. Gigantic billowing clouds became towering mythological beings celebrating our arrival, our discovery of each other, of the lives we were born to lead, of our finding each other again, here in Paradise.

"I must have done something incredibly right, sometime long ago, to deserve this," Julia whispered to me.

"We're so lucky," I replied. "Thank you, God! We will live here!" I said, half to Julia, half to the thousands of stars now appearing in the deepening sky. "This love, this awareness . . . we will live here! I know it."

"I do too," said Julia, as if we were making a promise to Spirit in a sacred ceremony.

"Julia, promise me you won't forget this day," I said as our ship dropped anchor in the moonlit waters of a perfect Hawaiian night. "And don't let me forget it either."

# Twin Souls

## John Maxwell Taylor

I met my twin soul under a dramatic set of circumstances. She came out of nowhere to perform the lead role in a musical I had spent seven years creating. I sang a song from the play at a spiritual conference. Afterward, people gathered around to say how much they enjoyed my singing, and suddenly *she* was there before me. I looked into her eyes for the first time in this life, and I heard an inner voice say, "This woman is perfect for you."

My twin soul told me that she also sang and was interested in spiritualizing the arts, and she mentioned that she was attending the conference with her husband. So much for inner voices. Yet as it came time to pick the female lead four months later, I remembered this woman and intuitively realized that she was the living embodiment of the character I had created.

I called her, and she took the role. Because I knew she was married, there was no thought of romance in my mind.

Rehearsals for the play began a few weeks later in my studio. There was obviously a deep friendship and spiritual connection between us. One day, I worked with her alone, and she sang for me her opening song from the show, a lovely tune about lost love from a previous life. As she sang, I felt an electrifying energy fill the room, and to my amazement, her spirit rose from her body and streamed out through the top of her head. It curved through the air and across the room toward me, coming to rest over my head, where it hovered like a golden cloud. I knew that this energy wanted to enter my body and that, if I gave my permission, this would indeed happen. I also knew that if I allowed this experience to occur, I would fall in love with my leading lady.

All my life I have seen the experience of love energy as God. To say no to this spiritual force seeking to enter my body would be to deny the divine. I also knew that I would be opening myself to a love that could never be possessed in the real world. I chose to surrender to love and live with the consequences, no matter how hard it would be for me personally. Upon my acceptance, the golden cloud descended into me through the top of my head, gently slipping into my body, right down to my toes, fitting into my spirit and form as if it were a sword entering a sheath that had long been prepared.

When the song ended, she sat down in front of me and said, "Your eyes look as if they could melt the world." They could, for our spirits were now one.

I made up my mind, right from the start, that I was not going to have an affair with her or interfere with her marriage. In some strange way, I knew that it was not a part of the plan that we should be together and have a life in the normal sense. This was a meeting on a soul level, separate from marriage, personal commitments, and the outer pattern of our lives.

Early on, I said to her on the telephone, "I will never hurt you." She told me later that when she hung up, she sat down and, inexplicably, found herself weeping.

I was helped in my resolve by three books by the Russian mystic Boris Mouravieff, who fled the Russian Revolution in 1917 and went to France, where he met his own twin soul, a ballerina then married to a successful businessman. These books, which came into my possession the week I surrendered to the flow of love, describe in detail what twin souls must do when they meet and one is already bound elsewhere. There can be no question of a sexual affair, because while we may have a right to sacrifice ourselves, we do not have the right to sacrifice the happiness of others.

This restraint is a test that forces the soul halves to leap across physical time and space to unite in spiritual transcendence. The karmic knots that bind their evolutionary patterns to others will eventually be untied, not cut, but this may not happen in the present lifetime. Loving without expectation of return leads to Christ Consciousness.

Everyone has a twin soul, according to Mouravieff, and these bipolar halves of a single whole will meet at least once in every lifetime. This meeting will be accompanied by a vibration unlike any other they have known, and will happen when least expected and in unusual circumstances.

Certainly, the production of a piece of musical theater is a pressure cooker for all concerned. The joy my twin and I were experiencing was offset by uncertainty about the future, and by performance anxiety. In the midst of all this, I became aware that the seven years of writing were now culminating in a production that required me, the male lead, to enact a mystical marriage ceremony on stage with my real twin soul every night in a major theater. That final moment each night when we were escorted into a beam of light center stage by our guardian angel was unforgettable. As our hands intertwined and we stepped into the light for the fusion of our souls into one being, the reason for our meeting was being fulfilled. We were participating in a dramatized union of our souls, a re-enactment of what had always been . . . our oneness in God. Each night, a sacred vibration would descend upon us as we stood there in the light.

When our time in the theater was ended, we had no legitimate reason to see each other again and parted, not without anguish. Yet time has eased the pain of separation. For me, the joy and love remain as the part of my soul that she entered and opened up to me.

If one soul is living in two bodies, it could mean that what happens in the life of one may instantly affect the other— mentally, physiologically, emotionally, and spiritually. Even if their connection is not apparent on the surface of daily life, the one is always working for the two through a connection rooted beyond but manifesting itself in time and space.

Experiments have shown that when a cell is divided and each half is placed in a separate location, if one of the halves is then altered, the partner half-cell automatically changes accordingly. This also happens with light waves (photons) when separation and alteration are induced. The shift in one instantly produces the same change in the other over a designated distance. If the Adam and Eve principle is seen as two waves of light emanating from the Godhead, and the return to Eden is seen as the ultimate reunification of those two waves into one, then the age-old split between man and woman has more than a hope of ultimate resolution.

The implication is that we are already one with our twin soul. Perhaps what we feel and know of love within ourselves, and the longing that drives us toward union with another, is actually a process beyond the popular psychological notion that we are complete within ourselves, and that when we fall in love we simply project our idealized masculine or feminine nature onto some poor mortal and give away our power. In fact, we are complete only when the presence of our outer counterpart is fully developed within us.

To have met and stood before that image in living form is for me an unfathomable blessing. Having experienced the perfection without, and released it into the Infinite, I feel I can now truly unfold it inwardly. My need to be together externally with my twin soul is gently superseded by a soul awareness centered in the heart of love; it can expand to embrace humanity as part of a twin soul's shared self. I believe that we are individualized light waves of love on the ocean of Infinity.

# The Look

## Stephen Freeman and Shawna Mullane

### Stephen's Story

In June 1994, I went to my first spiritual and healing seminar. It was held in Hawaii, and there were more than forty people in attendance from all over the world, including a woman named Shawna. Shawna and I talked, but I did not feel any obvious connection to her. I never sat with her at mealtimes. We both had our own lives in different countries.

The seminar was wonderful. As it wound down on the last day, we all headed to the local airport. I was going back to Montana, and Shawna was returning to Canada. All of us were saying our good-byes, and Shawna and I were talking moments before the shuttle was to depart, just two new acquaintances having a casual conversation.

Then it happened. Someone took a picture of the two of us together, and just seconds after that, as we were about to say good-bye and never see each other again, Shawna looked at me with the most incredible, penetrating, soulful, unconditional love I have ever felt or even knew existed. The moment seemed like an eternity. I lost awareness of my surroundings. It was just she and I.

I could see all the way down into Shawna's soul, and I knew she could see into mine. I felt totally vulnerable, as if my entire life were being revealed to a stranger. But at the same time, I seemed to know everything about her. Total recognition swept over me. I knew Shawna after all. A light breeze would have knocked me over.

I was dumbstruck and said, "Why are you looking at me like that?" She said nothing as she continued to pour her soul into mine. I was absorbed by our spiritual connection until I was jolted by the blare of the boarding announcement.

As we boarded our plane, I was still in a state of shock. How did I know this woman? How could I have found perfect love at the last possible second before never seeing her again? Why did this happen? What do I do now? I wasn't looking for this! I never expected to see her again, but a few weeks later we began to correspond.

My brief encounter with Shawna changed my life forever and opened my heart to a love more powerful than is humanly imaginable. Though we live in different countries, and in spite of all the barriers in our path, we know we were meant to fall in love again.

Since the time that we have both come to refer to as "The Look," we have both been regressed to past lives and learned that we have lived together and loved before.

## Shawna's Story

I have listened to the wisdom of dreams for as long as I can remember. Never was a dream so simple and clear, yet so powerful as one I had in November 1991.

I dreamed I was walking through a park at the edge of the ocean. I glanced over to notice a stranger approaching. Emanating from his face was a soft, translucent light. I became aware of a profound familiarity. My eyes were transfixed upon his image. I recognized his gentle energy, the way he moved. I recognized the language of his soul and his very being. I knew that we had shared many lives before, also that we would walk together again in this lifetime. I just didn't know when. Time is so elusive.

As we approached each other in my dream, we fell into a gentle embrace. The love that flowed between us was pure, unconditional, and without end. We did not exchange a single word, but we felt everything—past, present, and to be.

I recognized Stephen with one look at a small airport in Hawaii, a look that drew me deep into his soul, unfurling memories of ages past and connecting to our unfathomable love, which has lasted many lifetimes.

# Signs of Love

## Carol Tisch Allen

As a Vedic astrologer, I am a big believer in omens. Vedic astrology, an ancient system from India, teaches that there are signs around us at all times, pointing us where we need to go and revealing hidden truths and information.

I've observed many omens while in session with clients and at the important events of friends and family. Once, while doing a reading for a man at my home, I mentioned that the coming year would be very difficult for his love life. Just as the words left my mouth, my smoke alarm began blaring with deafening loudness. It had been set off by the incense I was burning on my piano—something I had done every day for years, never setting off the smoke alarm until that moment! I took it to be an omen that his love life would indeed be difficult. The universe was using the smoke alarm to concur with my reading. As it happened, the man called me a year later and confessed that his love life had been an uncharacteristic shambles all year.

I pay especially close attention to omens at weddings. They are such significant life events, so the energy is more intense.

I was in the wedding of a dear friend years ago, as the maid of honor. The couple had had a whirlwind courtship and didn't know each other very well. As the big day approached, the bride had more and more concerns about the impending nuptials. She loved her fiancé quite a bit, however, and decided to ignore her fears. As we stood in our fancy dresses moments before the ceremony, she handed me the box containing the ring she was to give her intended. I opened the box and discovered, to my great dismay, that the diamond was cracked! I had never heard of a diamond cracking and didn't know it was even possible! Aren't diamonds the hardest substance on Earth? I showed the bride. This symbol of her love for her groom was damaged, and I took this to be a negative omen for their relationship.

The ceremony went off without a hitch, yet there was another omen at the reception. The hotel had forgotten to place the bridge and groom figurines on the top of the cake. I decided to keep my mouth shut about that sign. As I feared, the couple had a very rocky time for a couple of years, even splitting up and planning to divorce for several months. Happily, they have worked through their issues and are reunited.

I recently attended the wedding of a high school friend. The couple had chosen to be married at a gorgeous country-club garden in the mountains. It was a beautiful, sunny day. The guests sipped mimosas under wisteria blossoms, chatting gaily about the happy twosome. All seemed well. As we guests took our seats, and the procession of bridesmaids and attendants began, a nearby siren wailed loudly. Oh no, I thought. A bad omen for the marriage. To my near complete disbelief, more and worse omens followed. As the minister requested the rings, a tiny girl with garlands in her hair toddled over to the bride and groom and dropped the pillow and the rings just as she reached them. While others in the audience chuckled, I bristled. Later, the couple lit two candles from one large candle and placed them on the altar as a symbol of their union. To my shock, a breeze picked up and the groom's candle blew out! The omens were obvious. The two had their work cut out for them. A couple of years later, I heard they were having a tough time.

I have seen positive omens too, of course! At the wedding of my sister, lovely butterflies flew around her and her betrothed throughout the ceremony. What thrilled me most was that a calico cat came from out of nowhere and nuzzled the feet of the minister during the whole service. Frogs happily warbled in a nearby creek. Ten years later, they are going strong.

Needless to say, I was curious to see what omens might occur on my own wedding day. My groom and I decided to elope to Las Vegas. We planned to have a spiritual ceremony the following summer for our loved ones, but didn't want to wait that long and felt we needed to do something legal.

Neither of us could believe we were actually going to be married in Las Vegas. Let's face it, it doesn't have a reputation as the most sacred, spiritual place in the world. Once we thought of it, though, we couldn't get it out of our minds. We decided just to have a great time and really play up the whole Las Vegas aspect. My husband is a big Elvis fan—he'd even played an obsessed Elvis look-alike in a film. He decided that we should get an Elvis impersonator to marry us—"The King" must officiate. For weeks, as we'd discuss our upcoming Vegas trip, he'd put on an Elvis accent and declare, "The King's gonna marry us, baby."

Once in Vegas, things started going our way. Our hotel room was upgraded from a regular room to an expensive suite. To our disappointment, though, we discovered that no Elvis impersonators actually perform wedding ceremonies. All we could find was an Elvis who would walk me down the aisle and then put on a three-song concert following the service—all to the tune of $160.

"Forget it!" exclaimed my groom-to-be. "Let's go on a helicopter ride instead."

So much for "The King" marrying us.

The big day arrived, and we decided to go to the International House of Pancakes for breakfast before heading to the courthouse.

"We're getting married today!" I announced to our waitress.

"That's wonderful," she enthused. "I got married at a little chapel here in Vegas twelve years ago and have been very happy ever since." Aha—a good omen.

Minutes later, as we hungrily gobbled our Swedish pancakes she arrived with a plastic bag. "This is for you. Someone left it weeks ago," she said, handing us the bag. "I've been waiting for a bride and groom to give it to." We opened it. Inside was a Nevada tourist license plate that read: WED 97. An excellent omen.

Hours later, we arrived at the Silver Ball Wedding Chapel. We were introduced to our minister, a very sweet older man who had been married for fifty-five years himself. While a video camera recorded the auspicious occasion, he led us through an extremely moving, poignant religious ceremony. Not exactly what we'd expected out of a cheesy chapel we'd chosen from the Yellow Pages! We both wept as he declared us man and wife. It was a very special moment. In gratitude, we shook the man's hands and asked his name.

"It's David King," he replied. We exploded in laughter. The King had married us after all! A most excellent omen.

Epilogue: Months later, after searching high and low, I saw the engagement ring of my dreams. My husband makes jewelry and had made our wedding bands, but I still couldn't decide on my engagement ring. (We never do anything conventionally!) I had gone into a friend's store. It wasn't a wedding store or even a traditional jewelry store, but there in a jewelry case was the perfect ring for me, and it cost far less than we had budgeted and was even half off! Knowing my husband would be thrilled, I bought it. A classical music channel was playing on the store's radio. As I was paying for the ring, the Wedding March from Mendelssohn's *A Midsummer Night's Dream* came on over the speakers. It was a beautiful omen declaring that this was, in fact, my true wedding ring and a positive sign for our upcoming midsummer spiritual wedding.

# Casting Spells and the Single Girl

## *Stephanie P. Gunning*

One summer evening a few years back, my good friend Alejandra and I went out for dinner in the East Village in New York City. At the time, I was recovering from the breakup of a two-year love affair. It had taken several months of serious willpower to disentangle myself from that relationship, but I was determined to move on.

Alejandra is Mexican and very expressive by nature. During dinner, she and I began lamenting the lack of passion and fear of intimacy we felt from so many men we met. We wondered if it was American culture or just our bad luck. During our discussion, I recalled a brief but unforgettable affair I'd had three years earlier with a non-American man. After six incredible weeks together, my French-Armenian boyfriend, Alain, had suddenly disappeared—literally without a trace. Overnight, his phone was disconnected and there was no one at his apartment. I was devastated. That heartbreak had left me feeling vulnerable and was largely responsible for my launch into the relationship that had just failed.

Time passed, but memories of my affair with Alain haunted

me, and though I tried to put it behind me, nothing seemed to match our romance. I had never been so open or felt so much chemical heat with anyone, before or since.

Then, two years after his vanishing act, Alain sent me a letter explaining and apologizing for his absence of manners. He told me that the intensity of what had happened between us had scared him and he had gone home to Paris for a time.

But by the time I received his letter, I was immersed in my new relationship and was committed to making it work. Alain and I got together for a face-to-face conversation one afternoon just before he left New York again to make a fresh start in Houston. Bye-bye, I thought. What bad timing we have. Though matters between us seemed resolved, a piece of me still wondered if we could have re-created the emotional connection we had once experienced.

Over the last year we had lost touch with each other, but now that I was alone once more, I was curious.

What would happen if Alain and I tried again?

Alejandra and I finished supper, and since it was languid and balmy on this particular evening, we decided to take a long walk toward home and continue our analysis. We found ourselves passing Enchantments, a witchcraft store.

Excited, I said, "Ally, let's go in. I want to buy a love spell." I had met witches and, in my capacity as a book editor, had read about their form of magic and ritual. I thought, Why not give it a try? What could it hurt?

We went in.

It was a few minutes before closing time, and the very tired looking saleswoman asked if she could help us. I giggled and said, "I'd like a love spell."

She rolled her eyes at me. I guessed that she got a lot of requests for this particular item. But I pressed on and said, "It's for a man I already know who has moved away. I want him to come back to me."

The saleswoman, who told us she was a witch, said, "Spells are created out of intention. Are you sure you want what you're asking?" I was a little embarrassed, but still high on the idea of my experiment.

"Yes, I want to do it," I replied. "Would you give me instructions?"

I thought, What are the chances that it will work anyway?

I was given a pouch with some deep red incense in it, a small vial of rose-colored oil, and two red candles. Apparently, red is the color of passion and love. My instructions were that each night for one week, I should anoint the candles with the oil, burn the incense, and light the candles while holding the image of my beloved in my mind as a focus of intention. During the week, I should move the candles closer together, an inch or so at a time, until they were touching, and then let them burn down completely. After that, the spell would be complete.

I've always been the sort of person who likes to try out face masks made of mashed fruit and oatmeal from the pages of women's magazines, and formulate new variations on old recipes in the kitchen, so I couldn't wait to get home and try the spell. Now I was cooking. I do a meditation practice, so I decided to incorporate this ritual into my daily half-hour routine.

The first few nights were fun. I followed the plan, smearing the oil on the candles, thinking of Alain. I didn't particularly enjoy the aroma of the incense, but I burned it anyway—I didn't want to sour the deal. I hadn't realized that candles burn pretty slowly. But I sat and watched as inch by slow inch the candles came together until they were touching. Then they fused. That was exciting. We are one, we are one, I imagined. Come back to me.

By day seven, unfortunately, the fused candle was only half burned. However, I was determined to see the spell through. If it doesn't bring my lover back, I thought, maybe it will bring me some other man. The eighth day, in the afternoon, I decided I was going to light the fused candle and burn it to a stub no matter how many hours it took. It burned and burned. After three hours, I got bored and just blew it out. I shook my head, thinking, Forget about it. That's enough of that. What will be, will be. I consoled myself that at least for a little while I'd taken destiny into my own hands.

But the next day, the phone rang. Unbelievably, it was Alain. "I'm back in New York. Actually, I've been here for the past six weeks. Do you want to get together?"

I was amazed. Obviously, my ritual had somehow connected me to the energy or truth of his return. And I felt sure that the very minute I had given up, blown out the flame, and accepted whatever fate would bring me had been the true moment of magic.

The spell worked, but not in the way I had expected.

Though we spent some time together, we couldn't rekindle our connection, and he moved away again. Alain's destiny was to leave New York, and I was only a detour on his journey, as he was only a detour on mine. This time we parted friends and with a sense of completion.

No more wondering about what might have been.

So I'm still looking for my soul mate, but these days I don't do it by casting spells.

When you cast a spell, you're messing around with what's meant to be or not to be, putting your will above the will of another energy. There are forces beyond explanation in this world, and though I had tapped into them briefly, now I treat them with respect.

Though I have to admit, I did save what was left of the incense and oil in a special place in my top dresser drawer, and the other day I happened to notice that red candles were two for $3.99 at the local supermarket.

Hey, you never know when a love spell might come in handy.

# First Meeting

*Monte Farber*

My first prophetic dream was really my best, for that is where I first "met" my wife, soul mate, and artistic collaborator, Amy Zerner. I was fourteen years old, staying with my recently divorced father, an Archie Bunker–like New York City police sergeant, in the family apartment on Argyle Road in Brooklyn.

I lay sleeping one steamy summer evening, tossing and turning in the grip of a recurring nightmare that had plagued me since childhood. In it, all the animals had escaped from the Prospect Park Zoo, where my father had worked as a patrolman, and they were making their way toward my mother, my younger sister, and me as a younger child. My mother took our hands and we all ran for the safety of our downstairs hallway, entering just in time as the elephants marched by slowly but menancingly, trunks holding tails like in the circus.

Suddenly, another dream burst in like breaking news. In it, I was sitting behind a beautiful woman with purple hair (!), massaging her lovely neck and shoulders. Now, that was big stuff for a fourteen-year-old boy in 1964. Even more amazing was that I actually felt the indescribable feeling of being in love with this woman, and also knew beyond a doubt that she loved and trusted me totally too!

In rapid succession I saw puzzling images of turning off a main road and up a hill with the sun shining through the trees, and then making the peculiar turn-within-a-turn that completes what I know now to be the end of the road to the home Amy and I have shared since 1975. I often think of that dream when I drive up that hill on a sunny East Hampton day, half expecting to see my fourteen-year-old dream body hovering in the trees. I even saw the now familiar view over my right shoulder as I back out of our driveway.

And then I woke up. I was in agony! I tried with all my might to go back to sleep and feel that incredible pure love, but of course I couldn't. I tried everything, but to no avail. I thought I could still feel the love, but only as a distant echo of the feeling in the dream.

Even then I knew instinctively that love was meant to be shared. I went into the tiny kitchen and, startling my father as he read the paper, excitedly announced that I had just seen in a dream the woman I would love and marry. Solemnly, my father put down his paper, looked at me with a pitying gaze, and said, "What do you know about love?"

Well, my first foray into prophecy may have engendered a lousy response, and I might not have known too much about love then, but since 1988, Amy, who *does* have purple hair, and I have had more than one million copies of our unique divination systems published around the world in nine languages. Just as Cupid is the child of Venus (art) and Mercury (writing), we think of our eight collaborations, which combine Amy's art and my writing, as our children. More important, for the last twenty-three years we have known and worked hard to build the kind of true love and mutually supportive partnership most people only dream about.

Happily, I have had many, many more prophetic dreams since that first one, some quite useful, but none as enjoyable. I have gotten so used to them that I can always distinguish the prophetic dreams from the "normal" sleep-dreams that fill my nights and naps.

And that recurring dream about the zoo break? It never plagued me again after I dreamed of Amy. Love does that, you know.

# Danny

## *Mariah Martin*

Last night, a friend and I watched the full moon rise over Kailua Bay in Hawaii. It danced between the ironwood trees and filled the night sky with golden light. We found a comfortable place to sit on the sandy banks and closed our eyes, then took turns listening to the sound of Spirit and channeling the Light Beings. I was full of joy. As I surrendered to my Light Guides speaking through me to my friend, my mind drifted back in time to another moonlit night spent with my soul mate, a Light Angel on earth, my first love, Danny.

He and I sat on one of the benches lining the beach near the lake where we grew up. The night sky was brightly lit by the full moon, but stars claimed an equal beauty. He was going away to France for a while. My heart was heavy with fear and a sense of aloneness. When Danny was around, I felt awakened and hopeful, at peace with being a sensitive person.

"Try to let go of your despair," he said. "I'll be back. Don't let them burden you. Listen to me. Someday you'll understand what I'm saying. Just listen."

He went on to talk about the soul. He spoke of our need to pay attention to how God speaks to us. He spoke about the connection that he and I had on an energetic level that time and space could never lessen. "Listen and you can hear our souls talking to each other. It doesn't matter if I am far away." I believed him.

That moment was like many others when Danny had quoted philosophers and poets like Sartre and e. e. cummings. He often spoke about the energy of light in all the wonders around us. We would spend hours staring at a flower, the bark of a tree, or snowflakes. "Just watch and let the flower speak to you. You will never be alone, I promise you." Being just a teenager, I didn't have a clue what he was talking about, but I loved him, so I listened and tried to imprint his words on my heart. "You have many gifts. You will be happier, I know it. Trust me."

When Danny said that to me, the future seemed full of possibilities, at least for that moment. My relationship with him lifted me out of the depression of my life.

The strict Catholic school I attended, where dreaming was not allowed and failure was ridiculed, felt like a prison. After school and during holidays, I worked in my father's diner. My best friend lived thirty miles away. Life in our small town was empty of anything lively or magical. When Danny came to our small town from New York City, my life became interesting, fun, full of dreams of the future and knowledge of the past. Magic happened in small, wonderful ways. I learned from him to trust my sensitivity, my love of beauty, my mind, my dreams, and my connection to Spirit. We would play games of finding the life force in things.

Not only was Danny sensitive, but he was also a young man with a genius level of intelligence and a photographic mind. I struggled in school. He taught me to close my eyes and listen to my teachers, to see stories in my mind as images and learn that way. He taught me to trust my flashes of intuition. Often when he came to visit, he would stand outside the front door until I sensed him being there. Little did I know at the time that he was teaching me to fulfill my gifts and have a good life using them. Our psychic connection was there right from the start.

We had met by chance when I was thirteen. One day, my sister and I had canoed several miles down the lake, and overcome by the heat, we pulled into a landing. There was a little candy stand by the lake that sold cold sodas and ice pops.

"How are you today, girls?" asked the older woman running the stand. "I want you to meet a young friend of mine."

Danny turned around. An electric charge went through me, and I couldn't look away from his radiant blue eyes. That was it, we were connected. He got into the canoe and came home with us to see where I lived. That night, he returned to my house with a bouquet of wild yellow roses. I always associate wild yellow roses with Danny. From that moment on, young as I was, he was the love of my life.

We were teen lovers in a time when there was an innocence to that kind of love. Being four years younger than him, I looked to him for so much. He became my comforter, my guide to adulthood, my psychic teacher, and, with his artist's soul, an inspiration to live life with gusto and sensitivity. Danny was a bearer of light, a teacher of soul truths, and a guide to my divine path, but when I first met him, the only way that I could let him in was as a romantic partner. Thirteen-year-old girls like me usually don't recognize soul mates. They want a dream boyfriend. Danny willingly took on the role he was to play in my life.

Through shared experiences with him, I was initiated into a large world here and beyond earth. Danny loved music and played in a band. I spent many moments enraptured by his drumming. I went to my first concert with him, the Modern Jazz Quartet. He felt called to God and, for a time, thought of being a priest. (I was relieved when that was over.) He also felt called to create and considered being a writer. Later he went to architecture school, and together we planned a house to be built in the woods. He introduced me to poetry by quoting poem after poem in English, French, and Latin. He contemplated the words of great philosophers and introduced me to the work of Teilhard de Chardin, the spiritual evolutionist. But most of all, he loved me. Danny kept me in his heart and was always there when I needed him, even during times when we were exploring other relationships, as young people do. I knew myself when I looked into his eyes or heard his voice.

Danny died when I was nineteen. He had spent some time studying in Paris and thought it would also be good for me to go abroad, to get out of the depression I felt at the all-girls college I attended. I was accepted into a school in Rome. One day his parents picked him up at the private school where he was teaching, and they were on their way to visit me before I left the country. A drunk driver hit them head on, killing Danny and his mother. The last time I had seen him, several weeks before the accident, he had talked about the years we had known each other and said that he wanted me to remember that no matter where I was, he would always be there.

"I will always be with you," he whispered in my ear as he kissed me before getting on the bus to go back to work.

Over the years since then, I have felt this love.

My work involves a lot of travel. When my children were young, it was difficult for me to be thousands of miles away from them. One day, when I was working far away from home in a small coastal town in Oregon, one of my children had a crisis moment. I felt consumed with anxiety. I prayed that God would help me find peace so that I could finish my work and go home. Being single, I was the sole support of my family, and it was important for me not to lose work. During a break, I went for a walk. It was late fall, and everything looked dreary and gray. The flowers had finished blooming, and the trees were losing their leaves. I felt enwrapped in the gloomy environment.

As I walked around a curve, a little voice from the angels told me to look up. There, before me, was a wild yellow rosebush in full bloom. A message from Danny. My mood lifted as the light filled me. He was with me as he promised he would be, and I felt flooded with love.

Everything at home worked out that time, and I was able to finish my work. I channel Light Beings for a living. Danny taught me to listen.

# Awakening to Love

## S. A. Forest

A quote by an "authority" on relationships finally propelled me to cast away any resistance or concern I had about going public with our story. I don't remember where I read it or the exact words, but the thrust of the statement was that people should stop looking for an "ideal" loving relationship, because it was an unattainable, impossible, unrealistic dream, a fairy tale. Two people just can't live that way, he said.

But I know otherwise. I've experienced that dream, that love, for the past sixteen years. So in case you don't already know it: the impossible is really possible, and the dream can be realized.

For years, loneliness tore at my heart, making life difficult to endure. The closeness, the caring, the intimacy, the continued physical presence of a loved one that I hungered for, was missing. What I wanted more than anything else—even spiritual mastery—was a loving partner, someone with whom I could open myself up totally and completely, with whom I could feel so connected that we would be as one. This is the fire that burned in my heart with a roaring, unquenchable desire.

Looking back, I see that the unbearable loneliness I was experiencing was tearing down the inner fortress I had erected to love, opening me up, readying me for the two major events that would shatter my quiet, simple existence.

During the darkest, bleakest, blackest moments, love entered my life. The first bolt of lightning hit one day about a year and a half after I moved from New York to Los Angeles. Echoes of a childhood spent in near isolation, plus an accumulation of the sheer physical loneliness I'd experienced since dropping out of the everyday world, reached a resounding crescendo, and I felt as if I couldn't go on anymore. I sat down to meditate in an attempt to ease the hurt and soothe the pain. Before I knew it, the walls of the room, as well as my body, dissolved. In what felt like an instant of Earth's time, I was in a universe infinitely more spectacular than any photos or artist's rendering the scientific community has produced, or that the imaginings of the special-effects units in Hollywood have created for the screen.

I'm not going to try to describe the event—which lasted for the better part of an afternoon—for there are no words, no reference points, for what I experienced the afternoon of January 3, 1981. What shook the very foundation of my being, more than anything else, was the distinct voice that was speaking to me from inside, different in tone, pitch, cadence, and feeling than the inner voice that was always chattering away in my head, the voice I had always assumed was "me."

This voice informed me that I had birthed him, actually birthed myself—and indeed, at one point it felt as if waves of contractions were propelling me along a universal birth canal until I was delivered into a cradling whiteness: brilliant, intense, and soft at the same time.

The deep, smooth, honey-toned voice went on to say that he was my Higher Self, my essence, that part of me connected to the force we call God, beyond the mind, beyond earthly conditioning and socialization, beyond fear and anger. He told me that he—rather I—it was all so confusing—was all-knowing, infallible.

I must confess that I did not greet the emergence of my "essence" graciously or respectfully. But this Higher Self—who, when asked his name, chuckled and identified himself as Alimar—was not only unflappable, but infinitely patient, compassionate, and, most of all, deliciously loving.

Nine days later, the second bolt of lightning struck. I walked into a room and met my beloved, Alexandra Light. The instant I set eyes on her, she owned my heart. In that first millisecond, I fell hopelessly, inextricably in love. Before we even exchanged a single word, I knew with unshakable knowing that she was the one I had been searching for my whole life. There was no need to get to know her, for it felt as if I had always known her, as if we had been together for years, not minutes or hours or days. But Earth is the stage for endless dramas, and the writers of this scenario whipped up a real tearjerker.

I soon discovered that Alexandra Light was involved with another man and that in three weeks they would be leaving to live together at his house in Colorado. Instead of becoming lovers, we reluctantly entered into a deep friendship. Alexandra was unique, the most original person I had ever met. She was a wild, free spirit, brilliant, funny, full of passion and life. She also had a knack for pushing all my buttons, for more often than not, it felt as if she were playing me as if I were the keyboard on a church organ. By the end of the three weeks, I vowed never to see or speak to her again. But the day she left Los Angeles was the saddest, most painful, most miserable day of my life.

In the months that followed, Alimar attempted to console me, but oh how I fought it. Even though his guidance was exceptionally wise, and would have saved me a great deal of grief had I listened, the skeptic, the one who still had one and a half feet rooted in the material-rational world, wasn't buying it. Even though my spiritual journey was deepening and evolving at an even more accelerated pace than before, not a moment went by when I didn't think of Alexandra Light, or feel the excruciating pain in my heart because of her absence.

Ironically, when she tried to call me, I wouldn't speak to her. My reasoning was that not having her in my life at all was less painful than limited contact on her terms. Despite arguments to the contrary, humans are not a rational species.

Nine months later, it was looking like the end of the world once more. I was going to have to move again, but now, for the very first time, no other alternative had presented itself. Two single bills bearing Alexander Hamilton's portrait and the number twenty in all four corners comprised my entire worldly financial portfolio. My only remaining possessions were a portable Hermes typewriter and a small set of ceramic drums. I had no home of my own, no transportation other than my feet, and no prospects, and the few people I felt a kinship with had left Los Angeles. Most important, I had no love in my life.

I wasn't frightened, just distraught. I was forty-two years old, and I was living like a teenage runaway. In society's mirror, I was an absolute failure. As for my Higher Self . . . well, where had that gotten me? Regrets and recrimination richocheted through the corridors of my mind like a squadron of heat-seeking missiles pursuing their targets. In response, Alimar lovingly told me not to worry, that everything would work out, but I discounted his sage guidance, still not sure that I wasn't making the whole thing up. Quitting had never been an option before. But now I was contemplating giving up all this nonsense and returning to Manhattan to see if I could pick up the pieces of my shattered career.

At the height of my despair, two major events occurred almost simultaneously. Shortly after my arrival in Los Angeles, I had met an agent at a meditation retreat who felt she could sell my two screenplays. After leaving them both with her, I completely forgot about them. Suddenly, out of the blue, she called to inform me that *both* properties had been sold for a substantial sum of money. That same afternoon, I was invited to a party as a reward for coming to the aid of someone in distress. At first I wasn't going to go. But at the last moment I took notice of an inner feeling that was urging me to relent. Fortunately, this time I listened.

The party turned out to be fun. During a lull, I was about to go outside for a breath of fresh air when the double doors swung open and Alexandra Light swept into the room and back into my life. I tried to disappear the moment I saw her, but my heart riveted my feet to the floor, and once she had my hand she wouldn't let go. Her relationship hadn't worked out, and she was free, but I still wanted to flee. Aside from all her other qualities, she was a beautiful woman, and men were constantly drawn to her. I didn't want the grief. A former lover once commented that I'm soft on the outside, but inside I have a will of iron. But even iron bends.

Alexandra Light and I spent a great deal of time together the next few days, still as friends, not as lovers. I kept telling myself that she would probably leave soon and be out of my life. But this thought was certainly no consolation. Alimar tried to give me guidance, but I was so hurt and angry I didn't give him a chance to speak.

Instead of leaving town, Alexandra Light rented a house in Malibu, sight unseen. When she finally did see it, she was so distraught that I took a great risk and told her about Alimar. And then I offered to see if my Higher Self would speak out loud to help her. That experience was so electric, it altered the course of our lives forever. Alexandra Light instantly fell in love with Alimar in much the same way that I had fallen in love with her. We agreed to spend the next thirty days together. Personally, I didn't think we would last forty-eight hours. But with Alimar in the picture, it was a whole different story. A short time later, Glorious Light, Alexandra Light's Higher Self, joined us, and those thirty days have stretched into sixteen years.

Alexandra Light is not only my lover and companion and journey-mate, but my teacher, my best friend, my birther and savior. Even after all these years, I am still in awe of her magnificence and brilliance. She is truly a glorious light.

But if you think it was all violins, smooth sailing, and they-lived-happily-ever-after, guess again. Both of us have extremely independent, strong-willed, passionate, headstrong personalities. Even though we love each other with every fiber of our being, without the sage, loving guidance and wisdom of our Higher Selves, we would never have made it through the early years (and some of the later ones). We would have gone our separate ways, and we most certainly would have spent the rest of our lives missing each other, longing for each other, living in regret and wallowing in memories of what could have been. A relationship on this level of closeness and intimacy, without borders or boundaries or outer distractions, has been the most difficult challenge of our lives. We've confronted our worst fears and our most powerful demons. We've been tested in situations that would have driven an irreparable wedge between most couples. But having Glorious Light and Alimar in our lives has allowed us to diffuse the destructive emotions, heal the damaged children and adults, and dissolve the barriers that keep people separate even when they are physically together.

After all these years, and all this time together, our love continues to grow and evolve. There are no mental or physical walls, no secrets between us, yet we haven't lost our individuality or our unique identities or the spark of joy and excitement that being together brings. We are rarely apart, yet we never tire of each other, never get bored or restless.

We lead a very, very simple, quiet, contemplative life. We laugh, we play, we have fun, we give guidance and work with our beloved students; we take care of practical matters, always with our main purpose, love and God, uppermost in our consciousness.

It gives Alexandra Light and me great joy and satisfaction to teach and guide others in a process we've developed to realize one's essence and to manifest and sustain deep, godly love. It is our hope that others may be inspired to connect with their Higher Selves and realize that eternal, everlasting, unconditional love is not only possible, but can serve as a vehicle for the biggest miracle of all, union with God.

# 6

# MIRACULOUS HEALING AND ANGELIC RESCUE

# A Healing Prayer

## Gennica Ivey

For as long as I can remember, I have had some type of medical problem, mainly with my eyes. When I was about four years old, doctors diagnosed me with a rare disease that left me blind in my left eye. This disease also left my left eye so damaged that it could no longer hold up my eyelid. I was sent to an eye doctor who specialized in prosthetic eyes, and he fitted me with a contact-lens-like eye that would hold my eyelid up. This eye boosted my self-confidence and did wonders for my appearance.

In my sophomore year of high school, I developed an eating disorder that left me deathly afraid of food. I was five foot one that year, weighing about ninety-five pounds. I thought I was obese. I had been taking courses to become a model, and in these I was taught to fear food. I avoided all my favorite foods, resorting to drinking water and eating oranges for lunch. This continued and got worse when my boyfriend of a year and a half broke off with me my junior year.

I was devastated. I figured he must have broken up with me because I was too fat. I dieted again, this time reaching an all-time low of eighty-nine pounds. My size zero pants no longer fit—in fact, they were much too big. My eating disorder had ups and downs all through my junior and senior years.

I was excited to finally be a senior. But once again, I had a health problem. This time it wasn't my weight; it was my eyes again. My left eye had become extremely light sensitive, so even the dimmest light hurt my eyes. My senior portrait was taken with one eye shut because it was too painful for me to look at the camera. I went to the doctor, and he prescribed medicine to numb my left eye because it was passing the light sensitivity to my right eye. I was okay for a while after that.

Toward the end of my senior year, I was having eye problems again. Intense pain racked my eyes. My left eye throbbed and watered like crazy. I was in constant pain, and I couldn't drive, write, or even look at people. I went to the doctor again, and he took out the contact and cleaned it. It made me feel better for about a day, but again the pain returned, and now it was worse.

One night I was lying on my mom's bed, trying to figure out what I could do to make the pain go away. Bored and discouraged, I thumbed through my mom's copy of *Hot Chocolate for the Mystical Soul*. I noticed there was a story about an eye, so I went ahead and read it. The author discussed her situation, and said that she had handled it by meditating and envisioning a bright light going into her eye, somehow healing it. I had never been a religious person, although I do believe in God. I put the story into the back of my mind and went to talk to my mom about what to do about the pain. Later that night, I was talking to my parents about God and how I didn't believe that He heard my prayers.

"If God listened to my prayers, He wouldn't have let this thing with my eye happen," I said.

"God gives you things for a purpose," they responded.

"Why didn't I get better after I got my blessing from Uncle Britt?" I challenged.

My mom responded, "When you got your blessing, we didn't know what was going on with you. Some doctors thought you had cancer and gave you only a few months to live."

I was quiet.

My dad spoke up. "Maybe God is trying to tell you something right now."

"Like what?" I asked.

"Maybe that you need to accept yourself the way you are. Not just with your eye, but with your weight."

Once again I was silent. Then I said, "So if I pray, God will help me and make the pain stop?"

"Not necessarily. Ask Him for the patience to endure the pain," my dad advised.

Later that night, before going to sleep, I got on my knees and bowed my head and asked for God's help in getting through this pain. I told Him that I really needed His help, and hoped He could hear me. I told Him that I knew there was a reason for this pain, and I understood it. I said good night, knowing I had done all that I could. When I closed my eyes, I envisioned a bright light healing my eye, and I saw myself free of pain. I fell asleep quickly.

The next morning, I got up and did my usual morning duties. Except that this morning was different from a lot of others in the past week. I was not grabbing my eye in pain. It felt fine.

I thought, Okay, so it doesn't hurt now. Let's see what happens at the end of the day. I left for school, hoping my eye would be okay. I went the whole day without its hurting, not even a little bit. And as I am writing this, I am still amazed but thankful that I have God there to answer prayers when I need Him the most.

I still have problems with food, but I am working on those because I know God is worried about me. He wants me to know it. And this time, I'm gonna listen.

# The Healing of Origins

## *Norma Jean Young*

For at least twenty-five years, I have been following a life purpose: to do whatever I can to integrate the family of humankind. As a very young woman, the enormity of this purpose drove me to want to house third-world countries with yurts and domes à la Bucky Fuller, and to dream of affecting the world positively in very large ways. As life pared me down to size, I finally came to a despairing rest that gave way to my feeling my extreme smallness—that I was one grain of sand in the grand design. It was only in such a state of surrender and deflated ego that Reiki came to me. With amazing simplicity, I felt the unifying force of Reiki.

One of my most challenging experiences was to go to a remote island in Indonesia to offer Reiki treatment and training to people who had leprosy. I had planned on going to Bali after training intensively in Japan, to have the best vacation ever. But in the Netherlands, at the World Reiki Master Conference, I met Ottie Tisscher, who had recently become a Reiki Master and was planning to return to Indonesia, where she was born, to offer Reiki to lepers. How could I do anything but ask to go with her? I was already scheduled to be there.

Ottie met me at the Denpasar airport in Indonesia, and we tried to prepare. She had the language and I had the teaching experience, so it was a fine team. We really needed each other. I was terrified. Even though doctors reassured me that leprosy is contracted only through open sores or cuts, I resolved to play it safe and not touch any afflicted people if I could help it. (I had been doing a lot of sword work in hundred degree heat in Japan, and I also had mosquito bites.) We flew from Denpasar to Timor and then to the Flores Islands.

Fortunately, we met Dr. Manik on the small plane. He was a doctor for the Department of Health in that region. When he heard what we were doing, he was moved to tears and asked if he could join us. He is a devout man, a convert to Christianity. He was a godsend; we needed him. He planned to handle his business and then join us in Lewoleba.

The tiny plane made a very rough landing in a cow pasture. Two smiling Indonesian women greeted us: Mama Isabella, the leader and vision-holder for the hospital and community, and Sister Juliana, a nurse and nun who was the single medical professional running the hospital. Sister Juliana took my hand immediately and walked close to me, swinging arms with me as if we were young girls and leaning into me. The best way to describe Sister Juliana is "velvet." Her voice was like velvet, her manner was velvet—obvious and lush. She and Mama Isabella loaded us into their "ambulance," which was a dented, rusty old step van.

When we arrived at the hospital, Sister Juliana took us into the stark meeting and eating room and warned us to be careful working with the lepers. She explained that they didn't know how to be with one another because they were not subject to normal behavioral consequences. For instance, even if they committed robbery or murder, they would not be welcome in jail. She wanted us to be a model for them, to show them how to converse and be together as people—to show them social skills.

We ate with them the food the two women had prepared, a kind of watery soup with fish that had been donated that day. My clear resolve not to touch anyone was met with an immediate challenge. A leprous man approached me and came very close, just standing and pouring sweet energy from his eyes into mine. I asked Ottie what was going on, and she said, "He is here to offer you his hand, Norma Jean."

There went all the *Ben-Hur* images of lepers. What do you do when someone does that? Obviously, there is only one response—you offer him your hand. From that moment on, I realized that I had to surrender to this experience and trust that I would be protected.

Then we went to Mama (a term of great respect, honor, and love) Isabella's home, where we would be living. It was a white, sprawling *Out of Africa*–style house set in a lush green jungle, and about a dozen people lived there with her.

The custom in Lewoleba is for people who have resources, be they respect or money, to take in or adopt those who have none, so this was a rather large compound of people living together. They were all people whose leprosy had been arrested, controlled with medication. Some of them were missing digits from their feet or hands, or their noses might be caved in. There were two men who were more severely crippled and distorted in their bodies; however, it was quite evident there was nothing distorted in their generosity toward us. They served us tea and cookies, all from a dirt-floor kitchen with an open fire pit outside.

This was when I informally gave Mama Isabella her first experience of Reiki. Up to that point, she explained, they had understood we were coming with an ancient herbal remedy for leprosy. Mama was deeply touched and said she had *never*, in all her years, felt something so deeply *received*. Nothing had been *given* to her like this before.

Ottie and I soon insisted on joining "the family" in the kitchen behind the house in the yard, and we started getting very close to these radiant and happy people. They laugh a lot. One woman sewed beautiful bags from a soft hand-woven fabric, hoping to sell them for support. Their artistry is so natural.

We were taken to be "checked out" by Father Eugene. As the island was predominantly Catholic, he was like the unofficial king. I felt that if he had not approved of what we were doing, we would not have been allowed to continue. We struck up an immediate and convivial relationship with this most happy, youthful-looking priest from Chicago, who had been there twenty years. He insisted we be honored guests at a blessing that evening in honor of the return of a family member to one of his parishioners.

Then came the time to present Reiki to the hospital patients themselves and see if they wanted to be treated or taught to do Reiki healing. This was one of the most challenging moments of my life. I was on a Catholic island, with a born-again Christian, to teach Reiki to lepers. The pressure built. Ottie kept nervously going out of the meeting room where the patients were gathering; I would fetch her and explain that since she was translating, she *had* to stay in the room!

Dr. Manik had arrived just before dinner. He was leading patients in singing—thank God! I was praying very hard for guidance. I began: "We are all children of God, all with our own life purpose, and we deserve to fulfill that purpose. We all have something to give. Reiki is the most sincere way I have found to do that."

Then I asked if someone would be willing to come forward and experience the Reiki treatment. This was a most definitive moment. We had come so far to do this; our success relied totally on their receptivity. I set a chair in the open and invited anyone to come sit and receive treatment. After a long pause, during which I felt my neck sticking out possibly farther than it had ever been, a man on crutches came forward. He smiled as Ottie and I put our hands on his upper chest, and then they all began to line up for treatment.

We could have stayed all night treating them. We then arranged a class for those who chose to learn how to do this treatment for themselves and one another. Twenty-four people came, including three boys. I have never taught Reiki so religiously.

Every healing Reiki circle became a prayer circle, singing Christian songs with Dr. Manik. We used the clinic tables for treatment. It was so moving to see the lepers treating one another, even if they didn't have complete hands. Their sharing each day was so heartfelt and moving that I would hold my heart constantly to be able to take in the enormous doses of feelings they expressed. They were given their lives back.

They had something to give. They were not untouchable; in fact, their touch had something to give. They were clearly radiant and overflowing with love and gratitude. This level of sincerity will be with me the rest of my life.

The Reiki effected many changes. The characteristic cough of Hansen's disease, or leprosy, diminished with several; their circulation and the feeling in their limbs increased. One woman, who lay lifeless in bed when we met her, suffering from an enormous goiter and many complications of the leprosy, recovered enough to get up to shower and resume her beautiful weaving in five days. A little girl's long-standing abscess, the size of a grapefruit on her neck, released and healed in days. A young man on crutches would walk a long way each day to have Ottie treat his oozing leg wound, which had been very resistant to healing; the healing occurred quickly.

There are fifteen leper hospitals in Indonesia, which is a very poor country. However, in the midst of this financial limitation, these people are radiantly rich. I am fed in the well of deep pure sincere Being by them. I am forever honored and supremely grateful for my time with them.

# Malignant Cancer Healing in Four Months

## *Jill Schneider*

In February 1975, at age twenty-nine, I was diagnosed with cervical cancer. I had no pain or other symptoms, and wouldn't have had any idea I was sick had my annual Pap test not come back from the lab marked "Class Five: Conclusive for Malignancy." A concerned nurse gave me the news and said I should come back for another test so they could double-check. I did, and spent the next fews days wondering whether I would die or ever be able to have children. Then the same results came back.

It's funny. There I was, young and seemingly healthy, hearing my doctor describe something hidden within my body that had the power to kill me. He described all the options at my disposal, invasive procedures every one, starting with cutting out a section of my cervix and hopefully taking all the cancerous tissue with it. But that might not be enough, he told me; I might still need a complete hysterectomy.

As I thought about what my doctor had said, I became convinced that the line of treatment he had outlined was all wrong for me. It seemed painful, complicated, and disharmonious with nature. Ultimately, I knew my life was in God's hands.

Through regular meditation I'd developed a strong center, and there weren't many things that could shake me up. I was a committed vegetarian, dabbled in yoga, and was curious about Eastern philosophy and medicine. I believed that treating the symptoms of the disease wouldn't be enough. The imbalance at the root would just find new territory to invade and destroy. I felt that the Pap test was telling me there was a stagnation and a depression within my reproductive system. Cleansing and rejuvenating the area made unqualified sense to me. So before I tried anything drastic, like surgery, I was determined to give my body a chance to respond to noninvasive natural methods.

That was twenty-three years ago, but I still remember with remarkable detail how I felt as I tried to explain my decision to my gynecologist. My heart was beating a mile a minute as I asked him whether I could try natural methods for a month and then be retested. He just looked at me and said, "Jill, I don't think we can work with you anymore." I left the doctor's office shaken, like a child who had defied the school principal and gotten expelled. This was the mid seventies, when patients didn't question their doctors. I was disheartened, but I knew I had to do what I believed was right.

At the time, I was taking a course called "The Theory of Oriental Medicine" with Ralph Alan Dale. I told Dr. Dale about my diagnosis, and on his advice I telephoned Michio Kushi, an authority on macrobiotics and the founder of the Kushi Institute in Massachusetts. Macrobiotics is a natural system based on the Asian principles of yin and yang and their presence in whole organic foods. It aims at restoring an energetic balance and wellness through diet and lifestyle changes. Kushi put me on an extreme diet that required me to eat nothing but cooked brown rice for ten days. Chewed many times in a relaxed and meditative atmosphere, the rice became a liquid that I visualized would bring loving, life-giving, and healing energy to my body and mind. Gradually I added other grains, vegetables, seaweed, seeds, beans, miso soup, and a small amount of fruit to my meals. At every meal, I breathed deeply and meditated on how the food was my healing tonic, my medicine.

Dr. Dale also referred me to a local Chinese acupuncturist and herbalist, whom I'd visit twice a week for an hour-long session. After the acupuncture, he'd take me to a little kitchen area and cook me sweet potatoes and herbal tea, then give me a hard ball of herbs—about a half inch in diameter—to chew on. On my own, to augment the macrobiotics and Chinese medicine, I placed heated castor oil packs on my abdomen for twenty minutes a day. I'd read that Edgar Cayce, the psychic healer, had used this method to treat cervical cancer.

After a month, I made an appointment with my mother's gynecologist. He wasn't any happier than my first doctor had been with my decision to forgo standard treatment, and wanted to perform cryosurgery, freezing my cervix to slow the growth of abnormal cells. I refused. The results of a new Pap test were better, though they still showed some precancerous lesions. Not normal, but remarkably improved. It was enough for me. I was convinced my cancer was in remission and that I was on the right path.

It amazes me how many people can learn that there's something seriously wrong with their bodies and then go on living the same sort of lives. We must do something to change the environment in which our diseases form. In my case, I felt an incredible pull to travel. So off I went with a few good friends to visit Peru and Venezuela.

On the trip, I kept up a macrobiotic diet, supplementing the brown rice I carried in my backpack with organic vegetables grown by the people whose villages we visited. Walking through ancient ruins and sleeping in primitive dwellings, I discovered a sense of clarity. Out of my familiar urban environment, I was at peace with myself and with the world. Breaking away from the routines and unhealthy energy of life back home was a major component in my healing.

When I returned in June, I felt so healthy that I was certain the cancer was leaving my body. The doctor gave me another Pap test, and this time the results were normal.

Cancer swept me into the reality of how temporary and precious it is to have a human body. Two and a half years after I returned from South America and received that happy diagnosis, I gave birth to my son, Aaron, who is now attending university. I have never had a recurrence of cervical cancer.

# The Angels Who Saved My Life

## *Doreen Virtue, Ph.D.*

Late at night, when I was a little girl, a strong and loving force would sometimes suddenly awaken me. In my darkened room,

I'd see sparkling lights and be surrounded by an unearthly love and intensely deep silence that let me know my angels were near. Then I'd fall soundly back to sleep, assured that I was safe and protected by great and gentle beings.

Over the years, as I pursued my doctoral degree, got married, and had children, I lost contact with the angels. While I still loved everything about angels, I stopped talking to them. Occasionally I'd hear a spiritual voice direct me to make changes in my life, yet because my life was so hectic and busy, I often ignored the wisdom of my angels' guidance.

That all changed on July 15, 1995. That day, as I was dressing for an appointment I had at a church in Anaheim, California, a male angel's voice above my right ear clearly said, "Doreen, you'd better put the top up on your car, or it will get stolen." In retrospect, it's odd that the voice didn't startle me. The communication seemed natural, even though at the time it wasn't a normal occurrence in my life. I was in a big hurry, though, so I considered the voice more an irritant than a help. My priority was to be on time, and nothing else seemed important at that moment. "I don't have an extra five minutes to put up my car top!" I protested mentally to the voice.

"Then have Grant put the top up," the voice firmly counseled. (Grant is my son.) My white convertible is ordinary-looking when its black cloth top is up, but with its top down the car is a bit showy. Clearly, the angel wanted my car to be unobtrusive so as not to attract the attention of a thief. Instead of being surprised that a disembodied voice was speaking to me and calling me and my son by name, I continued arguing stubbornly. "I don't even have time to ask Grant to put up the top!"

Driving to the church, I felt negative energy surround my car like a thick fog. I heard a voice say, "Someone has just spotted your car with the intention of stealing it." So I prayed for protection as I pulled into the parking lot and parked close to the church. But as I stepped to get out of the car, a man suddenly screamed at me to give him my car keys and purse. My angel's warning had been accurate!

I followed an inner directive from the angels to scream with all my might. Luckily, my shrieks caught the attention of a woman sitting in her car across the parking lot, and she leaned on her horn. All the noise caused the people in the church to come outside, and the car thief and his accomplice ran away. Thankfully I was unharmed. When I called the police to report the attempted crime, I learned that those same car thieves, armed with a gun and a knife, had been on a spree that day.

As a result of the attempted car-jacking, I learned my lesson about listening to angels! It was amazing that a disembodied voice had spoken to me and accurately known my future. This shattered all of my beliefs about linear time and let me know that I was being watched and protected. However, my brush with danger had left me shaken. I felt jumpy and unsafe in the aftermath of the incident.

When I asked the angels to help me heal from my trauma, they immediately answered that I needed to let go of judgment and anger toward the men who had tried to steal my car. They also told me I needed to forgive myself for ignoring their warning. The angels quickly assisted me to forgive and heal, and I felt a new inner peace.

In the end, it turned out that the attempted car-jacking was one of the most positive experiences of my life, and I am grateful that it happened! Not only did the event humble me and help me begin listening to angels, but it also led me to actively solicit their guidance and help. The more time I spent conversing with angels, the more easily I could hear their loving wisdom.

Shortly after that, I began helping my counseling clients in therapy sessions to hear their own angels. Today, I often act as an intermediary who delivers the angels' messages to my clients. As the former director of two inpatient psychiatric hospitals and an outpatient treatment center, I have used or witnessed virtually every therapeutic tool known to psychology and medicine. Yet the healing power of the angels exceeds any form of man-made therapy I have ever witnessed. These divine messengers have wonderful gifts from God to impart to us.

Angels have a different way of seeing ordinary situations. Their messages help us to shift our beliefs and thoughts to empowering and loving viewpoints. They teach us how to use our spiritual senses to see, hear, feel, and know the real world that transcends our world's illusory problems. I am so grateful that we are all loved, guided, and surrounded by angels. And now, whenever the angels give me a directive, I follow their advice!

# The Miracle Healing Power of the Body

## *Yonah Offner*

I was driving to my first professional ski contest. It was a crisp early spring morning, and there were no other cars on the road. As we wound through a windy mountain road, in an instant my life changed. The car swerved out of control, hit an embankment, and went off a cliff at sixty miles per hour. I was thrown out of the back window as the car rolled three times, coming to rest on and crushing my body.

You have heard the story of the classic light; I was having a near-death experience. As I moved toward the light, I felt a voice say, "You must go back."

As I looked back to see my body crushed from head to toe, pinned underneath the car, I kind of laughed to myself, "You must be kidding. I am not going back to *that* body."

I was moving closer to the light when I heard the resounding voice repeat, "You must go back." It was so loud I knew there was no mistake. I knew I had to go back.

As I looked at my body, I pleaded, "Only if I can walk again." Hours later, I woke up in a coma at the hospital.

I literally had to be in a coma to wake up to my life. I had been on a crash course anyway with sex, drugs, and rock 'n' roll. This was my wake-up call to get on my spiritual path.

The prognosis was very bleak. The doctors said I wouldn't walk out of the hospital, that I would be very lucky ever to walk at all. I was told to forget sports, I was lucky to be alive.

In spite of the prognosis, I was able to experience a miracle with my body, my mind, and my soul. After growing addicted to every drug in the hospital, I was able to begin a slow recovery. Slow, that is, until I met a woman who said she could help me. She said, "Come to the beach and do yoga with me."

I agreed, and the next day, through yoga and bodywork, I began my journey to understanding the human body's powerful ability to heal and repair itself. It wasn't until I was really able to deeply forgive the driver of the car that my healing accelerated.

I ran my first marathon less than two years after my car wreck. It was no accident. My body continues to improve every day, naturally and easily, without drugs or medication.

Today I'm on a spiritual path, speaking to audiences who want to "Feel Better and Be Your Best" on a daily basis, awakening them to the same simple techniques that saved my life!

# Angel in White

*Julianna*

In the summer of 1967, one week after the birth of my second daughter, I was rushed back to the hospital. Something was terribly wrong. The doctors worked on me for two days trying to stabilize my condition, to no avail. I felt a great deal of fear as well as pain in those few days, along with an overwhelming sense that I was about to die. Nothing like this had ever occurred to me, and I had always felt pretty indestructible. Then there came a point at which through the medicine and being frightened and exhausted, I just stopped feeling any physical pain. I remember my husband's panicked and fearful looks, and how I knew the news was not good. My family was called in, even a priest. I remember very little after that about the hospital, the doctors, or my family.

The one thing I do recall with compete clarity is the nurse who was at my side in those critical hours. She was so beautiful. Her face was surrounded by an unusual haircut unlike any I had seen before, with bangs cut in the middle, creating a heart shape that framed her illuminated, calm, knowing eyes.

The last thing I believed in then was angels. In my estimation, my life to that point had been filled with little joy or happiness. I wasn't even sure God knew I existed, let alone cared about me. And if He did care, then why on earth would He allow so much emotional pain to flow through my life?

Even after the doctors gave up on me, my nurse did not. I kept talking to her, telling her I needed to see my older daughter, but that she was away on a camping trip with her godparents and could not be reached. "Just let me live to speak with her, then I will go," I said. Even though I was far removed from a loving higher power, while this nurse was with me I had no fear of dying. My only concern was for my children.

Finally a new day dawned and my condition began to stabilize. I asked to see the nurse who had stayed with me, wanting to tell her how her presence had given me the determination to fight. For a week, I asked everyone who came into my room to please send the beautiful nurse with the heart-shaped haircut back to me. And they all told me the exact same thing: "We don't have anyone on staff who even comes close to your description, and no one nurse was here all night." Most likely, they said, I'd been delirious, reacting to the pain and medication, but I knew in my heart she had really been there.

Not until many years later, and after a lifetime of change and emotional repair, did I come to know beyond any doubt that my guardian angel had allowed me to spend time with her. During that night, she had showed me how to accept the unconditional love of a higher power that I'd had no idea existed. I can still remember the day, many years later, when the realization of her existence hit. All of a sudden, there was no question in my mind that she was as real as any human being walking the Earth.

Today I collect angel figurines of all shapes and sizes. For me, this is one way to give a face to my higher power. I have now begun looking with a new understanding at people with heart-shaped faces and an extreme glow in their eyes. There really are earth angels walking among us. We just have to know where to look.

# The Angel Bus Driver

*Ron Paul*

My car broke down at two a.m. in an area of Los Angeles that is considered very dangerous. Desperate, I got out and flagged down a passing car. The men in the car agreed to take me home, but after I climbed in the backseat of the two-door car, I knew I was in trouble. They began making derogatory comments and said they were going to take me to a park. I knew I was in danger of being beaten or killed, yet I was trapped in the back with no exit door. I asked the men to let me out of the car, and they refused.

I began to pray fervently. I said to God, "You've always helped me before. I need Your help right now!" At that moment, the car stopped at a red light. I heard an inner voice say, "Push the front seat forward and quickly climb out of the front door." I obeyed the voice, amazed that I was able to push the seat forward and escape.

The men in the car yelled and drove after me. But then a city bus drove by. I flagged it down, and the bus driver let me on. No other passengers were aboard. I explained to the driver that I was in danger. He offered to drive me home. The men in the car chased the bus for a while, screaming, but eventually they stopped. I reached home safely.

The next day, I called the bus company to thank my rescuer. But when I asked to speak to the bus driver, I was told that no one by that name or description worked for the company. I gave the bus dispatcher more details about the driver, including the street where the bus had picked me up and the time of morning when the rescue had occurred. The dispatcher emphatically told me that the company didn't run any bus on that route during the early-morning hours when I had been taken aboard the bus.

I then realized that God had divinely guided me to be rescued by an angel who miraculously manifested as a bus driver, and a bus, in order to save my life.

# My Guardian Angel Saved My Life

## Jill Bruener

The phone call came in the early-morning hours of New Year's Eve, 1977. I was twenty-four years old at the time. My mother, who had been diagnosed with leukemia and was not expected to live much longer, had been in the hospital for several weeks. The nurse who telephoned me told me that Mom had taken a turn for the worse and that I should come to the hospital as soon as possible. My mind raced as I hurriedly got dressed; I feared the worst and dreaded going to the hospital.

The air outside was cold, and I was blinking away tears as I made a halfhearted effort to brush the snow off my windshield. All I could think about was getting to the hospital in time to say good-bye to my mother.

The Cincinnati streets around me were virtually deserted as I pulled up to a red light. The drone of the wipers, back and forth, brushing off the light flurries of snow, was the only sound that broke the cold silence. I was distraught, and found myself praying. I asked God to give me the strength to face whatever situation I would find at the hospital. I implored Him to send His angels to be with me. Tears were streaming down my face, and the wetness stung my cheeks in the cold, dark air.

I was reaching for my purse to get a tissue when I heard a voice—it seemed to come from out of nowhere—speaking to me. It was a male voice, and it rang with a great urgency. "Lock your door! Lock your door now! Do it!" the voice commanded.

I was so startled that I didn't even turn around to lock my door. I just pulled my left arm up and back, pushing the lock button down with my elbow. My heart was racing, and I had cold chills all over my body. It was a shock to have an unseen person talk to me in my car, and the warning tone in his voice terrified me.

Not more than five seconds after I'd pushed down the lock button, a huge man loomed out of the darkness. He lunged at my car door and grabbed the handle, trying frantically to yank it open. As I looked out the car window, I couldn't see his face, but I could see that he was holding something shiny and metallic in his other hand as he continued to pull at my door handle.

"Hit the gas!" the warning voice screamed at me. "Go, go, *go!*"

In a panic, I stepped on the gas pedal. The tires squealed as the car shot forward. I didn't even look back as I took off down the street.

When I was safely away, I tried to calm down and sort out what had happened. I was quite shaken and was convinced there must be a man in my car. At the next light, I turned on the overhead light and looked into the backseat. I was definitely alone.

I remember thinking to myself, My God, where did that voice come from?

Then I knew. I felt a warmth and ease spread through my entire being. God had listened. The angel of comfort for whom I had so desperately prayed had indeed been sent, and he turned out to be an angel of divine protection as well.

For I am convinced that it was my guardian angel's voice that warned me and saved my life that day, so many years ago.

# Soul Mates

## Anne Wallace Sharp

Every now and then an individual comes along who makes a profound impact on our lives. A stranger . . . who becomes a friend . . . a person with whom a strong bond is quickly formed. It's as if we've known this person all our lives . . . and many lifetimes before. These people are our soul mates.

Sixteen years ago, I was faced with a devastating illness that took its toll on me physically and emotionally. Ironically, it was during the dark days of this crisis that Debbie came into my life. There was nothing logical about it. I barely knew her. We had worked at the same organization for years, but rarely communicated or spent any time together. When other friends were falling by the wayside, though, Debbie came to me and stayed, just when I needed someone the most.

Over the course of the next fifteen years, my relationship with Debbie grew and matured into one of those grace-filled friendships that come along only once in a lifetime, if at all. Debbie was there, supporting and loving me as I struggled through some pretty tough times, and I was there for her during her rocky times. We often joked that we'd been to hell and back with each other—and loved every minute.

During those same years, I continued my journey toward a spirituality I could embrace wholeheartedly. I grew weary of the religious aspects of my faith. I stopped going to church and sought solace in nature, for there I could see evidence of God everywhere. I believed that the animals, birds, stones, stars, and trees—in fact, everything around me—had spirit and lessons to teach me. I became aware of spirit guides and angels who were ever-present to me, offering me insight, protection, and wisdom. And I believed I had lived before—many life-times, in fact—and that I had chosen to incarnate in this lifetime, knowing what crises I would face and what lessons I needed to learn.

It was then that I realized I had known Debbie before and that our coming together years earlier had been preordained long before we were born. I knew that she and I were together for a reason, and that we had much to teach each other, and to learn.

When Debbie was diagnosed with terminal cancer, I found myself struggling to cope with a multitude of feelings and questions. I knew my faith and beliefs would be challenged. I felt phenomenal sadness and was terrified at the possibility of losing her. Debbie opted not to pursue conventional treatment but to rely on her own belief system to heal herself. I accepted her decision. If anyone could heal, it was Debbie.

The next twelve months were a horrible roller-coaster ride. As Debbie's physical condition deteriorated, we both suffered profound periods of doubt. But it seemed that when Debbie's faith wavered, my belief in her healing intensified, and vice versa. She considered cancer a "gift," and she talked about the lessons she was learning.

It was difficult, at times, for me to look at her disease as a gift. I felt helpless as I watched my friend weaken and deteriorate before my eyes. There was little I could do other than pray and walk with her on this stage of her journey and mine.

The final and crucial test of our faith and love for each other descended upon us like the fury of a killer tornado. The cancer had metastasized to Debbie's liver, and she woke up one morning extremely jaundiced. Her appetite vanished, and the pounds began to drop off at an alarming rate. She became weaker by the moment. I tried hard to believe in the possibility of a miracle, but I also faced the very real possibility of losing her.

I did lose her . . . but not in the way either of us anticipated.

Debbie was staying at my home and sleeping on my sofa. She awoke in the middle of the night with no memory of where she was, or of who I was. Sixteen years of friendship and memories had been eradicated in the matter of a few moments. Debbie was terrified, and I was unbelievably sad and scared.

We soon discovered how deep our connection really was. After several hours, Debbie's fear subsided. Somewhere deep within her was a memory of me on a soul level. I look back at that time with awe and wonder.

For a few brief yet unbelievably long days, our relationship grew and flourished. I was amazed at how quickly new memories were made. The basis of our friendship had always been trust, honesty, and love, and this new relationship was no different.

I soon realized that nothing of importance is ever truly lost. Despite Debbie's memory loss, I hadn't really lost my good friend. Our love was still intact. I knew then that I could cope with Debbie's death, if necessary, but I also believed that she would recover and heal.

And recover she did! In the short span of a few hours, Debbie's memory returned completely and the cancer left her body. I saw the jaundice literally disappear in front of my eyes, and I watched in amazement as Debbie healed in a matter of minutes. I had witnessed a *holy moment*.

The cancer is now gone, and in the months since that moment, Debbie and I have both found that our relationship is growing in intensity and meaning. Regardless of what happens in the future, our connection to each other is *real*. Death, illness, and other changes may separate us physically, but none of those can truly break the bond we have.

We are soul mates destined to journey together time and time again.

# Touched by the Divine

## *Roger Drummer*

As a triathlete living in Hawaii, I rode twenty-five miles of hills daily as part of my training regimen. I felt amazingly strong, and my legs were extremely well muscled. It was the spring of 1989, and I was preparing for a summer of cycling. My training came to an abrupt halt when a pickup truck turned into my path, causing an accident that changed my life forever. I was propelled into the windshield and over the truck, and landed on the roadway; I spent the next eight days in the hospital nursing a broken knee, torn tendons, a dislocated shoulder, and various soft-tissue injuries. Released from the hospital, I left for Ohio and spent three months recuperating at my parents' home.

My cast was removed, I could barely bend my knee and was in constant pain. I knew I would have to find a new vocation that didn't require much standing. I decided to go to Los Angeles to study Oriental acupressure. I thought surely I could earn a living doing Japanese massage, which is performed on the floor. I needed a source of income that didn't require being on my feet for extended periods of time. I enrolled in Shiatsu school but soon discovered that I was extremely fatigued and spent most of my free time at home, lying down.

During this period I came to realize the true extent of the injuries I'd sustained in the accident. Because I was in a constant state of pain and inflammation, I could no longer run, swim, or bike comfortably. My physical injuries were intense, but the worst injury was to my self-esteem and self-image. Before the accident, I had focused my entire life on the daily training for triathlons. Fitness was my life. To me, perfect diet and spartan health regime defined who I was and how others perceived me. Suddenly, my identity was gone. Because physical fitness was my sole source of pride, my already fragile self-esteem was shattered. I realized that my life had little if any substance. Years of exercise addiction had left me without any real relationships, few marketable skills, and a deep sense of loss. The ensuing mental anguish further depleted my energy and helped to create the tired, depressed person that I had become. My bicycle accident was the turning point of my life. I was left with chronic fatigue and nothing to do but look inward.

I traveled out to Los Angeles and settled in Venice Beach, a gathering place for many a lost soul. I was tired, depressed, angry, and physically a shell of my former self. In this emotional state, my sole expression in life taken from me, I spent most of my time in a state of hopelessness. I was extremely bored. I was living on disability pay and had very little expendable income. A fellow student told me about an herb shop in Venice run by a well-known herbalist and published author. My friend said that this herbalist often took on apprentices. I thought maybe I could learn something about Chinese herbs and supplement my income by becoming an apprentice.

I began visiting the shop daily in order to read portions of the owner's book on tonic herbs. My plan was to read his book for free and to be seen regularly, thus gaining acceptance as a likely apprentice at the shop. Actually, I had very little interest in Chinese herbs. What really brought me to the store on a daily basis was that I had nothing else to do. My life was pretty empty.

My plan worked. I had read most of the book in a month and had been noticed. In the summer of 1990, I began my apprenticeship, performing all the menial labor at the store. I was the dishwasher, janitor, and stock boy. The store owner, Ron, had started his own apprenticeship this way, learning from a Korean Taoist, and he was quite happy to pass on the tradition. I was rarely spoken to and just went about my tasks. Little did I know that I was being tested. I had to show my desire to learn by doing the daily grunge work for no pay before time would be spent teaching me.

One day, Ron was brewing a special tea for his closest friends. I overheard him talking about it and could feel his excitement. He was preparing a *shen* tea to be served after closing. In Chinese herbalism, *shen* translates as "Spirit," the radiance of a human being. *Shen* herbs are relaxing and stress-relieving, allowing us to step back from life and gain new perspective or wisdom. These concepts were all new to me. I didn't really understand *shen*. How could you gain wisdom from an herb? Besides, with my chronic fatigue I thought that relaxing was the last thing I needed. Yet I was curious. Ron's enthusiasm convinced me to check it out.

Although I hadn't been invited, I stayed after closing and made myself useful. Serving everyone tea, I managed to drink three cups myself. Unimpressed by the taste, I left early to walk home. Ten minutes later, about halfway home, a voice spoke to me from the heavens: "Don't worry, everything is fine." I found myself looking to the clouds to locate the source of this voice. Suspicion started to creep in, and I thought surely someone was playing a practical joke on me. Checking behind and under every car in the vicinity turned up nothing. Thoughts of *Candid Camera* danced in my head. Confused, I resumed my walk home.

I hadn't gone far, maybe twenty steps, before I heard again, "Don't worry, everything is just fine with the world." The voice was powerful, and once again I found myself gazing upward into the clouds, searching for its source. In that instant I knew that God had spoken to me. It wasn't so much a thought as a realization. I just knew. Some inner intelligence, hidden perhaps deep in my cellular memory, was telling me I was in the presence of the Divine.

A tingling sensation engulfed my entire body. I felt an awareness of every cell of my being, as if I were being made new, alive for the very first time. Totally calm, relaxed, and in awe, I continued walking. The air seemed sweet, as if I were eating it and being nourished by it. I felt the existence of an energy, previously unknown and untapped, lying dormant within me. I knew that the world was indeed "just fine." I was exactly where I needed to be, and everything would work out. I knew that the problems of poverty and chronic fatigue that plagued me were temporary yet necessary lessons that would work themselves out over time. I spent the evening at home, alone in my room, in quiet contemplation.

This feeling lasted the better part of four days. I felt a heightened sense of awareness and an ability to understand the deeper meaning of every situation I encountered. I began to wonder if this was how it felt to be enlightened. I felt radically alive, peaceful, and fully in the moment.

A week later, as the intensity of my experience began to wane, I tried to gain insight into what was happening to me. When I shared my story with a few of my fellow tea drinkers, they all laughed or made references to drug use. Strangely, I alone had had any reaction to the tea other than mild relaxation. Realizing I would have to figure this out on my own, I stopped sharing my experience. I did, however, continue to work at the shop and learn more about herbs for *shen*.

As my health improved and my awareness expanded, I began to feel that somehow I had been chosen to be an herbalist. I was part of a cosmic event that I didn't fully understand. I realized that life could be exciting and mysterious, that ordinary people could have extraordinary experiences, events usually reserved for mystics or spiritual aspirants. I had been touched by the Divine, and life had taken on a whole new meaning.

Yes, everything would be just fine.

# My Journey to Love with Jesus

## *Ben Woodson*

WEDNESDAY, OCTOBER 2, 1996

That morning, I kissed my wife, Lucy, good-bye and boarded an eight fifty-five plane to Miami. I remember sitting in the seat thinking only of Lucy, of how much I really loved her and how much she meant to me. I realized I hadn't said that to her in a long time, and felt sad. I needed to tell her how much I loved her.

My brother, Ed, picked me up at the airport, and it was good to see him again. As we drove to Grove Isle, I thought about how it had been only sixty-three days since I was diagnosed with multiple myeloma, an incurable cancer of the plasma blood cells that attacks your bone and eventually weakens your immune system. I didn't focus on the shock I'd felt when I'd been given the news of the cancer, but thought only of how blessed I was to have so much support from my family and friends, especially my sister and brother. I felt so much unselfish concern and unconditional love from so many.

THURSDAY, OCTOBER 3, 1996

After a full day at Grove Isle, Ed and I drove together to Key West. We shared things we had never shared before, stories about our father and mother, our family and the past. I could feel us growing closer by the moment. It was a great trip with lots of love. At about nine-thirty that night we arrived in Key West. I felt tired but full of joy. Sometime between eleven-thirty and midnight, I turned off the TV and the lights and fell asleep.

FRIDAY, OCTOBER 4, 1996

In the wee hours, I felt the need to go to the bathroom so I pulled myself out of bed and walked into the bathroom. Upon returning to bed I noticed the clock on the VCR. It was two-forty. I crawled under the covers and turned over on my left side, facing the door and the curtains. My eyes were wide open. I wasn't sleepy at all.

Suddenly, I felt there was someone in my room. It was a strange feeling I had never experienced before, a presence that was strong and overwhelming yet warm and exuding the greatest love I have ever known. I knew that someone was standing behind me, beside the bed. I was not afraid. Love was all over the room.

I turned my head from the pillow and looked over my right shoulder. There, standing beside my bed, was Jesus Christ—in body—whole, complete, tall, warm. He was dressed in a white gown that looked pressed and starched. His gown was thick and full. I thought that I knew what white was, but I didn't until I saw His gown with my own eyes. The gown was the whitest of white. It was beyond white.

His face was warm, surrounded with full, light brown-blond hair. His eyes met mine with the deepest, warmest gaze I had ever seen. He reached down and took the covers from the edge of the bed and fell in behind me. I was frozen. I felt the mattress sink and move. I never moved.

He put his arms around me. I felt Him all around me. I turned my head to the wall. He moved His body closer toward me, and then His spirit was inside me. He became one with me. I never moved. I was never afraid. In fact, I started laughing. Then He spoke to me: "Don't worry. I am with you now. I have always been with you, you just didn't know. Everything is going to be all right. I have plans for you, and you will understand."

The warmth and fullness started to flow over me even faster now. I was so at peace, laughing, smiling, loving. He continued, "Go about your life and follow your heart, and you will know what I want from you. Be natural, be yourself."

I felt so happy and so full. So warm. So complete. Never in my life had I felt that way. We both laughed and giggled like newborn children. I knew that everything was going to be all right forever and ever, till the end of time. I was called to be part of something, of what I don't know, of a love I had never experienced.

I didn't sleep the rest of the morning. I didn't move, and the smile never left my face. I was so at peace, like never before in my life. I just lay there so full of warmth. I had never felt these feelings before, a love that was so magical.

I don't know where the time went, but suddenly it was five-thirty, time to shower and go to work. While driving from Key West to my office, I called Lucy. I told her that something had happened to me that morning but that I couldn't tell her about it on the cellular phone. I would tell her later that night.

When I arrived home, Ed was waiting for me. We ate dinner, talked, and laughed together. While we were lying on my bed watching TV, I turned to Ed and said, "You know, something happened to me this morning and I need to tell you about it." I was telling him the story, word for word, as I've set it down here, when all of a sudden I began to shake and cry. I could not get the words out of my mouth. I was hysterical and crying in disbelief about what I was saying. It was and is too overwhelming for mortal words to describe or explain. I felt exhausted, drained, weak, and tired, and I fell asleep. I slept long and hard.

It is interesting to note that October fourth has a religious, historical significance to thousands of people around the world. It is the celebration of Saint Francis of Assisi, a day to acknowledge the physical appearance of Jesus to Saint Francis and the appearance of holes in Saint Francis's hands and feet.

SATURDAY, OCTOBER 5, 1996

The next morning, I had a massage, then went into my bedroom and read from my daily devotional, *Our Daily Bread*. I had forgotten to read it on Friday because of all that had happened, so I turned to Friday's devotional and read a story, "He Called Me," about a three-year-old girl who communicated with Jesus on the telephone. It also said that if you hear a personal call from God, you must answer in the affirmative and respond with simple faith. Selected Bible passages for the day were Romans 8:28–39.

I was shocked and fascinated. I opened my Bible and began to read those scriptures. As I read, I started crying and shaking. The selection spoke directly to my heart and what had happened.

Jesus Christ most definitely left me a message that morning, by His presence with me and by God's written word. It is something I will always be able to hold on to and follow on my path through life. It is a signpost pointing out a way to follow my heart.

My journey continues with a mission that is growing stronger and stronger day by day. I feel so much power out there. I can feel it all coming together. He called to me! And He is calling to others to awaken to their hearts and follow! He wants me to be some part: He wants all of us to be a part. He wants me to call others to His love.

From the day of Jesus' appearance to me, I felt a tremendous lifting of stress, confusion, perceived problems, weight, sickness, and pain. I felt that whatever it was that had caused my cancer had left my body. It was no longer in me. I had been purged and flushed of the things in my body and mind that had brought this cancer to me.

I continued to be treated for the cancer, and I underwent various levels of chemotherapy. On May 7, 1997, I underwent high-dose chemotherapy in preparation for the collection of my stem cells in order to have a bone marrow transplant. After my stem cells were collected, the doctors were very pleased with the results of my blood work, which continued to show normal levels of protein in the blood and indicated that the cancer had gone into some sort of remission. The tests continued every two weeks, then every month, and for over a year they continued to show normal levels. The doctors have been very surprised, and have told me that there is a small group, less than 5 percent of multiple myeloma patients, that responds well to chemotherapy, and that a full transplant is not necessary for me at this time.

Well, I have thanked them for all this information and have gone on living my life and following my heart. I know who cured me. When God appeared to me through Jesus Christ on the morning of October fourth, 1996, He took away everything that had caused the cancer. The healing process could then begin.

God is in each of us right this minute, and we have in each of us the ability to get in balance and open the channels for our bodies to heal themselves. We should never ignore the wonderful things that God has created through modern medicine, but in order to effect a thorough healing we must take charge of whatever it is that is ailing us and follow our innermost feelings to perfect the individual healing that each of us must go through if we truly want to be healed.

I have never felt so full of love and so blessed as I do today. I feel I am overflowing with God's love. Relationships have become so important to me, and nothing else really seems to matter very much. All that I want to do is share God's love with others and be a light to others by giving them the peace and joy that I have in my heart and knowing—truly knowing—beyond any doubt, in every cell of my body, that God, through Jesus, walks today as He did two thousand years ago. He is in each of us, He is us, He has always been here with us, and He will always be with us, forever and ever.

# The Voice

## Lisa-Marie Lacroix

The one point I would like to make extremely clear before I begin this story is that I was a very apathetic person at that point in my life. Because of trauma I had sustained as a young child, I had locked down my feelings, and I found it a much safer way to live my life. This way, no one could penetrate my emotions and hurt me.

I was the lead vocalist in a rock band, traveling throughout Canada with six guys in a big yellow school bus. I was far too audacious and would walk alone at night through the worst districts in the city to get home from a party. My playmates would often be falling-down drunk, and I'd refuse to catch a ride with them.

The music pounding out of the stereo system was deafening as I made my way through the gathering of faceless strangers. I held my beer bottle close to me with my thumb firmly positioned over its mouth. I always held on to my drink, never allowing a window of opportunity to someone who might spike it with acid or something. Invariably I would nurse a single drink all night. I was put off hard drinking after witnessing the antics and mishaps of friends. I am the kind of person who likes to keep her wits about her at all times.

I was making my way from the living room to the kitchen at my girlfriend Laura's house, looking for Reed, the guitar player I had recently started seeing. Squeezing my way past some glassy-eyed souls, I caught sight of him leaning against the refrigerator, smiling contentedly as Laura shamelessly groped him. I didn't have any place in my life for trash like that, so I made my exit.

Outside, the crisp October air felt cleansing. We usually

have snow by then in Winnipeg, and I was glad we didn't that night. I had approximately one and a half miles to walk to sanctuary—my parents' house. I was almost halfway home, walking down a very pretty and familiar street in the middle-class district where I grew up. The streetlights cast dark, sweeping shadows across the manicured front lawns. I was infuriated and swearing to myself about the kind of guys I hooked up with. The sound of my boot heels echoed on the sidewalk.

My self-absorbed thoughts were brought to a sudden halt by the sound of a very loud engine tearing down the street behind me. Then came the voice, a male voice in panic beside me. From the left side of me I heard it say, "Run!"

To my right, car tires were slamming to a screeching halt. It was all happening so fast, yet it seemed strangely slow. I was not the type of person to just run, so I questioned the voice: "Why run?"

This time the voice was full of panic. "Run, you're almost out of time!"

Now, there was no body attached to this voice, but I felt compelled to listen to it. As the passenger door of the car to my right flew open, I tore off to my left through some sleeping strangers' yard. As I rounded the end of the bungalow and came into the backyard, the voice yelled, "Fall on the ground, you don't have much time!"

If you have ever been chased, you know that the last thing you want to do is lie on the ground! Instinct automatically tells you to keep moving. Against my better judgment, I fell firmly onto the ground. The voice spoke for the final time: "Don't move. Don't look. Don't breathe."

I had a hard time holding my breath with my heart pumping so fast. I thought for certain my heart would burst in my chest. As I lay so vulnerably on the cold, damp grass, I wanted to be somewhere, anywhere, other than there.

My pursuer ran right alongside me. He was so close that I could feel the ground shake beneath his feet. I wanted so badly to look up at him, but I kept my head down as I had been instructed. Then once again I heard the sound of the loud engine and screeching tires from the back lane. The driver and my pursuer must have planned to rendezvous and abduct me there. Now they were confused, and I heard them talking, trying to figure out how I had disappeared. I listened to them share their loathing of me, and silently I questioned, Why? Then miraculously, a car door slammed and I heard the sound of that engine moving into the distance without me.

I couldn't get to my feet fast enough! I was trying to comprehend what had just happened to me, and I looked down at where I had been lying. It was the only section of the backyard that was protected by shadow. Suddenly I heard the sound of someone running down the street. Cautiously I peered around the corner of the bungalow, and remarkably, there was Reed. He was running down the center of the street. I called out his name, and we ran to each other.

I asked him, "Why are you here? How did you find me?"

He said that he had seen me leave the party and had come after me. When I was nowhere to be found, he heard the sound of the screeching tires in the distance and instinctively followed it.

As he walked me the rest of the way home, I revealed to him all that had happened. I wasn't quite sure he would believe me, because I didn't really believe it all myself. The last few blocks we walked in total silence. Reed, I assume, was trying to figure out if I was defective, while I myself was silently thanking the voice.

A few weeks later, I was visiting my friend Jade. She lived with her father not too far from where my parents lived. I had not told a single soul other than Reed what had happened to me that night, so what Jade then revealed to me left me speechless.

One morning a few weeks earlier, she told me, her father had taken their dog for their usual run along the floodway, a deserted region behind their residential area, and they made a startling discovery. There in the middle of nowhere was a young woman. She was stumbling around aimlessly, trying to conceal her battered and naked body with trembling arms.

Jade's father immediately removed his jacket and wrapped her in it. He understood her fear and explained that he had a daughter about her age at home. He insisted that she accompany him home and that they immediately contact the police. She silently nodded and cautiously followed him.

When the police arrived, she reluctantly told them her story. She explained how she had been abducted the night before by two men in a car. Grief-stricken, she spoke of how these monsters had raped and beaten her, and how they had abandoned her like a piece of garbage.

Were these the same two men who had tried to hurt me? I can't say for certain, though deep inside me I know it had to have been them. I wonder if this young woman had also heard the voice before it happened. Why was I miraculously spared these horrors while she was subjected to them? As I look back, I have come to realize one very significant thing: the voice knew me better than I had ever known myself. I certainly was not quite as tough as I had thought.

I thank God for sparing me and sending me the voice.

# For He Is the Light and They Shine Through Him

*Michele Kufner*

About eight years ago, I started feeling as if I had a chronic case of the flu. I had headaches and stomach pains, and my joints ached all the time. Some days the pain was more intense than others, but the feeling of being ill was constant. I had no appetite. Eating—just swallowing—caused me great pain. My weight dropped to eighty-seven pounds.

I was diagnosed with chronic fatigue syndrome and fibromyalgia. My symptoms were so severe that many of the doctors who examined me thought I had other complications as well. They prescribed a variety of painkillers. As I was allergic to most of them, my doctors were constantly switching me from one medication to another.

Despite the painkillers, most of the time I was unable to get up from a chair by myself. I hurt so much that I had to be carried to the shower as many as four times a night, and I would sit under the hot running water just to get some relief. I could barely drive my children to visit their grandmother, a short one-hour trip, and once there I remained bedridden for three days until I could build up enough strength to drive us home. Some days I was able to go into work for a few hours. Other days I wasn't.

I began to feel that I was going crazy. My life was a constant cycle of pain and exhaustion. Little things like washing dishes, cooking dinner, and even just getting out of bed each morning became major efforts and were sometimes impossible. I had no quality time with my family.

As I couldn't even get out of bed, my eight-year-old son took care of his three-year-old brother most evenings, cooking dinner. Had it not been for my family, I don't know how I would have gotten by. Had I not had children, I know I would have allowed myself to die.

One evening when everyone else in the house was asleep, I swallowed several handfuls of pain pills, haphazardly mixing them together. I'm not really sure how many I took. I later found myself on the bathroom floor vomiting, shaking, and sweating. It felt as if I were coming out of my skin. At some point I started to pray: "Please, God, help me. I can't live like this, but I don't want to leave my boys." I had reached the end of my tolerance. I simply couldn't be sick any longer, but I didn't know where to turn for help. I finally fell asleep on the floor and was awakened by the morning sun coming in through the bathroom window. I didn't tell my family what had happened.

That day I stayed home from work, feeling sick and exhausted. Lying on the couch, I turned on the TV. A talk show was on. I wasn't sure why, but I felt compelled to watch it. Dr. Eric Scott Pearl and a panel of medical doctors were discussing how so many of Dr. Pearl's patients had been healed of unusual afflictions. One man described how as a result of a session with Dr. Pearl, he regained the use of his legs. Video footage and a photograph were shown of the man at various points prior to the healing. Dr. Pearl explained that the healings were brought about by a "higher power" that to the best of his understanding seemed to come through him. I knew that Dr. Pearl was telling the truth, that he was for real, and that I had to see him. I called the television station and was given the number for his office in Los Angeles.

I phoned and asked the receptionist if the doctor could fit me into his schedule. I called my parents and told them what I had seen, and how excited I was. Although they were skeptical, my mother said she and my father would help with the expenses. She decided to go with me, and six days later, we were on a plane headed for Los Angeles.

The forty-five minute taxi ride from Los Angeles International Airport to West Hollywood seemed an eternity. I could hardly wait to see the doctor. My first appointment was scheduled for that afternoon, April fourth, 1995.

When I met Dr. Pearl, I was comfortable right from the start, knowing somehow that I had been sent to him. I knew that God would take it from there. My first session began in a quiet room with dim lights and a soothing atmosphere. Dr. Pearl lightly placed one finger above my heart, and I immediately fell into a light sleep. I wasn't entirely asleep, though, because I was clearly aware of the movement in the room and sounds in the outer office. Dr. Pearl held his hands over and above my head, and I felt a warmth in and around my body. The energy level in the room was very intense.

At one point, the doctor left me alone for a moment. I had a strong feeling that someone else was in the room, even though I knew the doctor was not there. Then I heard the soft voice of a woman. She told me that her name was Parsillia and that she was my guardian angel. Parsillia told me that I would be healed. The physicians had done all they could, but Parsillia's presence told me that my life was beginning again.

My body became intensely warm all over. The most painful areas of my body became hot, then returned to a comforting warmth, feeling much better. At one point I felt Dr. Pearl standing by my left side, but when I opened my eyes I realized that no one could possibly have been standing there, as the treatment table was against the wall. Someone with a very comforting presence *had been* standing there, however.

My second session, on April fifth, was just as dramatic. Parsillia returned to me, and I felt the presence of other angels as well. Again several areas of my body became hot, then relaxed and warm. Several times, Parsillia repeated that I was being healed. I had so much energy after the session that my mother and I went shopping. It shocked me when I heard my mother calling me to slow down; for years, everyone had been forced to slow down for me.

In my third session, I fell directly into a light sleep even before Dr. Pearl came into the room. Parsillia told me that they would be working on the cause of my headaches and the sharp, stabbing pains I had been having in my head. She said they would cure them that day. I experienced warmth in my right cheek and then throughout my entire face, and was told that I was being filled with love, peace, and patience.

During my fourth session, the angels told me that I was healed and would gradually notice other changes. I was given messages for my father and my former mother-in-law. I was also shown some beautiful gates, which I assume led to heaven. There was singing all around me, flowers of colors I had never seen before, and happiness everywhere. I was told to spend more time with my sons, especially my oldest. Parsillia told me to keep in contact with her. She promised me she would be there for me.

It has been a few years since my first visit with Dr. Pearl, and my life is still changing. Things returned to normal—quite quickly, and quite fully. And in case you're wondering, I want you to know that *I am healed*. My condition is not just in remission. More important, I have my life back and my children have their mother back.

I couldn't find any happiness or purpose in life when all I could concentrate on was fighting my illness and pain. Through Dr. Pearl I was able to regain my family, my purpose, my happiness, my life. My feelings for him can best be summed up in something one of the angels said: "For he is the light and they shine through him."

People can talk, people can wonder, people can debate whether healings of this nature truly occur; whether they are mind over matter; whether they would have happened anyway; and whether there really are angels. Ask me. I know.

# Destiny

## *Norma Jean Young*

It was a destiny day for Jacque Scott. She lay in the intensive care unit of the hospital she and her husband had created as a paradigm-shifting model of health care—with a blood clot in her lung. This hospital that she had transformed into a truly healing and beautiful atmosphere, and which had been featured on Bill Moyers's *Healing and the Mind* television series, now held her as she faced a critical crossroads. Her heart had stopped the day before, her breathing was labored and required oxygen assistance, the pain was great and wearing her down, and the medical staff, who were her close friends, were deciding if they should place her on a respirator. She seemed to be losing ground.

I was visiting Mid-Columbia Medical Center that day to give two in-service presentations on Reiki touch therapy. I had met Mark Scott, Jacque's husband and CEO of the hospital, at the American Holistic Nurses Conference. He had presented the keynote address, and I had offered a workshop entitled "Reiki: The Ultimate Mother Meeting the Crises of Our Time, Inside and Out." I was a good meeting, one that acknowledged my longtime interest in the Plane Tree Hospital Model (so-named because Hippocrates taught under a sycamore, or plane tree). I had been carrying the slides and portfolio of the Plane Tree Hospital Model with me through twelve countries, sharing this hope-giving health-care system as I initiated people into their own ability to heal and bring wholeness through their hands. Mark acknowledged that I had many years of experience with energy healing, where as he was just beginning—and I had better come see him at his hospital.

So there I was in the hospital, having driven from Seattle, as Jacque faced her crisis. I offered treatment to Mark first, so that he could evaluate whether it might benefit Jacque. He visibly calmed as I treated him in total silence in the group meeting room. He gave the okay for me to treat his wife.

I entered the darkened room with the head nurse, who was Jacque's best friend, and placed my hands on the affected lung, talking softly to Jacque. "There is enough breath for you. There's room for you. It's your choice; you can go either way."

Within minutes, Jacque said, "You're taking the pain away." I continued to hold my hands over her lungs, and her capacity to speak easily increased steadily. We watched her regain herself quickly and become replenished. This woman who had been at death's door was assuredly filling with life force. Within an hour, her breathing was as clear as mine. Within three hours, she was joking and planning her next vacation, well on her way to recovery.

The next day, Jacque was out of the intensive care unit. Indeed, this had been a destiny day for Jacque.

# Early-Morning Angel

## *Judy Martin*

The virtually scripted, peaceful endings that follow the disastrous situations during our early lives truly make one wonder who upstairs is keeping such a watchful and loving eye on us as we go through the perils of growing up. Is there just one guardian angel who comes to the rescue? My humble opinion is no. I believe there must have been a flock of them watching over me during my teenage years; and one of the flock sometimes came to me in my dreams in an unusual form.

Throughout my life I have been fascinated with the Vietnam War. As early as I can remember, I had dreams about it. Often, I would be in a dugout or running with a blond-haired man who always wore a red bandanna. I called him Bob. It was a common occurrence for me—in the dreamworld, that is.

During my teenage years of evening exploration at the various hot spots on Long Island, my buddies and I would take over the dance floor. Waves of people would part as we made our way across. We were fearless and innocent at the same time. Driving home at night, the girls and I were generally very careful. But one night, I decided to leave a bit early because I was upset at seeing a former boyfriend having too good a time without me. The experience to come would both rob me of my feeling of safety driving home on the nighttime highways alone and would teach me that some angel is doing an early-morning shift whenever I hit the road.

I had left the club with a girlfriend, who walked me out to my car.

"Judy, are you sure you want to leave?" Cathy asked. "Come on, I'll take off in about a half hour."

"I've got to be at work early," I replied. "I'm not in the mood to stay."

"Love ya, drive carefully," she yelled as she ran back into the club.

And so there I was, alone in my old Pontiac, with a sick feeling in my stomach. I had a funny feeling that night. It was very dark in that parking lot, but it was even darker on the Southern State Parkway as I headed home. I was probably driving faster than I should have in my rush to get home.

It was a cool spring night, and worth the effort of rolling down my windows to let in the fresh air. A really bad song came on the radio, and I was compelled to change the station immediately. Unfortunately, my concentration was thus broken as I was about to exit the highway onto a side road.

"Bang!" The noise was so loud it made me dizzy.

I had hit a curb. My tire blew, and I careened across all three lanes and back again before my car made an abrupt stop at the foot of a light pole.

I said a quick prayer of thanks that my face was not attached to the pole in front of me and that I seemed to be alive. I knew I was okay, as every muscle in my body was shaking. The shoulda, coulda, woulda's of safe driving went through my head, and I found myself alone on the highway at three-thirty in the morning, miles from the nearest exit. I was frightened and began to cry.

Debating for several minutes, I decided that a young woman on her own in a dead car at night, even in a well-lit area, was not safe. But ahead was only a pitch-black road, with just a few scattered lights. I waited in the car for about twenty minutes, watching cars race by. Too scared to flag down a car, I began to doze off in the driver's seat when I was startled by a beeping car whizzing by.

I could stay put no longer. Figuring it was about two miles to the next exit, I decided to make a run for it; in retrospect, that was probably the wrong thing to do. I quickly exhausted myself, realizing that my days at the gym weren't worth the monthly fees I was paying. Alone on a dark road I was a sitting duck, so I kept up as good a walking pace as I could. I could just see the lights of the exit in the distance when suddenly a car came to a screeching halt beside me.

Shocked at the sight of a beat-up old Rambler, I started to run. The car pulled up beside me, and the window rolled down. This was it. I was in deep trouble.

"Young lady, you shouldn't be walking alone this early in the morning," the driver said in a joking manner.

I was terrified, afraid to even look in his direction. He continued next to me, driving at a snail's pace.

"I know you are scared, but I want to help you," he said in a loving tone.

I looked at him. He was an older man in a crisp white T-shirt, and his arms were covered with tattoos. He had longish blond hair and was casually smoking a cigarette. In fact, he had a pack of them under his sleeve. This guy looked like the perfect ax murderer, but he seemed to have a sincere attitude.

Wavering over whether I should get into the car, I decided I could make the next exit, so I picked up my pace. The car continued next to me. The man didn't say a word but instead put on a Doors tape. The lyrics blared from the speakers. I kept walking; the song became like a chant in my head.

*Judy,* I thought. *Get in the car.* I argued against my gut feeling that it would be okay. The music was loud, and all the signs indicated a dangerous situation. The Rambler followed me, and then I was galvanized by a loud screech of another car behind it.

"Hey, sweetheart!" screamed a young man from a car filled with howling, drunken fools. Decision time. These frat boys were taunting me, and one even got out of the car. With that, my fear was more than I could handle.

"Get in the damn car . . . now," said the older man, spitting out his cigarette onto the pavement.

Quickly reacting, I jumped into the car. Out of the corner of my eye I could see that the frat boy had just about caught up with me. My driver didn't say a thing. I hardly looked at him. When I did, he threw me a sincere smile. I also noticed that he wore a red bandanna around his wrist.

I thought, *Where the hell is he taking me?*

Much to my surprise, he answered my question, though it had never come out of my mouth. "Silly girl, I'm taking you to the next exit like you wanted," he replied. "What is your name?" he asked.

I told him, though he conveniently skipped telling me *his* name.

"Wondering about the tattoos?" he said proudly.

Well, yes, as a matter of fact I was. But I kept silent as he started to tell me his story. He had been a soldier during Vietnam. When he told me that, warmth came over me. Suddenly I wasn't afraid of him anymore. The feeling was unexplainable. He said very little after that.

Within minutes, he pulled off at the next exit and into a gas station. We had driven at least five miles; it would have been quite a walk. He slowed to a stop and just kept smiling at me. I grabbed the door handle, wanting to jump out to end my fear, but it was jammed. A stream of fear ran through me as he got out of the car. The tattooed Vietnam veteran appeared at my door and pulled it open without incident.

"Gets stuck sometimes. I oil it, but it just gets stuck," he said, almost apologizing. He opened the door with a refreshing "My lady." As I was getting out, he offered me his hand. On his forearm was a large tattoo with dark arrows through it. In bold letters it said, BOB.

Upon seeing that I felt as if I were in a time warp. Was this the Bob I had dreamed of? I felt suddenly compelled to start a conversation. I thanked him again and told him I was going to phone my dad to come get me. I called from a phone both and had a quick conversation with my dad, while Bob leaned against his car smoking a cigarette. I felt very lucky, I explained to my father, that someone had helped me out. Hearing my father's voice drained my fear. I turned and hung up the phone.

I walked out of the phone booth, and Bob was gone. I had turned away from him for only an instant, but I guess that's all an angel needs to fly away.

# Logic of the Heart

## *Gary Holz*

Ten years after being diagnosed with multiple sclerosis, I had been reduced to living in a wheelchair. My condition was rapidly declining, and there was no feeling in my body from the chest down. My doctors gave me less than two years to live.

One night, I set out to escape my depression by going to a local jazz club. There I met a stranger with whom I shared my desperate situation. She told me of certain aboriginal healers in the Australian outback who might be able to help me. As my own Western doctors had assured me that I would soon die, I saw that I had nothing to lose by seeking out a new and different form of treatment. So I cashed in all my frequent-flyer miles for a ticket to Australia.

My friends and family thought I had lost my mind, and not one of them would agree to take the trip with me. On the airplane, I was forced to sit in my wheelchair without a head support, catheterized and uncomfortable for the entire lonely eighteen-hour flight. Nobody spoke directly to me except the flight attendant, and then only when necessary. Finally, the plane landed in Brisbane at three in the morning.

From the airport, I called the phone number I'd been given. A man's brusque voice answered and told me to go to a certain hotel and wait. Totally exhausted, I checked into a room, where I slept for several hours. I was picked up at the hotel later that day by a one-armed, one-eyed aborigine, who then took me for the ride of a lifetime out into the outback.

I spent an entire month in the desert outback with a healer named Trista, who taught me to discover the amazing personal power to heal myself. Under her tutelage, I learned that my own past conditioning and thoughts were what had created my illness. Day by day, I began literally to change the cellular memory of my body to initiate the healing process. And remarkably, by the end of the month, I no longer had symptoms of multiple sclerosis and for the first time in over a year had taken several steps out of my wheelchair.

Back in America, I was filed by a new sense of purpose. As a result of my extraordinary experience, I pursued and obtained a doctorate in neuroimmunology and opened a wellness center in San Diego. I am a full-time healer these days, using the same techniques I learned form the aborigines. Believing that the power to heal lies within each of us, I teach patients how they can get to the root cause of their own diseases and heal themselves.

# Protected by Angels

## Gerald Jampolsky, M.D.

When I helped start the Center for Attitudinal Healing in Tiburon, California, in 1975, I didn't realize that I myself would be healed so deeply.

At the time, I was killing myself with alcohol, yet I was afraid of death. I thought that my only reality was my body, and that when I died, that was the end of life.

The Center was founded to help children with life-threatening illnesses, yet my inner guidance told me the following: "The children who will be coming to your center will be wise old spirits in young bodies teaching you and the other volunteers another way of looking at life and at death. They will help you let go of your fear of death."

Greg Harrison was the first child to die at our center. By the time he arrived at the Center, he's endured about eight different series of drugs for leukemia, and all of them had made him quite ill. Greg, his family, and his physician finally made a decision that there would be no more drugs. Shortly before he died, Greg attended a group meeting at which I was present, and another eleven-year-old child asked him, "What is it like to know that you are going to be dead in a few weeks?"

As the meeting's facilitator, I tried to think of a way to smooth over what seemed to me an unanswerable question.

While I was trying to figure out something to say, Greg spoke. With an air of great peace and tranquility, he said, "I think that when you die you just set your body aside, which was never real in the first place, and then become one with all the other souls. And sometimes you come down and act as a guardian angel to someone."

Immediately I sensed that Greg was going to be my guardian

angel. I could feel the power of this small child's teaching, urging me to look at life and death differently.

It was the beginning of my own transformation.

Over the next few years, quite a number of children at our center died, and it was my good fortune to be at the bedside of many of them when they made their transitions. My fear of death was shrinking steadily, and I felt the truth of my initial inner guidance about the Center.

About five years after Greg died, I had a miraculous dream that made me cry with joy. The dream took place at the top of a hill. All the children who had died and I were holding hands and dancing with glee in a circle.

Then, all of a sudden, the children started to float up into the sky, waving and laughing. Finally they all turned into light, leaving me there. I knew with all my heart that I was not alone on the top of the hill. I knew that their light, their true selves, and my light were joined forever . . . and ever. I felt a new and exhilarating sense of freedom.

Today I feel that Greg and these other children are watching over me—that they are truly my guardian angels. They protect me as God protects me and remind me that my true identity is a spiritual one. Now when I pray I don't ask for things or certain outcomes—for me, praying is thanking God for all the blessings that have been bestowed upon me.

I had an experience some time ago that confirmed this sense of protection and blessing in my life: I drive a 1985 Renault convertible, and I park it outside about a hundred yards from our house. A couple of years ago, in the middle of a severe storm, someone knocked at our door and said that a giant tree had just fallen right on top of my car. I rushed to see the extent of the damage.

The tree had not hit the canvas top of my convertible but had landed on the trunk. Under the tree's weight the car had sunk about a foot into the ground, which was covered with mulch. When we finally got a truck with a pulley to lift the tree, the car came back to ground level without a single mark on it. The workmen gathered around, scratching their heads, at a loss to understand why there was no damage. Then one pointed to the rear fender, where there's a bumper sticker I like very much.

It reads: PROTECTED BY ANGELS

There was no other explanation.

# 7

# DREAMS, PAST LIVES, AND OUT-OF-BODY EXPERIENCES

# A Setup in Time

## Triana Hill

I was born on the lobby floor of the Queen of Angels Hospital in Los Angeles. My Hungarian Jewish immigrant mother had been deserted by her husband, and didn't have insurance or money to cover hospital charges. I lived my first sixteen years in a small, run-down one-room shack in Venice, California. We had no hot water or refrigerator, and I slept on the floor.

My mother wanted me to be a "a good Jewish girl." My grandfather was a rabbi, and my mother was devoted to her religion. However, when the subject of religion was brought up, I would walk away. I didn't want to be Jewish or of any religion. To my mother's frustration, I refused even to honor the Jewish holidays.

My first sixteen years were very difficult and lonely. My mother scrubbed floors to make a living, and there were times we didn't have enough money for food. I never went to a movie, rode in a car, or ate in a restaurant. I ate with my hands, and didn't even know how to use cutlery. I was very introverted, considered myself ugly, and basically only believed in one thing . . . survival!

My biggest goal in life was to be a secretary when I finished school. I graduated at age sixteen, went out on my first date, and shortly thereafter got a marriage proposal, which I accepted because I would finally be able to sleep in a bed. I had no idea what love was! My husband and I were not compatible, so I decided to get a divorce. We had two children, whom I ended up raising on my own with no monetary support from my ex-husband. I got a job as a secretary and struggled financially, never having enough money to raise my children the way I would have liked.

At the age of thirty-three, still not believing in anything but survival, I had an experience with my daughter that changed my entire life and belief systems. At that time I was still not religious. I was not spiritual, did not know what metaphysics was, and believed that you live and you die and that's it!

On a Sunday afternoon, my daughter Kim and I had both gone to the beach, she with her French-Canadian girlfriend, Louisa, and I with Troy, a male acquaintance. Troy was very good-looking and charming, but for some unknown reason my daughter and I didn't trust him, so neither of us shared much time with him.

Troy and I had just gotten back from the beach when my daughter returned home with her girlfriend. When Kim came in the door, Troy yelled out at her, "Stop, don't move!" He ran into the kitchen, got a wineglass, and, holding it over her head, put his hand on his heart and exuberantly shouted, "Alibistro!"

My daughter just stood there with a stunned look on her face that matched mine, and then she walked out of the room. I went over to Troy and said, "What on earth was that all about? Have you lost your mind?"

Looking embarrassed, he answered, "I don't know what came over me. I don't believe we have past lives, but suddenly I knew that she and I had shared one together. That's what prompted my actions. Maybe I am going nuts!"

Troy, Louisa, and I sat and talked for an hour about what had just happened, but none of us could make any sense of it. Then, realizing that my daughter had never returned to join us, I asked Louisa to go find her and tell her she wasn't being very sociable.

Louisa returned almost immediately and, quite frightened, announced that Kim was lying on my bed, clutching her stomach and crying hysterically. I ran to the bedroom and found

Kim sobbing uncontrollably. I thought maybe she was ill. I kept asking her, "Are you sick? What's wrong with you?"

She couldn't hear me! I didn't know what to do, or whether I should call an ambulance. In desperation, I put cold, wet towels on her forehead.

Still sobbing, Kim finally opened her eyes and said, in between sobs, "Mother, we live other lives. I just experienced a life where you and I were sisters and I was about to marry a count . . . and . . . and . . . in this lifetime he's Troy! You both betrayed me, and I killed myself by putting a dagger in my stomach."

What she was saying made no sense, and my only desire at that moment was to calm her down. I convinced her to come into the living room, got her settled, and brought her a cold drink. I asked her to please tell us what she'd just experienced.

She took a deep breath and started speaking, not in English but in French! She and I had never been to France, and she had never studied the language.

Looking astonished, Louisa, who did speak French, said, "Kim, you don't know how to speak French, and you're speaking perfect French!"

Kim answered her in French.

I was in shock, as were Troy and Louisa.

Kim proceeded to tell her story, a poignant and tragic one. In the seventeenth century, she and I were sisters in the south of France. In 1654, she was in love and engaged to Dominique le Conte de Montigue. She did not know that he was also having an affair with me, and that I was carrying his bastard child, until she overheard us talking about it in the garden one day. She silently declared vengeance on both of us.

She convinced her fiancé to tell the government that I had committed treason and to have me burned at the stake, which he did. The day after the execution, she got him to drink wine that she had poisoned and he died shortly thereafter. Then, realizing that she had killed her only sister and the man she loved, she no longer wanted to live and killed herself.

Kim also spoke about the Plague and many things that

were transpiring in France at that time. Finally she said, "I'm tired. I have told you my story."

As she said that, I suddenly felt hatred for her. I loved her as my daughter, but I was simultaneously experiencing the other lifetime, when she had killed me and my unborn child. I heard myself screaming at her in French, and I knew exactly what I was saying.

At that point Louisa said, "I'm leaving. It was shocking enough to hear Kim speak French, but now you're speaking old-world gutter French, and nobody can do that unless they were born and bred in France."

I begged her to stay and translate my side of the story, and she did. When it was over, all of us were stunned. Our reality had been shattered!

My daughter and I didn't talk much about the experience over the next few days, but then we saw a television program called *It's All in the Mind* hosted by a doctor named Thelma Moss, who was the head of the parapsychology department at UCLA. The program was about reincarnation. I realized that we were not the only ones in the world who had memory of a past life.

I called Dr. Moss and told her a little about our experience. I asked if we could come to the university to talk to her and gain some clarity on why we had had this experience. Dr. Moss agreed to let us see her the following week.

We spent several hours with Dr. Moss, and she told us that our experience was the most unusual story of reincarnation she had ever heard, primarily because Kim and I had simultaneously flipped into the same lifetime, each receiving the same information. Then she stated that the most startling part of our experience was what she called "a setup in time," because someone was present who knew and could translate the French.

We finished giving her all the details, and she said she would do research on seventeenth-century France and get back to us. We said our good-byes and headed for the parking lot to make the seventy-mile drive home.

As I started to get into my car, I felt compelled to return to

Dr. Moss's laboratory, though I didn't know why. The feeling was so strong that I had to go back. Her door was closed. I knocked on it, and she called out, "Come in, Triana."

I entered and asked her, "How did you know it was me? Your door was closed!"

She answered, "I sent you a telepathic message to return, and you received it."

I asked her what "telepathic" meant, and she explained it to me. Then I asked, "Why did you want me to come back?"

She said, "I want to test your psychic ability."

I thought the idea was ridiculous, and I proceeded to laugh uncontrollably. I finally replied, "I don't believe in that garbage."

She said, "Triana, you are very psychic."

I answered, "How can you say I am something I don't even believe exists?"

She said, "I can tell by your energy body."

Feeling very stupid at that point, I asked. "What's that?" and she explained.

I finally agreed to be tested, feeling sure that she would discover that I was not psychic! When the test was completed, she told me that I was in the top 5 percent of all the people she had psychically tested in twenty-five years, and she wanted me to do psychic research with her.

I was totally confused. I had felt weird when I first went to see her and weirder when I completed the testing. I just wanted to forget everything that had happened and be normal. I thanked her and told her that I would be in touch, though I had no intention of contacting her again.

For two and a half years I did not tell anyone about my experience or attempt to use my psychic abilities. My life was a struggle and very difficult financially, as I was making only four hundred dollars a month as a secretary and raising two children on it.

I then thought about my psychic ability and came to the conclusion that I might somehow be able to utilize it in business and thereby make more money to take better care of my children.

I went into the very competitive field of executive search. I used my psychic abilities to know whom to call and how to convince them to change companies when they weren't even looking for a job. All of my global business was done over the telephone!

I opened my own corporation in the seventies, when very few women headed their own businesses. In a few years, I became number one in the world in my field and was honored in *Who's Who in American Women*. I continually wondered if everyone was psychic and just didn't know it, like I used to be. I wanted to find out. So I closed my corporation doors and started teaching Breakthrough—Beyond Conception® empowerment workshops all over the world.

In the past twelve years, I have taught in sixty-five countries. Students have opened their intuition through my processes; they have stopped using their programmed logical minds and taken quantum leaps in their lives by using their unlimited intuitive minds. My life today is devoted to helping people find and utilize their full potential and to realize three things: one, anything is possible; two, just because you haven't experienced something doesn't mean it isn't true; and three, we are the greatest miracle of all.

# The Dream

## Melissa Giovagnoli

My grandmother, whom we called Baubie, was the most important person in the lives of my two sisters, my brother, and me. Growing up in a dysfunctional family, we found great comfort in our grandmother's hugs and kisses. She had a special place in her heart for me because I was the martyr of the group, constantly choosing to go without whenever my father said, as he often did, "How are we going to afford that?" When my grandmother visited us in our little tract house in Cleveland, she would silently hand me a bag of licorice before giving goodies to my sisters and brother.

I grew up seeking Baubie's guidance. Dad's florist shop was connected to our house, so there was little privacy for a young girl. Baubie's apartment was a place of refuge when the storms at home became unbearable. My grandmother always had wonderful food to eat, and we would cry and talk and eat my troubles away in the comfort of her warm kitchen. My family was always in some sort of crisis, so I found myself taking bike trips to Baubie's house almost every day. But as the years went on and I got involved in school activities, I visited Baubie less and less. I got caught up in becoming popular and getting the kind of grades needed to get into a good college.

Time flew by, and soon I was off to school. Once, when my grandparents went to visit my uncle in California, my grandfather had a serious stroke and was put in a nursing home there. Rather than come back to her apartment, Baubie decided to sell her things and move out to be with him. We kept in touch through phone calls and letters, but I was still preoccupied with getting ahead, making sure now that I found the right career. During this time I fell in love with Steve, who is still my husband after twenty-one years. Baubie came to the wedding. She was so happy. It was her big day, and all her family was with her.

A year later, she came to see us in our first town house. Together, she and I painted one of the old brass lamps she had given to Steve and me, and we sat up until the wee hours talking about her life as a little girl growing up on a farm in the outskirts of Cleveland. She had the best stories, and she always came up with new ones each time we found ourselves engaging in these marathon storytelling sessions. Just before she left to go back to California, Steve took a picture of Baubie and me on the front stoop of our town house. Baubie looked at the camera while I leaned over sideways and kissed her cheek.

Two weeks later, I had a dream that Baubie was going to die. Ever since she'd suffered a heart attack five years earlier, I'd been concerned about her health, but she'd looked so healthy on her latest visit that I really had no reason to be concerned. Nevertheless, I felt a strong urge to call her. I didn't want to worry her, but I shared the dream and waited for Baubie's response. She said, simply, "That's okay, honey. We all have to die sometime. And remember, I told you it was wonderful that time I had my heart attack. It wasn't scary at all. In fact, I felt a real sense of peace come over me, even with all that pain."

We talked about the dream for more than an hour. She assured me that she would be fine and that I need not feel sad when she died. She would be going someplace better, and she would always love me and be there waiting for me. I didn't share our conversation with my family—or with anyone, for that matter—at that time.

Only seven days later, though, I received a call at about six p.m. from my father. He began, "Hi honey . . ." But before he could say another word, I said "I know. Baubie's dead." He confirmed the fact and hung up shortly afterward. I went immediately to our small living room window and looked out at the night sky.

I didn't cry. I didn't have to. We had already said good-bye.

# Story Number One

## *Laura Alden Kamm*

*During my near-death experience in 1982, I had what is now commonly referred to as a life review. What follows is a portion of what I experienced.*

I recall seeing a particular scene from my childhood. I was about five or six years old at the time, and my best friend, Sue, and I were doing our usual investigating around the neighborhood on a beautiful day in spring. I thought it would be great if we could find a robin's egg, hatch it, raise the bird ourselves, as I dearly loved robins and had always wanted to have one for a pet. Well, it didn't take us long before we found a nest cradled on a neighbor's ladder that hung horizontally on the side of their garage. I was the taller of the two of us, so it was my job to reach into the tightly woven nest and grab an egg.

In our search for adventure, and the egg, we had forgotten all about the mother robin, who suddenly came darting at my hand and head, chirping frantically and flapping her wings. Sue and I ducked and dodged the parental squawks, but somehow I still managed to hang on to the egg. Dashing away with the tiny cobalt shell in my hand, we headed toward Sue's backyard, positioning ourselves on the picnic table and ready to play midwife to this baby robin. Bit by bit, we gently chipped and peeled away the protective layers of the shell.

As I watched this scene play itself out before me during my life review, feeling the excitement pounding in my heart as I glimpsed behind the membrane of the egg and spied the tiny bird, I felt the same excitement I'd felt as a child all over again, only more so. I watched as Sue and I peered through the fragile layers, and I also watched and felt as our excitement bent into dread. This miniature bird didn't look anything like what we thought a robin should look like. It was emaciated and featherless, and soon it was dead. I watched as Sue and I sat there, as little girls, regarding our deed with horror.

As I stood in the midst of this near-death experience, I felt huge amounts of remorse and consternation well up inside my being. I felt not only my own pain and sorrow, but Sue's as well. Beyond that, and much to my surprise, I felt and truly absorbed the mother robin's panic and sorrow as she searched to no avail for her baby. The worst sensations were that of the baby robin itself. As I stood there gazing upon the scene, I could feel the energy that was once inside that small, helpless creature leave, never to return to that place and time again.

Surrounded by several loving guides, I continued to stand there watching the scene play over and over again. I felt their love and attempts to comfort me, yet I was mortified. I recall returning my focus to the scene playing out, where I watched as Sue and I gently laid to rest the pieces of the eggshell and the dead baby robin in the flowers that hugged the border of Sue's backyard. The silence spoke volumes as Sue and I parted company and I walked back up the hill toward my home, passing the neighbor's house where our mischief had begun.

Again I felt an overwhelming sense of remorse and loss. I was devastated, and the heaviness of this burden brought with it significant amounts of awareness concerning the inter-connectedness that I have, that we all have, with all things. This new awareness smoldered deep within me, constantly re-minding me, even to this day, that all things are a part of life's web of existence.

Days later, after I regained vital signs and woke from my coma, it was determined that I needed to have brain surgery to correct some abscesses that had developed in my right occipital lobe. I was rolled into surgery at eight the following morning and awoke from the surgery eleven hours later in Neuro-ICU. A huge white turban of gauze was wrapped around my head.

The morning after surgery, the nurses in Neuro-ICU were all chattering to me, telling me that I just had to see *"this."* They rolled my bed over to the window, and there on a tree branch was a robin. However, this was no ordinary robin. He was an albino-headed robin. Everything about him was just as a robin should look and be, but his head was pure white, looking as if it were wrapped in surgical gauze—just like mine. The nurses teased me that he and I were twins.

Little did the nurses know of my near-death experience, my life review, and the scene with the robin that had been re-played to me from my childhood. Nonetheless, I knew why the albino-headed robin was there. He was confirmation that I was being guided, protected, and cared for from a divine place, and that everything was going to be all right. I stayed in Neuro-ICU for three days following the surgery.

My little robin sat on that tree branch night and day for those three days, never moving. After I was moved into an-other room, one of the nurses came in and told me that as soon as I had left the ICU the robin had flown away.

# One Sunday Morning

## *Victoria Bullis*

On a wintry Sunday morning in 1990, I was sitting up in bed, trying to meditate. I was still sleepy, and having a hard time concentrating. My mind kept wandering, mostly to a recent conversation I'd had with some Native American friends about near-death experiences. In their tradition, those who return from the journey say that they've crossed over a river, rather than having gone through a tunnel.

The entire topic of being able to glimpse "the other side" had fascinated me for some time. I was reasonably sure, but not entirely, that the accounts I'd heard were accurate, but I was also open to the scientific theory that near-death experiences are a product of one's brain patterning during some trauma. Or perhaps it's a combination of both.

I can remember how I was thinking, at one point that morning, that it would be fantastic to make either journey happen— to go across a river or to travel through that tunnel. At that very moment, I felt extremely strange, and with a *whoosh* found myself just inside the base of a vortex! I actually seemed to be half in and half out of my body; an inner part of me, my soul, was trying to drag my body up with it, into gorgeous swirling lights. Consciously, I said, "Oh my God, I'm going to die, here and now. And I'm not ready!"

My soul, still attempting to lift up my body, responded, with obvious annoyance, "Oh, for heaven's sake, you're not going to die! We're just going to the Light for a while!" At that, this deeper part of me pulled us away and began twisting around and around, becoming a whirlwind.

Bright colors, especially blues, pinks, and violets, pulsated from the tunnel walls in streams and twinkling lights, like sparklers on the Fourth of July. The colors at the base were vivid, growing more pastel the higher we climbed. I say "we" as I was in touch with both my conscious self and my soul at the same time, almost as though we were two separate entities. Chills of a type I'd never known began to encompass me as I felt us getting closer to the rim; they were chills of unique excitement and pleasure, not fear or concern. My final conscious thoughts, as we readied to cross an invisible but very real barrier, were of nervousness that I'd left my body back on Earth. I hoped I'd be able to return to it.

Suddenly I felt a popping sensation, and was immediately propelled into a sense of weightlessness, pure bliss, contentment, and harmony. And I was completely at one with each of those vibrations. I had an instant and total knowingness that this was exactly as it should be on the physical plane too, and also how simple it could be to achieve it. I also felt sadness that we lose these qualities once we arrive here as humans.

Although I didn't see anyone around me initially, I sensed that the area was filled with warm, encouraging beings, and I felt totally at peace. I knew to wait, that something would start happening in a moment or two. Presently, people whom I didn't recognize approached me. I knew instantaneously that they were friends and relatives from other lives, and one by one they gave me little nonverbal messages of encouragement for my current life. Some of the messages were even humorous, although I consciously received only the gist of them, not literal words. I noticed all my guides encircling me, and how much they were enjoying my awe at all this. Then, from off to the right, I saw Winston Churchill approaching me! Although I recall saying something like "Oh, wow, I've always admired you," I somehow didn't find it strange to find him there.

Telepathically, Churchill shared with me how hard it had been for him to let go of what he had felt were mistakes and bungles that cost a lot of lives during World War II. In a split second, I was able to take in everything he himself had seen when he'd reviewed his life, and also how he'd finally come to terms with himself. When I asked why he was sharing this information with me, he disappeared! Intuitively, though, I know I received an important message on some deep level.

Using telepathy, I stated that I wanted to choose a few historical figures to talk with. I heard back, "One." A flood of famous people crowded through my mind, and I got so confused I couldn't make a decision. Agitated, I related that I needed help, and suddenly Thomas Aquinas, the great theologian of the Middle Ages, appeared. I was disappointed at first that it wasn't someone more glamorous, but then I was totally embarrassed that he could hear my thoughts. He laughed, and said he just wanted me to know how necessary it is at this time to leave behind our worn and outmoded notions of what being spiritual should look like. Then he, too, disappeared.

All of a sudden I realized I was being drawn back to the top of the vortex, and found myself sending a hurried good-bye to everyone. I received back messages of love. In an instant, I was down at the other end of the tunnel and, with a jolt, in my body again, still sitting upright in bed. I had brought with me the incredible rainbow colors from the tunnel journey; they were whirling around me and flowing through my body.

I remained motionless for a very long time, afraid that the bliss and beautiful lights would stop if I got out of bed. I was in a trance most of that day, overwhelmed with feelings of amazement and euphoria.

Even though in meditation I've since been able to re-create going up through a tunnel to a higher dimension, I've never been able to relive the intensity or astonishing sensations of that one January morning. Every once in a while I regret not having had a longer time "up there." However, I'm a little afraid of wanting to attempt it in quite the same way again, as I have a feeling that next time will be *it*!

# Mr. Prime Minister

## *Roberta Johnson*

I kept having dreams about the Israeli prime minister, Mr. Netanyahu, and I couldn't figure out what they meant, so I went to a psychic. The dreams had no romantic overtones to them; they actually left me with a quiet feeling of serenity and peace. But the psychic couldn't tell me what the dreams signified.

In the first dream, I was having a picnic lunch with Mr. Netanyahu in a very lush green setting overlooking a lake. There were lots of people around us, including many children. I knew that these people were Mr. Netanyahu's family, but I still didn't know the significance of the dream.

The second dream that I had was the same as the first.

In my third dream, Mr. Netanyahu and I were at an elaborate banquet having dinner together.

The fourth dream was even more puzzling. Mr. Netanyahu and I were standing in a very beautiful office that had mahogany furniture. We were discussing a problem that we were going to tackle together.

The last dream occurred in March. In it, Mr. Netanyahu and I were walking hand in hand, accompanied by a large entourage. Suddenly, a large man came up to us and gave me a huge bear hug, his arms completely encircling me. I was very comfortable and content with this. When I awoke, I felt happy and giddy, although I still didn't know what these dreams were about.

Feeling extremely frustrated by then, I went to see a friend of mine, the Reverend Catherine Alsbury. I told her about the dreams that I was having involving Mr. Netanyahu, and she told me that she thought they meant that I was going to go to Israel for some reason. She also told me about two meditation exercises I might try in order to find the meaning of the dreams for myself.

The first exercise involved sitting quietly at a table and closing my eyes. I was then supposed to pretend that I was at the table with Mr. Netanyahu and ask him why he was in my dreams and what he was telling me. I was a little skeptical of this type of meditation, but being desperate to know, I took it very seriously and tried it. The second exercise was to meditate on the country of Israel and ask it why it kept coming to me in my dreams. Once again I did the exercise and took the meditation very seriously.

The next week was Holy Week, and we were encouraged to stop by the church to pray, meditate, or talk with the minister if we felt like it. So on April seventh, I went to the church, sat in a pew, and begged God to please tell me why I was having these dreams and what they meant.

On the very next day, I received a phone call from an old friend and former co-worker with whom I hadn't spoken in three years. We both do therapeutic work with seriously ill children, and now she is working for a volunteer group called Operation Smile. She asked me if I wanted to go to Israel that June to do therapeutic play and medical teaching with Arabic children in the West Bank who were having reconstructive surgery.

Well, you can imagine my surprise and relief! Suddenly I knew what the dreams were about. This was what I was supposed to do!

I am now planning to go to Israel on June second. Although I am stressed and scared about the adventure, I know that our efforts will be an instrument of peace and harmony. I see the message of my dreams very clearly now, and I hope that I will have the opportunity to meet Mr. Netanyahu while I am in Israel.

# Soul Travel

## *Charles Lewis Richards*

When I was a junior in college, I went through a period of transition and questioning about the true purpose of life, death, and the hereafter. This led me to research and study various religious and spiritual disciplines.

Growing up, I had never been one to easily accept the word of authority without proof. My curiosity expressed itself through a keen interest in life sciences, hobbies, music, and the usual sports. Yet by the end of my sophomore year of study, I was in an existential crisis. A part of me demanded to find meaning in the mysteries of life and death—answers that had to come through direct personal experience.

My research led me to pursue a method of spiritual development that hinged around a technique called Soul Travel. Sure, I had read in holy books about journeys that spiritual figures had experienced beyond the body in the heavenly realms. I had also read about near-death experiences. Yet could the average individual do this type of thing? I had to find out.

The idea of having a personal adventure in the heavenly realms, free from the limitations of time or space, seemed like the ultimate spiritual adventure. My excitement at such a possibility was like a fire within. Soul Travel promised to open doors of insight and meaning, without any props, austerities, or years of isolation. After doing various exercises for about six months with little success, I asked, as if to challenge God, for an experience to show me the truth of the worlds beyond life.

One afternoon I decided to take a nap on my sofa. While lying there, I reviewed in my mind a particular Soul Travel technique. It involved, among other things, the singing of a spiritual sound called HU. While drifting off with the sound of HU in my mind, there came a sudden alertness and an awareness of being in the midst of a lucid dream. I had read about this, but it was not what I understood to be Soul Travel.

Immediately, I began to apply the Soul Travel technique. While doing this, I heard what sounded like a loud motor running in my left ear. Lying on my back on the sofa, I reasoned that it was impossible that this sound was coming from anywhere but within, so containing my excitement, I continued with the technique. Suppressing my curiosity to open my eyes and look to the left was difficult. Yet my fear of breaking the momentum of whatever was happening kept me going.

Suddenly I felt the strong sensation that my body was rapidly dropping downward through the sofa and floor, as if I were lying horizontal on a roller coaster that was quickly descending. Then there was a rapid and powerful ascent.

During this time, the motor sound transformed into the

rising sound of very loud flutes swirling and fluttering so intensely that my initial concern was for my eardrums. But a feeling of bliss accompanied the flutes, and the thought came that this was an inner, nonphysical sound that would do me no harm.

My ascent continued, and I began to see threads of brightly colored light, so bright and pure that my first impulse was to protect my eyes. Again the feeling of safety overcame my brief fear.

What happened next left me awestruck. Suddenly a world opened up in which every atom seemed to vibrate with life, energy, and love. The sound of swirling flutes had reached a crescendo and seemed to emanate from within and all around me. It was pure excitement and bliss.

I found myself standing in a world where the clouds in the sky swirled and flowed with a mixture of the purest and brightest colors one could imagine. The experience was more real and intense than anything imaginable, and suddenly I understood the statement "As above, so below." The physical world of my body seemed insignificant and so far below.

My thought was: This is proof, indeed, of the worlds beyond and the kingdom within. No books on religion, no philosophy, no church or priest, could substitute for this experience of majesty and reality.

Standing there, I wondered at my own appearance. Holding a hand up in front of my face, I was surprised and amused to see its shape composed of glowing light.

I then thought of my body lying there on the sofa in my apartment, and I wondered at the length of my stay. Instinctively, I decided to return to my apartment and imagined myself back in my body. It was like falling into the void. Immediately I found myself gently floating back into my body on the sofa. It was as if my soul were repositioning itself back in my physical body.

At first, the white walls in the room appeared to reflect the motion and colors of the other realm, but quickly they became solid and normal. At the same time, the sounds of swirling flutes began to gently fade into the distance, leaving behind that other reality.

When all this had ceased, I got up to check the amount of time I had been lying on the sofa. It had been approximately fifteen minutes, though it felt much longer. My ecstasy could hardly be contained. I wanted to tell my friends immediately.

As I reflect back on it now, in an instant, during that experience, I knew for a fact that death was merely an illusion and that life would go on with even more beauty and understanding at the end of my time here on Earth. It was also clear that all life is sacred and that we are all here to give support, comfort, and insight, when possible, into the full potential of our spiritual nature as soul.

In the years since, I have had many more Soul Travel experiences here and in the beyond, but that was my first. It changed my life forever.

# The Day I Met Princess Diana

## Bevey Miner

I had just finished blowing out my birthday candles. This was an evening of celebration for me, though I was having a little trouble feeling that turning forty was cause for celebration. Forty seemed a turning point, a mile marker that pointed up the swiftness of life's passage. Was I halfway through the journey? Perhaps more—or maybe less? Certainly I was no longer young. I had decided to celebrate anyway, and my girlfriends and I were gathered for a slumber party—forty-year-olds can still have slumber parties—when we received a phone call telling us to switch on the news.

When we turned on the television, we were stunned to learn of Princess Diana's death. Sensational commentary from reporters and vivid footage of the car wreck were part of every news report, and these images affected me strangely. I could not stop looking at the mangled car and staring at the backseat where Diana had sat. I sat transfixed, watching the television as they played the same scene over and over again that night. I couldn't bring myself to turn the TV off.

That night I had vivid dreams. I saw the accident happening—the tires screeching, the car's impact, the sound of metal crunching. I was somehow close enough to see the terror in Diana's eyes and the fright on her face. My dream allowed me an intimate view of her emotions: I could almost feel her fear. I was able to witness everything as if it were in slow motion. I did not see anything beyond the moment of the crash, though the dream-accident repeated itself continuously throughout the night.

The next morning, I felt drained by the trauma of my dream, and the images of the accident stayed with me throughout the day, though they did not overtake my emotions so intensely. That night, I had the same dream, but not as repetitively or descriptively. The following day, I could feel the horror of Diana's death fading, and I went about my daily work routine and didn't think about the scene again.

That evening I had plans with Charles, a friend of mine who had been a spiritual guide in my life during the previous year, a rough one for me as I struggled with corporate pressures and simultaneously coped with a divorce and the challenges of single parenthood. I had begun to search for ways to create harmony in my life, instead of the total exhaustion I was feeling. Then I met Charles, who is a psychologist, and he introduced me to meditation. With his help, I was transformed and gained an understanding of this practice and my abilities. Meditation was just what I needed to carry me through this stressful time, and I found myself very adept at it.

We decided to meditate before going out to dinner. This was routine with Charles. We struck our familiar poses, me on the couch and him in the chair. It wasn't long before the scene of the car accident appeared, this time more vividly than ever. This time, in fact, I was seeing the accident through Diana's eyes. It was in slow motion, the volume of the sound impossibly loud. I began to weep and started breathing rapidly. I did not want to have this scene appear to me, and I even cried out not to be taken there.

My voice aroused Charles from his own meditation session, and he quickly came to the couch to comfort me and ask me to explain. After I told him my story, Charles suggested that I meditate again and ask for the trauma to end. He urged me to request help to get beyond this incident.

Reluctantly, I began to meditate again. Almost at once, I found myself sitting on a rock on a beach. Standing next to me was an old Asian man. He had white hair and a white beard and was dressed in a white robe. He radiated a deep serenity, and I asked him to help me. I told him that I couldn't bear this experience. It was too much for me to feel the pain and fear that Princess Diana had gone through and to know that she had been fully conscious throughout the entire experience. I realized that my own vaguely realized fears about death and suffering were being brought to the surface for me to face.

He was silent for a moment. I waited for him to reply, to say magic words that would free me from my sorrow, but when he spoke, he simply told me to look off into the distance.

As I looked through the fog toward the end of the beach, I noticed a figure walking. She was wearing a white dress that blew in the wind. Her gait was slow, almost as if she were moving in slow motion. She appeared to be beautiful, even though I couldn't see her face. As she came closer, I saw that it was Princess Diana. She looked radiant, peaceful, and happy. She said in a soft voice, with her lovely British accent, "Don't worry about me, I am okay. I am at peace."

I looked at the Asian man. Smiling, he said, "See, she will be fine."

My heart almost floated from my chest, as a heavy burden seemed to have been lifted from me. I felt joy to know that she would live on in another dimension, whole and free.

The accident, the pain, and the terror—they were all finished. Diana's life on earth was over. But I still had mine ahead of me, and after that, I knew now, there was nothing to fear.

# Caroline

## Ginna Bell Bragg

In the fall of 1976, a dear friend gave a party for my twenty-ninth birthday. He said, "I have invited a woman from Ojai. You are sisters, and it's time you met."

What I expected I do not know, but when I walked into the room, I met my mirror image. Her name was Kern, and she later took the name Caroline, married Charles Muir, and became a respected teacher of Tantra Yoga. But that is another story. Back then, she was simply Kern, and our meeting was profound and deeply moving.

Our mutual friend was right: we bonded instantly, somehow knowing each other in the deepest sense. We spent the evening talking, looking into each other's eyes, forgetting there was a party going on in the background, and knowing only each other's presence. We were dressed somewhat alike, in the flowing fabrics and soft pastels of the seventies. Our hair was the same color, our faces the same shape, our bodies created out of the same mold. A big difference was the color of our eyes: mine were the brown of my Indian heritage, hers were a bright and brilliant blue.

The evening flew by in a flash of excitement. I had found a soul sister. If you are a woman, you know what I mean. It's not every friend who qualifies for this place in one's heart. I knew I would tell her everything, that we would be friends for life. I invited her and her husband for dinner the following night.

After the soup and homemade bread, the salad and choco-late mousse (I remember the flavors well), we sat in front of the cracklng fire and told stories of our lives. We talked of our children, our dreams, our work. We discussed our grand-fathers, both of whom had been successful businessmen. Mine had founded the Bonne Bell cosmetics company, hers was an inventor of veterinary drugs. Caroline stopped my story and said, "Well, this is funny. When my father was in the Army, and we were living in Carlisle, Pennsylvania, we lived next door to one of the Bell sisters."

The flesh on my arms stood in Godbumps. I paused. "Well," I said, "that could only have been my mother!"

After much more excited discussion, my new friends left and I went to bed in a state of agitation. It was too late to call my mother, so I waited anxiously until morning.

The phone call went something like this: "Mom! Does the name Mary Cusack mean anything to you?" Mary Cusack was Caroline's mother.

"What? What do you know about Mary Cusack? I have been looking for her for twenty years!"

"Oh, her daughter is my new best friend!"

"Little Caroline? What? What? Tell me everything!"

And so I told my story, and then took Caroline to see my mom. The reunion was very moving, with Mother telling stories of how "little Caroline" used to take the cotton ball soaked in White Shoulders perfume from its hiding place in my mother's blouse and hold it to her nose, and how the parents of us two— one not yet born, one a year old—had lived in the same apart-ment building and played bridge some nights until midnight.

For me, the most moving part of the story was when my

mother told of the evening that she and Caroline's mother, Mary, had discovered that *their* parents had been dear friends, too, had traveled together before our mothers were even glints in the eye, and had lost contact after a time. Our mothers then met entirely on their own, some twenty years later, in an Army apartment building in Carlisle, Pennsylvania.

And there's more: Caroline's grandfather—Mary's father, my grandfather's friend—had also been in business with my great-uncle, before any of the grandparents knew one another.

Over the years, as Caroline and I have grown and changed and become mature women, we have stayed close. We are true sisters. We wondered at one time whether there'd been some shenanigans between our parents, but we've decided that no, it is of the soul that we are bonded. Our connection goes deeply into the histories of our highest selves, and the bond between our families is beyond our comprehension

# 8

# SPIRITUAL AWAKENINGS

# The Chinese Dragon Box

## Nancilee Wydra

My first memory of life is the day a gift box arrived from my Uncle Willie. Willie was a bombardier during World War II and had been shot down several times over enemy territory. He survived, in part because of an underground network that guided stranded soldiers to safety. Though he was thankful for the Resistance's efforts, I believe he really thought his good fortune was due to the bargains he struck with God as he parachuted into enemy territory. As he descended, he negotiated. On his third trip down, his contract to survive included being more attentive to his family—which meant us, because he had not yet married. My family received a box a month for the rest of Willie's life.

I don't know if my first memory was of the first box to arrive at our doorstep, or just one in the long string that arrived at our home until this tradition abruptly ended. In 1961, Uncle Willie was in a head-on collision, and the flap of his automobile's glove compartment door smashed his skull. The collision, caused by a truck full of drunks, ended Uncle Willie's life one month before what would have been his long-awaited retirement from the military.

I remember my mother answering the doorbell one afternoon to receive a box from the mailman. The plain brown paper did not allude to the drama of the dazzling azure-blue silk box hidden inside. Rolling aside what seemed like miles of wrapping paper, my mother held aloft a rainbow of colored threads that crisscrossed the lustrous blue silk surface. The extraordinary embroidered image was one I had never seen before.

"A dragon," my mom intoned in answer to my question as her hand extracted a thin sheaf of paper. Mysterious symbols marked a profusion of black lines across the paper's surface. I remember feeling upset that she couldn't read me the story of the symbols. I don't recall a great deal more about that day except that I remained transfixed by the box and spent a long time rubbing my chubby childhood cheek across its softness. My last vague memory is of the vibration of a parent's heavy footsteps as I was lifted and carried to my room.

The dragon box sat atop a high shelf in our living room until we moved three years later. I don't recall seeing it after that, and my mother can't remember exactly what happened to it. She guesses she gave it away to one of the legions of friends swarming around her life.

I didn't think about that box until many years later. Setting out on an adventure that for me paralleled the experience of the knights in King Arthur's court, I sought to uncover my Holy Grail. The first step was to leave the safe and familiar. Shedding financial security and a marriage of twelve years, I voyaged away from my home to discover my life's purpose. Needing a place to regroup, I sought to find dwellings that would make my heart sing. My choice seemed to be between a plain house on an uneventful plot of land or something else. I found something else.

Even I called myself crazy when I made an offer to purchase the ragamuffin house, without running water or a flush toilet, perched on five pristine acres. This cabin was the weekend escape for a city family. After the grown children had scattered across America, the parents, now well into their eighties, decided to sell. Certainly there were not crowds standing in line to acquire it. Yet I saw magic. Majestic old trees grew on gentle slopes leading to the edge of a meandering stream. The cabin, perched at the edge of a meadow, faced the warming southeastern sun, while the hill to the north buffered cold winds. I knew it would be a while before I could install the conveniences that were lacking, but still I couldn't refuse the siren's call. Nor could I explain it to family or friends.

My son and I moved in one warm April day, just as the daffodils were unfolding from their long winter's rest. The place had come filled with the debris of twenty-five summers of accumulation. Pots and pans, blankets, faded photos, and other paraphernalia were strewn everywhere. Armed with plastic bags, a shovel, and a rented Dumpster, I stepped inside to rid myself of the former owners' history. Yet trash has the capacity to archive a life, and it was not too long before I learned that the husband had been in the Air Force in World War II. So I was not exceedingly startled to come upon a faded silk box, similar to the one from my earliest childhood memory. The crackled, yellowed paper with the faded calligraphic imprint intrigued me. The kismet of finding this family's relic (or was this one ours?) stimulated me to uncover the message lodged in this coincidence. Maybe here was the affirmation that I had a chance at unearthing my authentic self. After all, I reasoned, the box was a happy reminder of the start of my life. Perhaps this replica heralded another happy beginning.

To uncover the meaning of what I now recognized as Chinese characters on the paper inside the box, I went to visit a friend, Lee, who had been born in Singapore.

Carefully extracting the fragile yellow paper I had tucked in my wallet for safekeeping, I handed it to Lee. "Wind and water, as it is above, so it is below," Lee translated, and then went on to tell me that such a box was typically a gift to a family when they moved into a new home. The dragon, he explained, is a symbol of protection and good fortune.

"Feng shui," he explained, "is an old custom about how our home can bring us luck or disaster. It is how certain places are better than others, and how an appropriately situated home can augur good fortune."

In that moment, I knew I was being shown my Holy Grail, and I sought afterward to uncover all that there was to know about this person-place connection. The risk of leaving the safety of my middle-class life was being rewarded with a re-connection to my essence. Lodged deep down in my earliest memory of place was the key to unlock a door to happiness.

I made sense: we are guided to thrive in this universe because it is in the best interest of nature to keep perfecting all species; maximizing our potential keeps our species in top form.

You really do know who you are. If you need reinforcement, dig inside your memory banks and dislodge the piece of the past that leads you to the center. In the memory is the soul of our contentment. Hold your memory up to the light, and you will never fail to see your way.

The magic of my life unfolded in a memory of place. What influenced you in your memory of place, as the Chinese dragon box in mine did me? Remember how you felt, and you will understand what message is being communicated to you. You cannot escape feeling the message.

# The Pond

## *Thomas Youngholm*

Reflecting all that fell into its sight, the deep, clear pond captured the rich blue sky, billowy clouds, emerald green trees, and a tiny portion of Mount Shasta. With no one around for miles, I contemplated what had brought me to this place.

When I was younger, you would never have seen me pick up or even read a book like this, never mind write a story for one. I was a "guy," and proud to be of the logical, rational, and practical persuasion. Several years ago, though, I began to experience mystical events that changed my perception of the world. But like a morning fog that gradually dissipates with the rising of the sun, the impact of those mystical events slowly faded with the onslaught of everyday realities.

Then, over a period of a few months, I experienced being with my mother, who was struggling painfully with breast and lung cancer. I was also out of work. After my mother's death, I took a much-needed vacation. Not knowing where I wanted to go, I just packed my car and headed north on Highway 101. Two days later, when I saw the magnificence of Mount Shasta topped with snow, I decided to camp out at its base. The trees, with their expansive reach toward the limitless sky and their roots driven deep into the earth, enveloped me with comfort.

The next day, a man told me about a special place where I could see actual drawings, petroglyphs, from hundreds, or maybe thousands, of years ago. He scribbled a map onto a used napkin and insisted that I go. Following the child-like treasure map, I drove south on Interstate 5 and exited at the Railroad Museum. Heading up a hill, I turned left at a fork in the road and proceeded a half-mile before parking my car. Hiking down a steep, narrow trail that dropped precariously into a small valley, I was to listen for running water. When the small stream became visible, I was to look for three huge granite boulders on which the petroglyphs were etched. Miraculously, I found them, and indeed I was thoroughly intrigued. My mind filled with all kinds of possibilities about their meanings, their origins, their creators.

So there I was on a hot afternoon, by myself, sitting on a long, flat slab of granite. I gazed upstream and watched how the melted snow squeezed between boulders and earth and tumbled over rocks. At my feet, the stream formed a tiny but deep pond before it narrowed, once again, continuing its journey toward the ocean. Sitting cross-legged on the smooth boulder, I stared out over the clear pond.

All of a sudden I heard a buzzing by my head as a thin blue

stick with wings flew haphazardly around me. The dragonfly flitted in front of my face and then landed on the knuckle of my left thumb. I was dumbfounded and astonished by the boldness of this creature. The dragonfly momentarily dashed off to the edge of the pond and then flew back, landing on the exact same place on my thumb.

The silent exchange lasted only a few minutes, but it seemed like a lifetime. I felt as if I'd been "touched." I can't explain what that really means, except to say that I felt intrinsically connected with this beautiful insect. As silly as it sounds, it was the deepest connection I'd ever felt with anyone or anything. That remembrance, though, stimulated my previous feelings of disconnection and loneliness. With no job, no intimate relationship, and both my parents dead, I felt engulfed by life's hard realities.

When the dragonfly flew away, questions flooded its absence. How had I allowed my previous mystical experiences to escape me? Why hadn't I focused on staying connected with nature, with myself, with others? As the winged creature flew by once again, I heard a gentle answer to my questions: "Because you have allowed life's illusions to fill your awareness, your consciousness." That soft voice resonated from a room somewhere deep within me, a room that had just been opened by the touch of that dragonfly. As I allowed my thoughts and experiences to sift through me, I reminded myself that it was always my choice where I focused my awareness.

The sun slid out from behind a cloud and sent beams of light sparkling across the pond. I wondered how nature in its simplicity could arouse such awe. As I continued to gaze over the reflective pond, a translucent shimmering caught my eye. I thought it was a butterfly swimming under the water. Immediately, I dismissed the illogical observation. With that thought, the aberration disappeared.

Disappointed, I let go of my rational mind and brought my attention back to the silvery particles of light. After a few minutes, to my amazement, not one but several of the creatures appeared. The only way I can describe them is to say that they looked like butterflies—butterflies with diaphanous wings studded with dancing sparkles of sunlight. Most of them glided over the surface, but two undulated beneath the water. As the magical creatures played before me, I felt my lips curl into a boyish grin. It was the knowing smile of a child whose beliefs in fairies, elves, and magic had just been realized.

When my logical mind interceded again, the water fairies immediately melded into the random sparkles of sunlight and disappeared. I spent the next couple of hours playing hide-and-seek with these sylphs, or whatever one wants to call them. As I watched and even waded in the pond, they appeared and disappeared with the change of my focus.

It's difficult to tell you what I experienced that afternoon. That's a bit embarrassing for me to admit, because relating such things is now my career—I'm a visionary writer and speaker, so I'm supposed to be able to transmit the mystical into form, into words. But the truth of the matter is that the full essence of my mystical moments, or anyone else's, is impossible to capture. That's because they reside out of reach of the logical mind, beyond the limits of our words, preconceptions, and beliefs, just a dream away from our understanding.

Can a picture of the Grand Canyon unfold one's experience within its majestic walls? Can a video of childbirth demonstrate the depth of love and connection a woman feels as she gives physical life to a soul? Can any words ever fully express what it's like to be touched by a fairy, an angel, or the Divine? Those moments are such personal experiences, yet they are available to all of us.

It's been six years since that mystical afternoon. Sadly, I have to say that a dragonfly has never again landed on me, and I have not seen those mysterious, sparkly creatures again. Since that time I have lived a roller-coaster ride of memorable highs and lows. And yes, I have had a few other mystical twinklings. Yet there are few moments that have clung to me with such clarity as that hot summer afternoon by the cool pond.

What I can tell you is that there is never a time when I hear or see a dragonfly that I don't feel a deep connection. And when I notice the glittering dance of sunbeams or moonbeams on an ocean, a lake, or a puddle, a big boyish grin always comes to my face. With that sense of connection or with that smile, I'm reminded of the thin veil that separates the "real" world from the mystical one. I'm reminded of how the slightest change of focus can bring magic to any of my ordinary moments.

So now, when I'm caught up in everyday realities and find myself face-to-face with a clerk or a co-worker, a friend or a foe, a loved one or a boss, I try—I'm not always successful, but I try—to feel the dragonfly sitting on their words and see the sparkling water fairies swimming in their eyes.

# The Art of Listening

## *Ellen Lieberman Weil*

Toni Mack, a powerful, loving, vivacious woman, was my first spiritual teacher. She was a strong catalyst for personal transformation, and we spent many hours together during my five years of training. There were times when her teachings were very soft, and gently instructed, and times when she was harsh and fierce. One of the first and possibly most important universal truths she taught was that I was responsible for everything that happened in my life. Somehow, in order to grow and evolve, I attracted every situation I was experiencing.

One day, she felt I was ready to learn more about metaphysics from one of her teachers. She gave me four of his audiotapes, along with clear instructions on the order in which I was to listen to them. That night, I played the first tape. The next day, she called me at work, and I told her which tape I had listened to. I quickly found out I'd listened to the incorrect tape. *"You just don't listen!"* she said in a frustrated, angry voice. "I notice this about you. You're often half listening and half in your head, thinking about something else. You need to work on it."

"But I find it hard to listen all the time," I replied. "And I see that part of it has become a habit of tuning people or things out, and I tend not to listen even when it's important for me to listen, such as when you're guiding me."

"No. You don't get it. It's *always* important to listen—to everyone—all the time. You must become more present."

"But I don't feel that way," I retorted. "There are plenty of times when someone is saying something to me and it's absolute nonsense. Either they're not making much sense, or they're talking on and on about something irrelevant to me."

She paused, then responded, "You miss lots of valuable teaching with that attitude. You end up tuning out the most important stuff. Also, everyone deserves to be heard, as you do. It's okay to set boundaries and end a conversation abruptly, if that's appropriate, but you must open up to connect with people and hear what they have to say. I want you to start practicing the art of conscious listening, right now. This is your exercise for the next month. No matter who's talking to you, *listen fully. Do not tune them out* . . . and don't get caught up in your mind, figuring out what you're going to say to them as a response. . . . Just hear what they have to say first. Also, don't interrupt people and finish their sentences for them."

That conversation put me in an emotional tailspin, partly because of the intensity of her energy, but mostly because I knew she was right. I was not a very good listener, which indicated that I was often not that grounded or present. I wanted to change, to bring more light and awareness into my being.

That same evening, I went to a restaurant with some of my co-workers. We were at the bar, waiting for a table, when a tall, broad-shouldered, muscular man walked in wearing a T-shirt that read YOU DON'T LISTEN across the front *and* back! I gasped as I stood there, partly stunned, partly laughing, staring in joyful wonderment at this profound messenger that the universe, in all its comical, brilliant glory, had sent to me.

I take responsibility for having attracted the perfect messenger—a stranger in a T-shirt—to create such an impact on me that it would become easy to change . . . and I did. Now I am one of the best listeners I know, and I feel more present, loving, and concentrated, often hearing important pieces of information that other people miss.

Remember, God gave us two ears and one mouth so that we can listen twice as much as we speak!

# In the Wind

## *Lani DeFelice*

In the late seventies, just out of high school, I joined my sister and two women friends who were renting a small house on a farm in northeast Vermont. We had a big vegetable and flower garden, and spent the summer working and playing in that beautiful countryside. We practiced yoga and meditation, went on an extended fast together, and took to learning about different spiritual views, from Native American beliefs to the teaching of Jesus in the New Testament and the Essene Gospels.

The summer came to a close and we said good-bye to our little home in the country. Deborah, Terri, my sister, and I bought bus tickets and headed south, eventually ending up in

Key West, Florida, where I put my newfound faith to the test. I decided to follow literally the teachings of Jesus, and not worry about what I should wear or what I should eat, but to trust completely in the Creator to provide for all of my needs. I chose to live on the streets, sleeping wherever I could lay my blankets and eating whatever I found or was given to me. It was for me the beginning of a five-year spiritual odyssey in which I was taught that the power of a loving, open heart and a mind centered on the Creator can bring incredible magic into your life.

Folks lived on the street for many different reasons, but one thing we all had in common was that we ended up in jail occasionally. There is a law in Key West against sleeping out of doors, and if the police find you, they arrest you and put you in jail for a few days, hoping to convince you to leave town.

One morning, word got around that a friend of mine had been jailed the night before. At the time I was wearing a pin-on button that had been given to me as a gift. It was a copy of a painting of Jesus' head by Raphael; I loved it and wore it always. My friend who was just jailed liked it also and told me so whenever we met. I went to visit him in jail and was moved to give him the button for comfort. He pinned it right on and walked back to his cell with a big smile on his face.

Back outside, with nowhere particular to go, I asked Spirit to guide me. I had a notion back then that I called "being in the wind," allowing my intuition to guide me wherever it chose. So following my inner voice, I went down this lane and that until I found myself in front of the town's health food store. It was a great little store, and the folks who ran it were kind. Out front was a "free" box, where people put used clothing, books, and such items they wished to pass on.

My intuition clearly told me there was something in the box for me. Following my inner guide, I reached in, and the first thing I pulled out was a gray T-shirt. Turning it around, I saw printed on the front the same picture of Jesus that was on the button I had just minutes before given away.

My heart overflowed with love and joy. I remember thanking the spirit world for acknowledging my efforts to be a fully present and loving human being. Needless to say, I wore that T-shirt until it was so full of holes it wouldn't stay on any longer.

# Oneness: The Experience

*Eugene C. Marotta*

On August 3, 1995, I had an experience that changed my life forever. It was a beautiful morning and the sun was shining. My appreciation of the loveliness around me was moving to a much deeper level. I began, with unusual clarity, to notice details and an orderliness to things that I had never noticed before. The sunlight was being cast upon each individual leaf of the trees in an absolutely perfect way. Each seemed placed in a planned way so that all the leaves could bathe in the nurturing rays of the sun.

Suddenly I began to fill with an indescribable emotion. It wasn't just one emotion, actually, but a combination of many positive feelings: appreciation, gratitude, awe, wonder, love, elation, bliss, and much more. My body felt light and tingly, and I had the sense that some aspect of myself was rushing up through my body and out toward the leaves of the trees that were in front of and above my head. At that instant, the leaves seemed to be moving toward me. I heard myself utter a strange sound deep from within my being, something like *Ahhhh.*

The next thing I knew, I was no longer there, and the leaves and the trees were no longer there.

In attempting to explain what occurred that summer morning, I can only say it was an experience of oneness. Distinctions were gone: no me, no leaves, no trees, no process of seeing. The feelings and emotions that led up to that point all merged into a feeling of perfection, virtually impossible to explain in words. It was as if I simultaneously experienced all of the most positive, pleasurable, uplifting feelings, sensations, and emotions I had ever felt before, multiplied by a factor of infinity.

I had no sense of time. To this day, I don't know whether the experience lasted a second, a minute, or an hour. I felt an unquestionable knowing that there is absolutely nothing to ever fear or worry about. In that moment, it was crystal clear that everything was perfectly okay, it always was, it always is, and it always will be. I felt more loved, cared for, and understood than ever before. I experienced a sense of expansion beyond description. What I tasted was nothing short of perfection. If I try to describe it as a place, it has to be Heaven. If I describe it as a being, it has to be God. But it was all and none of these things at the same time.

At some point, the distinctions began slowly to return. Awareness of myself, the chair I was sitting in, and the trees and other things around me began to come back into view. For about half an hour afterward, I felt as if I were walking on a cloud. Everything was beyond delightful, beautiful and perfect. At the time, I remember thinking that I was experiencing the world as Jesus or other enlightened beings must have. My feelings were of overwhelming love and appreciation for everything.

Unfortunately, after a short period of time my normal awareness returned. The experience was over but never to be forgotten. It was and is, by far, the most profound experience of my life and has changed me irrevocably. I can never return to where or who I was prior to it. I was given an incredible gift, a taste of the truth, of ultimate reality.

I've since come to learn that my experience is not uncommon. Mystics, saints, yogis, monks, and many others have been writing about mystical experiences for all of recorded history. Now I also realize that this so-called mystical level of consciousness is available to all of us, and that it can become a perpetual state of awareness, not just a once-in-a-lifetime experience.

Since that day, my priorities in life have changed. Raising my consciousness and working to assist others in their awakening has become my consuming passion.

# Among the Stacks

## *Jill Bruener*

Doing spiritual work can become burdensome at times. As a spiritual counselor, one can become overwhelmed by personal problems and the problems of others. I experienced that feeling in 1997. Things didn't seem to be going too well, and I was beginning to question my role in life. Was I truly walking the spiritual path that God had directed me to walk? I went into my prayer room, as I do every morning, and as I prayed, I told God and my angels that I felt abandoned, and I wondered if they were still around or if angels really did exist. It seems foolish now that I was having a pity party for myself and trying to second-guess God. I have learned not to do that anymore. A trip to the local bookstore changed my life forever!

My husband, Roger, and I decided to go the movies. We arrived a few minutes early and went to browse through the nearby bookstore. I headed right for the religion section, particularly the section titled "Angels." I was always looking for new books on angels. As I approached the section, I noticed a tiny old man wearing a rumpled brown trench coat and a funny-looking little brown hat. He was quite short, and a few wisps of snow white hair had escaped from his hat and fell lightly on his shoulders. He looked very unkempt, and even though it was warm outside, he was dressed in winter apparel. He was simply standing there teetering back and forth from side to side.

I began to scan the shelves for new titles, and then I thought back on my morning prayers, when I had questioned if angels existed. If they did, I thought, then mine must be taking a vacation. How dare my angels ignore me!

About that time, the funny little man turned to me and smiled. He had the kindest face I had ever seen, and his blue eyes twinkled and sparkled. He reminded me of someone I knew. Perhaps it was his hair. My father had had the same beautiful snow white hair and blue eyes. Yes, that must be it. He reminded me of my father, God rest his gentle soul. I was looking at the lines in his face, framed in that snow white hair, trying to determine how old he was. He looked ancient, yet his eyes danced with the youth and enthusiasm of a toddler exploring the world. He seemed to study me for a second, contemplating what to say. It was one of those awkward moments when you don't know whether to keep eye contact or look away. He started nodding his head yes as if acknowledging some sort of wisdom. Then he looked at me and said, "You know, there really are angels. Trust me, I know."

I didn't know what to say. I finally managed to nod my head in agreement and mumble something like "Yes, I know. I even teach a class about angels."

His grin only broadened slightly. He tilted his head to one side as if sizing me up, and then he said, "No, really. There really are angels. You've been doubting if yours are still around, but trust me, they are. They haven't deserted you, and God loves you very much. Trust me, I know."

Oddly enough, I did trust him. He was so wise.

While I was in the midst of this conversation, Roger had been standing in the next aisle. Keep in mind that Roger is six foot eight, so he could see over the racks and had a view of the whole store. He wasn't more than a few feet away, and he heard bits and pieces of the conversation.

Well, by this time I was getting a little anxious. How in the world could this gentle, sweet little man know that I was fussing with God and my angels, and had been questioning their existence that very morning? I started to say something, but he held up his hand and stopped me.

"I know, I know. All humans have doubts. But there really are angels and they're always around you, and God loves you. Remember that. Your guardian angel is always just a few feet away if you should ever need him."

I was trying to digest all that he had just said. There was something oddly familiar about his essence. All of a sudden I felt comforted. I felt loved and protected. I felt ashamed for having doubted God. I was so emotional that I wanted to cry and laugh all at the same time. With that, the odd little man started to walk off, just as Roger was walking around the corner of the aisle. I felt the need to talk more with the little man.

"Wait!" I shouted. "Roger, stop him!" But as I tried to follow the man around the corner, he vanished! "Roger, where is he?"

My husband scanned the entire store, but the odd little man seemed to have vanished into thin air. We were toward the back of the store, so he couldn't have slipped out the front door that quickly. I had been only a step behind him, and from Roger's bird's-eye view he could see the entire store and the front door, but the man was nowhere to be found! We ran to the front door and looked up and down the sidewalk, but he just wasn't there. We asked the people at the front desk if they had seen the little man in the trench coat leaving, but they just shook their heads no like we were crazy.

I looked at Roger, and Roger looked at me. Then reality set in and I laid my head on his chest and began to cry. I felt so blessed. I wasn't worthy of what I thought I had just experienced. Then the Bible verse came to mind about being kind to strangers because you could be entertaining angels unaware.

I am convinced to this moment that my guardian angel appeared to me that day disguised as that little old man dressed in that shabby brown coat just to let me know that he was around and that all I had to do was trust and believe.

# Angel Unawares

## *Kathy Juline*

The door opened slowly, creaking as old wood tends to do. A beautiful face appeared out of the darkness as the musty smell of close air wafted toward me.

"Yes?" the elderly woman said. Even though she did not smile, she seemed to me in that instant to be one of the kindest souls I had ever encountered.

What made me approach her front door that sunny spring morning? I had dreamed recently of a house such as hers. It was an old wood frame house, with a porch at the end of a straight sidewalk and two columns supporting a shingled overhang that sheltered the front door. Blue paint on the concrete porch, a huge oak tree, and weather-beaten fencing around the backyard—all these details from my dream stunned me as, taking my daily walk, I turned the corner onto Diamond Street.

The moment I saw that house, I felt a strong impulse to knock at the front door.

Wearing a wondering expression, yet almost relieved, as if she had been expecting me and I was late, the elderly woman spoke softly. "Yes? Can I help you?" Using a cane for balance, she held herself in a stooped position. Mystified suddenly at my decision to knock, I had no idea what to say to her. Why was I there? Then some words tumbled out.

"Your house—it's nice," I said. "I was just walking by and I wanted to tell you that I like it. What a beautiful tree, too. Have you lived here long?" It felt to me that both of us knew in our hearts that liking her house was a metaphor, a kind of code, for something much more significant, something inexpressible.

"Yes," she answered. "I have lived here a long time, since before the war."

After we talked awhile on her front porch, she invited me to come in. Patricia—that was her name—told me about her childhood in Nebraska, of the times those distant decades ago when her family had no money because of droughts or dust storms or crop-eating insects. She told me how she would watch horse-drawn carriages lumber down the road, a strange longing filling her. Then there was the day she finally got married, and then she and her husband moved out to Southern California in the thirties. She showed me her collection of dolls, all finely dressed in clothes she herself had made, down to real patent leather shoes. And I saw pictures of her only child, a daughter, now past retirement age but movie-star beautiful in her youth. Patricia's husband was killed in the war, and she had lived alone ever since her daughter left home. Now, agoraphobic, she ventured out only to the metal mailbox that was nailed to one of the columns on her porch.

"If you don't go out, how do you get your groceries?" I asked her. I offered to do her shopping, and for as long as she continued to live there, every week or so I dropped off at her house a sack of things she especially liked—tiny LeSueur peas, strawberry ice cream, russet baking potatoes, fresh eggs, peaches in season. In return, she offered to pray for me and for my two daughters, whom I brought with me occasionally on my visits. My girls were preteens when Patricia and I first met, and she continued to ask about them even as they graduated from high school and went off to college. Though Patricia's body ached painfully with arthritis, she never failed to be a fountain of hearty strength from which I drank.

I bought her a few groceries and a book now and then, but what she gave me cannot be so easily purchased. Or can it? Does a treasure lie right in front of us all the time? Perhaps guardian angels hover about everywhere, in whatever unusual forms and under whatever unexpected circumstances we discover them. I thank God for the dream that made me stop that day to knock at my neighbor's door.

# The Awakening

## *Asandra*

This story of my awakening begins twenty-four years ago, when I was sixteen. I grew up in an average home in middle-class America. My upbringing was neither deprived nor dysfunctional. I was free to express myself creatively and had good friends. But in spite of this, there was a dark shadow growing at the core of my being. Overwhelming me was a relentless feeling that there was not enough love in this world. It was not familial or romantic love for which I was yearning. It was a deep sense, even at a time when most teenagers are focused on other concerns, that something significant was missing from my life. As this emptiness grew within, I made a quiet decision to exit this world.

After making an unsuccessful attempt to die by swallowing a large dose of tranquilizers, I slipped into the darkest despair I have ever known. I felt trapped in a place I did not want to be, yet I could not find my way out. That is the last memory I have of my old life. . . .

I cannot recall how much time had passed since that incident, but my next memory is of sitting on the front lawn of my house absorbed in a book of inspirational prose. I looked up from the book and, for the very first time, saw life vibrating around me. Every leaf on every tree was imbued with the life force of God. Every blade of grass, every creature, even the wind blowing through the leaves, had God's love as its essence. My spirit was filled with love! Joyful, divine, infinite love. It was a bliss I hadn't known was even possible.

I cannot explain exactly what happened. Somehow I had shifted into an altered dimension of reality wherein I could see and feel with precise clarity. The experience was of entering an infinite realm where the love of the Creator is all that there really is, and everything seems to be dancing in the joy of that knowledge.

This moment of ecstasy did not stop. Every day, for months on end, I would be filled up spontaneously with the overwhelming experience of God's divine love. It poured forth from my being, in an unconditional fashion, toward everything around me. I know that I was whole, complete, and one with God.

My higher faculties opened up. If a friend complained that she was not getting along with her mother, I could hear the voice of her spirit saying, "I need love." I would open my mouth, and wisdom beyond my years would eloquently spill out. I looked around me and knew that the divisions and barriers that man has set up are an illusion. I knew that everything belonged to God. Naturally and effortlessly, fear, pain, and separation disappeared. The magic of God's love had entered my spirit and I was truly free.

These mystical experiences continued for an entire year. Although they eventually faded away, my spirit had been changed irrevocably. And in the year to follow that, a spiritual teacher in human form entered my world, showing me how to keep alive my connection to the divine. Magic had found me, and I was open to embrace what has come to be an extraordinary journey, my life.

I feel blessed to have been shown a higher reality at such a young age. This knowledge carries with it a responsibility to honor the truth and to help others along the way. It will never leave me. It is the truth of who I am.

# Oma

## *Jacqueline Forsyth-Rubinstein*

Everything in life happens just the way it's meant to happen. We can't stop destiny; we can just be more open to learning from the experience and thus to become richer in the knowledge. There is no standing still in life; there is only moving forward in the hopes of bettering ourselves. Life is a game, and we all need to know the rules in order to play. It is all in how you play it. These are just a few of the sayings by which my grandmother lived her life.

On Mother's Day, 1998, I called Oma in Holland to wish her a wonderful day and to thank her for being in my life, for she was the one who always knew the answers to all my questions. This was the woman who had given birth to my mother and to two other daughters, the last of whom was born in a Japanese concentration camp in Indonesia. Oma was imprisoned with her three little girls for four years. That is where she overcame the fear of hunger, torture, and many illnesses, including gangrene, all without knowing if she would ever see the love of her life again. He was imprisoned in a men's camp in a jungle far away. This is just a small part of who my Oma was.

We talked about my three children. I was constantly seeking her advice. She was a master of communicating, in the simplest terms, how I should deal with every situation. When she would speak to me, my sense of being overwhelmed with life would dissipate. She would break through all the distractions and convoluted factors we pile upon ourselves, and get to the bottom line and the essence of life—what is important, what is a priority, and what would ultimately matter when all was said and done.

She called me the day after Mother's Day and told me she was concerned for my health. She knew that I had traveled to Europe twice in the previous three weeks and I had contracted bronchitis. She scolded me for once again taking on more than I could handle, and said that I needed to simplify my life. She had called to tell me she had gone out with one of my aunts, and then ended the conversation by telling me she was nearing the end of her life. "Honey, I'm tired."

I became alarmed. "What do you mean, 'tired'?" I asked, not wanting to hear what that meant.

She said, "I know it's time for me to go. My mind is in great shape, but my body is old and tired. That's what makes it really hard, honey."

I responded by saying, "That's the most selfish thing I have ever heard." She laughed, and I continued, "This isn't about you, Oma, this is about me and my needs. I need you." She told me then, as she had told me so often before, that she would always be behind me. I said, "Just because you raised three children and helped raise eight grandchildren doesn't mean you can leave the fourteen great-grandchildren."

She argued that she would have more time in death than in life, that once she passed on she could truly watch over us. In spite of the positive words, I felt the life drain out of my body. I had no reserve left, yet I knew that within the next few days I would get on a plane for Europe and leave my three children behind for the third time in five weeks. There was no question in my mind. I had to be with Oma in her last few days. She was not even sick, but we both knew that she would be leaving us soon.

Within two days of that conversation I received a call from my cousin in Holland saying that I should come as soon as possible. Thankfully, my mother, though unaware of Oma's fragile condition, had left for Europe that morning. I drove the few hours to Los Angeles and was on the next plane. From that moment on I prayed for guidance and the strength to be the instrument I was meant to be. The flight lasted fifteen hours, and I prayed the entire time. I knew I had to be there for my grandmother and also to serve as a source of strength for my mother and her two sisters, whose relationship had grown strained over the years.

When I walked into my grandmother's small, compact apartment, I immediately saw the relief on my mother's face. I also saw my grandmother's eyes well up with tears. She looked me in the eye and said with a big sigh, "You're here." For her to have the core of her family surrounding her was the essence of her being.

My prayers were answered. From the moment I walked into my grandmother's apartment, God's love and light were guiding me. I was the instrument that I was meant to be. I instinctively knew what to do. I sat by her side, and I knew my job was to take her through her death. I massaged her. I had strength that I knew came from beyond. I could pick her up, although she was five foot ten, I could change her, bathe her, and give her medicines and morphine. My job was to make her comfortable. She did not have to tell me what she needed—I knew. Then she would smile.

My mother and I prayed, my aunts prayed, and as her family, we became one. The force of our love for her made all of us even more powerful. We all slept in her small bedroom, on the bed, on the floor, wherever we could, just to be close to her. It was an honor to be with her in that room. As difficult as it was is also how wonderful it was. We didn't even really sleep, because there was so much energy.

We did need a nurse at some point to help us, so we called a local service, even though we knew Oma would not be happy with someone she did not know. The doorbell rang. There stood a beautiful Asian woman who wanted to know if this was the Mrs. Carpentier-Alting who had lived in Indonesia and Suriname during and after the war years!

"Yes," we said with shock.

"Oh," she said, "I can't believe it." She had known my grandmother from both those countries.

When we brought her to my grandmother, they both smiled, and my grandmother said, "Oh, Joke, my darling. Are you here to help me?"

As Oma had always said, you get out of life what you put into it. Here was her loving friend from the past, Joke, who had showed up on her doorstep to help look after her. She even remembered me from the time that I had lived with my grandmother in Suriname. It just all seemed to be so right. Joke sang spiritual songs to my grandmother from Suriname and Indonesia—all the things that my grandmother had identified with her past.

The next day, my grandmother seemed so much better. She was talking to everyone and asked for all the grandchildren to come by. She gave to everyone an insightful piece of advice to take away. This was done with love and lightness and without any solemnity.

We were all in her bedroom, which opened onto the living room—her family and all her loving and loyal friends. There must have been twenty-five people. She was lying there, with her eyes closed most of the time, when all of a sudden she said, "Jacqueline, make sure everyone has a glass of wine." I did so. She asked, "Does everyone have a glass of wine now?"

"Yes."

"Cheers to you all. May you have happy days ahead of you." Everyone clinked glasses, and from her bed, Oma smiled. My mother, my two aunts, and I were massaging her, and she opened her eyes and looked at me and said, "What a wonderful thing to be massaged from one life to the next. I love you all."

That night, everyone left but my mother, one of my aunts, a friend of seventy years, and me. Oma started to go downhill. Once again, the higher being took over. At one point she asked, "How do you know what to do?"

I responded, "I don't know what to do. This is God's will working through me."

As the night progressed, my grandmother's pain increased at a rapid pace. To me, the amazing part was that as long as I stayed in the light, I was never frightened that I would not be able to handle things for her.

The next day was a terrible one for Oma. She was racked with pain, and at one point her blue eyes turned a vivid cobalt. She raised her arms to the ceiling and asked God to please take her. She then turned to me and said, "Help me, please help me."

I held her in my arms and said, "Hold on tight. I will help to take you to the other side."

She said, "I know you will." I gave her some more morphine, and she thanked me. She then said, "I need you to hear me. Life is *very* short. So do not waste it." And this from a woman of ninety-three! She then went into a deep sleep. I could see her releasing herself from her body.

We all stayed by her side that night in a sort of twilight sleep. At four in the morning, the four of us awoke simultaneously. We held hands and stood around her bed and started to pray with her, and at eight minutes after four she took her last breath. Oma's final gift to us was to let us see her to the other side. From the moment she took her last breath, her face became young, relieved.

We called the doctor. I felt it was only natural that I help dress her in the outfit she had chosen, and to do her hair and makeup as I had always done whenever she stayed with me. It was her wish to look her natural self.

If someone had told me a few weeks earlier that I would be doing any of this at all, I would have never believed it; but when it came time, it was the most natural and rewarding thing I could think of to do for someone I loved. Through this experience, I have tried to appreciate every day that God gives to me, and be grateful for the experiences that I have had. From this experience, my two aunts are now friends again, and my mother and I have become even closer. The whole family has grown closer and more loving.

At her funeral, we played her favorite song, "Climb Ev'ry Mountain," and I read these words: "Dear Oma, as your grand-children and great-grandchildren, we too will try to climb every mountain and follow every rainbow until we find our dream, just as you have always taught us to do. We thank you for all your wisdom and all your love. We love you, and we say good-bye to you."

As my mother and I were preparing to leave my grand-mother's apartment after we had taken care of all her things, we stood and had a prayer and thanked her and God for the ex-traordinary experience we had just had together. We thanked her for letting us be with her there in the apartment, and at that moment my mother opened a drawer we thought we had emp-tied. In it was a small, worn book titled *Thank You for Being Here*. There was a marked passage. It read: "There is a school of life through which we all wander. There is no standing still in it, and there is no returning. There is no repeating, we only keep going forward to a new light and to a new insight. Every minute we are a little different and every minute we under-stand a little more, and every minute we hope to be a little better."

Good-bye, Oma. We will miss you.

# Freedom

*Mariah Martin*

It was a peaceful day. The field outside my Vermont country house was in full bloom with wildflowers. My life was finally reflecting the positive outcome of hard work and success in my profession as a therapist. I should have felt contented, but instead I was irritated by the presence of an old feeling.

For as long as I could remember, I had a feeling that Earth was not my home and that no matter what I did or what I achieved I would never belong here. As a young child, I climbed trees and lay in the top branches waiting for "them" to come and get me. While other children would pray at night for God to protect them, I would pray that God would come and take me home. I felt disappointment each morning when I woke up in my bed and was not somewhere else called 'home." As a young teenager, on starry nights I would gaze at the stars looking for "home."

I learned to be quiet about my homesickness. When I was about seven, I tried to teach my girlfriends to lie perfectly still on the lawn, breathe deep, and levitate. My mother found out and rushed me to the priest. I felt isolated, different. Although I wanted to go "home," for years I worked to normalize myself and fit in.

That day in Vermont, I was irritated that with such peace and beauty around me I would still have the longing to go "home." I sat in my favorite rocking chair, closed my eyes, and prayed that God would help me make peace with being here on Earth.

After a few moments of trying to quiet my mind and connect with God's light, I gave up and opened my eyes. The world no longer existed. Everything, as far as I could see, was swirling masses of light. For a second, I thought there was something in my eyes. I felt them and blinked. When I looked again, everything was still masses of swirling lights, only now each form, both inside the house and outside in the field, was outlined just the way I outlined pictures with crayons when I was a little girl. The inside of the forms was light swirling colors, and the outside was a deep, thick, solid color. I shook my head and tried to see the solid forms as one, inside and out, but the contrasting light image wouldn't change.

Strangely, I wasn't scared. My soul voice guided me to just watch and observe.

My eyes grew heavy. I closed them for a minute, fully expecting to see the normal scene when I opened them again. But it wasn't there. The outline had disappeared and everything was just moving masses of light. Nothing existed, nothing at all except colorful light moving around everywhere.

I felt an incredible sense of peace in my bones and cells. The presence of God was all around me. I stared at the swirling light until once again I had to close my eyes. The scene in my head was also of light. I lost track of time, but later I was amazed to learn from the clock that the dance of outline and moving light had gone on for more than an hour.

The intensity of the experience exhausted me. I fell into a very deep sleep. When I woke up, a new feeling rushed through me. I was in love with Earth. I felt as if the light had swirled through me and washed away the homesick feeling. The peace of the day was, at last, the peace I felt in my being. Freedom! Freedom to enjoy my visit to Earth, to love being alive here and knowing other humans. But most of all, I could experience the freedom to be myself, a visitor exploring human nature.

God didn't take me away from this world, as I prayed when I was a child. Instead, She taught me that this world is also of the Light. I now look up to the starry sky and know that "they" are there in the stars, enjoying Earth through me. I am home in the vast connected world of Spirit's light.

# The Night George Went to Be with Jesus

## *Sophie Coors*

My son George was filled with a lot of spirit and spunk. He was a natural athlete and a natural clown. He fished, hunted, and played tennis and racquetball. From his youth he was afflicted with cystic fibrosis. He hated his treatments and his bouts in the hospital, but he never asked, "Why me?" He had a real joy of living and was always the life of the party. He went through the usual teen escapades, but managed to graduate from high school without too many setbacks. He went off to college, but after a year he had to come home for daily treatments. He was now twenty years old, and the real battle against CF was just beginning.

My mother had a stroke and died six weeks later. We were all in shock, but still didn't turn to God. In fact, we stopped going to church, and went instead every weekend to a family cabin on a nearby lake. We worked together as a family with no outside interests and no phone, but we seemed to forget the Lord was still there. I ran faster and faster from the loss of my mother and the truth that my son's days were numbered. My husband and I couldn't seem to communicate about our son's long-term illness.

As he sensed his road becoming more and more narrow, George was searching and seeking. One day, he and two of his friends found God! They were on fire with the Holy Spirit, so they joined a Baptist church and attended every church meeting in town. I could see that George's strength was coming from somewhere, but all of this was not for me. His faith became strong, and he began to lead others through prayer groups, calls, and ministering.

We kept hoping for a miracle, but time was running out for George. We went to Houston for an interview for a heart-lung transplant, but were turned down.

On Thanksgiving 1984, we held a huge family reunion at our cabin. We had just rebuilt it after a tornado had partly destroyed it. George was very thin and weak, but managed to give a beautiful blessing and thanks to God for our family.

The first of December, he entered the hospital for his final battle against CF. He battled for two months with a huge amount of courage and bravery. He was so close to God, so compassionate to others, and so filled with the Holy Spirit. Christmas came, and he was able to spend only an hour at home before his fever pulled him back to the hospital. He was on oxygen and growing weaker, but was still strong in spirit. His friends from church came every day and laid hands on him for healing. He was healed for three beautiful days and went before the church to thank them and God. He felt he was going to be spared so he could lead others to God. It still had not dawned on any of us that we were going to lose him.

On Sunday, January twenty-seventh, George and I were watching Adrian Rogers preach on TV. His sermon seemed to be meant particularly for George (they had become close in the last few years). Adrian always ended his sermon by asking those who want to give their life to God to come down the aisle. I raised my hand without realizing what I was doing, and gave my life to God. George's eyes filled with tears as his mission was accomplished! I felt such love and peace, but I didn't fully understand it.

That night, as usual, we had close friends to visit. George quietly laid his head down on the bed table, and they all thought he was gone. He suddenly sat up and said, "Fooled you, didn't I?" He was joking as usual.

My older son arrived, and then it was just us: my husband, my two sons, and I. George asked to hear his favorite song, "Shine Down Your Light." He was having trouble breathing, and I could feel him slipping away. The room slowly started to fill with light, and George said in a strong, clear voice, "I can see Heaven; you will never have this chance again to ask questions. I feel so filled with wisdom and love. The light is so unreal and God is here! I have been so stupid— it is *so* simple—I am healed and whole again." With that he was gone, the light faded, and it was over.

The funeral was a celebration, with friends singing and telling us all about God's love for everyone. We were all filled with strength that kept us from breaking, and so many were led to God that day.

The last four and a half years, we have been growing in our faith in God. The Holy Spirit, through George, has filled us all with a peace that passes all understanding. We have tried to minister to others, especially at the hospital George spent so much time at; and we in turn have been healed by helping others.

Thank you, Father, for sending George to lead so many back to you. "It is not the length of our days but the depth of our lives that counts."

# Birth of a Book

## Mary Ann Halpin

My art has always been a reflection of my life. It has been a journey of fascinating self-discovery, sometimes joyful, sometimes painful.

My photographic work consists primarily of shooting portraits for the entertainment industry. For years I was struck with the insecurity that I constantly encountered from women about their body image. They never seemed to feel perfect enough, and there were always discussions of using plastic surgery to correct one flaw or another. This attitude haunted me. So I decided to express my feelings about it through a series of figure studies of a variety of women's bodies.

The first model who came to my studio was a pregnant woman. I was amazed at how comfortable she was with her body. It was so refreshing! She was goddess-like in her joyous expression of her swollen body—so full of baby. I was so moved by her. What a gift! What a miracle that a woman's body can do this! I finished my figure study series and did an exhibition. Over the next few years, I started photographing pregnant women as goddesses.

While I photographed a very pregnant friend, Cassandra Peterson, the actress who does the character "Elvira," I was telling her of my book idea about women in recovery at a mission on Skid Row. She suggested that I call her friend Sharon Hays at General Publishing Group. The following week I made that call. Sharon explained that although they wouldn't be interested in the Skid Row idea, they would consider my pregnancy book. I told her I wasn't planning on doing a pregnancy book. She was sure Cassandra had told her I was. Well, I said, I would get back to her when I was.

Disappointment followed, because I was convinced that the mission project had such great merit. I couldn't understand that someone would not want to publish it. However, after a week went by, I heard a voice in my head say, "If you don't do this pregnancy book, someone else will!" Wow, was I not listening to my creative muse? Luckily, my muse had gone to Cassandra. Thank God she was listening for me! I immediately called Sharon again, and told her, "Yes, I am working on a pregnancy book, and I will keep you posted." With that comment, the journey accelerated.

A few months later, I attended a lecture by Dr. Wayne Dyer.

As I was standing in line beforehand for the ladies' room, I recognized Dr. Dyer walking toward me. He looked as if he had just come out of a blissful meditation. Our eyes met, and he greeted me with a warm hello. I thought, What a nice moment and a great bit of bliss from this spiritual being! How curious that out of hundreds of people he stopped to connect with me. During the lecture, he talked about his seven children. His wife, Marcelene, was writing a book about spiritual birthing.

The voice came to me again: "This is the woman to write the foreword to your book!" I was listening this time. The next day, I put together photos and a letter and sent them off to Dr. Dyer, asking him to give the package to his wife. She called me from Florida a week later. I explained to her that I didn't have a publisher firmed up yet. Marcelene reassured me that she was confident I would get one, and she would be honored to write the foreword of my book. We became great phone friends. She has been a wonderful emotional and spiritual support through the whole project. Marcelene's wisdom and insight always shift me to a new level of awareness.

The energy of the project was now flowing swiftly. I had twenty-five images and was ready to get a publisher. I sent out twelve packages to publishers I believed would understand this book. I received twelve form rejections. Finally, I called Sharon Hays at General Publishing and we had a meeting. To my amazement, Sharon and the other woman with whom I met were both pregnant. I knew this was an omen. On January second, 1997, I received a call from their editor. They loved the project and wanted to get on it immediately.

I needed to have around seventy different images ready to go by July for a release date in October. My work was cut out for me. The next few months were surreal. The dreams I had, the women I met, and the two births I witnessed were among so many miracles I experienced.

Laura Robinson Ettlinger, a beautiful actress, called about being in the book. She explained that she was due to deliver her baby that week but was determined to be included. I told her it was impossible, as I was booked that week to photograph five different pregnant women and there wasn't any time available. She pursued the issue anyway, showing up that afternoon at my studio door in all her pregnant glory. What a vision of strength and beauty!

By this time in the project, I knew that whatever presented itself to me was meant to be. That voice told me, "Photograph her tomorrow." I was photographing a pregnant woman in Kabuki makeup that morning, so I scheduled Laura in the afternoon. She lived only a few blocks away from my studio, and we agreed that we would photograph her in her garden. Laura was having a home birth, so if she went into labor it would be fine.

Well, you guessed it. The next morning, her husband, Mark, called and said that Laura had begun contractions. I asked her if she still wanted to do the shoot. She said, "This baby isn't coming until dinner." We arrived at around two in the afternoon and began shooting at three-thirty. Laura was having intense labor pains, and we would have to stop every now and then till they passed. Two hours later, she said, "This baby is coming now."

We went to her bedroom. While Mark called the midwife, I did energy work on Laura. I kept visualizing the baby coming swiftly and easily. Laura told me to stop because she felt the baby coming. I reversed my energy flow, and the baby seemed to slow down. The midwife arrived at six o'clock. She examined Laura and helped her into a pool of water set up in the corner of the bedroom.

That morning, as I'd been packing my camera bag, something had told me to bring fast film. I had had a feeling I would be photographing a birth in low light. At seven thirty-five, Julia was born in water. The room was filled with love and magic. All of Laura's women friends were in the room for support. Her husband and the midwife were in the pool with her. I took photographs. It was a miracle!

This is just one of the extraordinary experiences that created the birth of *Pregnant Goddesshood: A Celebration of Life* . . . my baby.

The book was released in October 1997, and I was not quite prepared for the reaction that it inspired. My journey as an artist has been accompanied recently by much controversy. The goal for the project had been to create a book that would make people feel—I don't like to create art to match people's furniture. However, it seems that there are many book buyers and TV producers who are afraid that these photographs might offend someone. The book has stirred up strong emotions about the taboo of pregnant women. As a result, and through the support of the many women who love this book, I am exploring the concept of "Freedom of Vision," especially when it's "art from the heart." It will be interesting to see where this next chapter leads me.

So I remain in the Goddesshood, photographing my journey as the mystical celebration of life continues. In my heart, I truly believe we are chosen to create certain projects in our lives as contributions to the healing of the planet. Of course, we must be listening to our creative muse to know what they might be!

# Recognizing the Answer

## *Wendy Lagerstrom*

A wise and remarkable teacher once told me that Spirit has three answers to our prayers and requests, and they are:

- Yes.
- Yes, but not quite yet.
- I have something better in mind for you.

I find that I have lived most of my life wanting to hear only the first answer to my prayers.

A couple of years ago, after much soul searching and growth, my partner, Ray, and I decided to find a place to live together. So feeling a deep sense of rightness, we began the search for a house in the country.

We are practical people. We did our homework, checking out neighborhoods, bulletin boards, and papers, and talking to friends. We went the extra mile of hiring an agency that does the searching for you, cross-checking your wants and demands against local newspaper ads and many other sources. Each day, Ray and I would take turns calling the agency to hear the latest possibilities.

I felt confident that as we had held the whole question up to Spirit for guidance and direction, we'd find our little country house within a few weeks, a month at most. As the lease on my old place was coming due, the timing would then be perfect. I was ready for that first answer, "Yes," to just roll into place. . . . Right?

Wrong. A month went by, and nothing materialized that met our needs. Anything that came close to our dream was either snatched up before we could blink or would require forfeiting too big a chunk of our wants. I began to worry. Why weren't things working out? We'd done our part, now why wouldn't the powers-that-be cooperate?

Ray kept a more optimistic view than I, and even went off confidently to attend a conference, sure that something would materialize. I was responsible for calling the rental agency each day in his absence, but one busy day at work I simply forgot. I decided to get a newspaper and check the new ads myself. And there amid the listings was one we hadn't heard about from the agency that sounded rather interesting. I called the number, made an appointment to meet the rental manager, and off I went for yet one more viewing of one more house.

I arrived at the little country house to see a couple walking down the driveway, and much to my surprise I recognized the man as an old friend, Peter, whom I hadn't seen in months. We greeted each other with a hug, and he introduced me to the wonderful new lady in his life, Ginny, who just happened to be the rental manager. Well, Ginny and I hit it off beautifully, and Peter told me to look no further, that this was the place. Then he instructed Ginny to look no further, to rent to us! Our search was over.

There I stood, humbled by the gift of these events, the seeming accident of getting a newspaper that one day, finding an ad that dear rental agency had not passed on to us, and of finding Peter and Ginny as our contacts in a tough and competitive rental market. The answer of "Yes, but not quite yet" made total sense now with my freshly acquired 20-20 hindsight. However, my lesson was not yet complete.

During the visit, Ginny shared with me her present battle with breast cancer. I mentioned that I do energy healing work called Reiki, and asked if she would be interested in a free session. The answer was yes, and we began the next week. Ginny responded positively to the treatment, and decided to continue with six more meetings to support her through her chemotherapy and radiation therapy at the hospital.

I'd been wrestling with my own questions and doubts about Reiki. I'd had great responses, but my left brain just couldn't make peace with the idea. All told, the results of this whole story are indeed remarkable, for Ginny is now doing great. Her hair thinned out only a bit and then filled back in, while the cancer has not been heard from since. Because of this experience with Ginny, my confidence in the Reiki work has grown, and I've moved forward to develop a practice. And yes, it's true, Ray and I feel grateful daily for our lovely country house with sheep grazing nearby and a large variety of birds feeding and nesting in our garden.

I try to keep all this in mind now when I send a question out to Spirit. I remind myself of the three possible answers, trying to stay open to how they might materialize. And then I work on embracing these two great truths:

1.  I am not in control of the big plan of things.
2.  Thank goodness I'm not!

# Lightbulb

## *Tracy L. Shaw*

I was going through a very stressful time, having been accused of a theft I did not commit and simultaneously trying to figure out if the gentleman I was dating was the right one for me. I felt he wasn't, but he was so nice, it was hard to figure.

I'd been single for a couple of years—single meaning no live-in or steady dating partner—and I was really quite comfortable with it. Working two jobs never really gave me time to feel lonely, and I enjoyed my solitude when I did have it. But I awoke early one morning and felt really *alone*. I had just been interviewed by the authorities and was scheduled to take a polygraph test to prove my innocence. It would have been nice to have someone to hold me. It wasn't a sexual need—I just wanted a nice comforting arm around me, a hug to push the worries away.

I found myself speaking this need out loud. "Wouldn't it be nice to have someone here to hold me?"

A voice in my head answered back, "Yes, Rick could be here." Rick was my dating friend.

I replied out loud, "But he's not the one," and snuggled down into the covers a little more. Almost immediately I found myself in that place where sleep and dreams meet, that in-between dimension. I heard a door open, and a presence came in.

Now, sometimes when this happens I feel fear, and I tell the presence that if it is here in the name of Jesus Christ, it is welcome to stay. Most times it stays, sometimes it leaves. This time, though, I was not experiencing any fear at all. I felt the presence come in and lie down beside me, and put his arms around me. He gently kissed my forehead and held me.

I asked him out loud, "Who are you?"

And he replied (now don't laugh too hard), "You can just call me lightbulb." (He was very serious.)

He stayed for a minute or two, then left. I felt very warm, comforted, and peaceful. That was all that I had asked for, a hug.

I immediately thought to myself, I must put this in my journal. But as I felt myself get up, write it down, and call a friend to talk about it, I realized I was still dreaming. I awoke and was so sure I had written it down that I checked. I had not.

As I sat up, fully awake now, to begin to record the dream, I silently asked Spirit what the message was. I got a twofold answer. One, "the lightbulb" had obviously gone off over my head (like in the comics) as I fully realized that Rick was not the one for me. Two, the presence, "the lightbulb," was just that—Light. Divine Light, the Holy Comforter Himself, had visited me and answered my heartfelt prayer for comfort.

Thank you, Jesus.

# Contributors

**Jeremiah Abrams,** therapist and author, is the director of the Mt. Vision Institute and the Vision Training, a certification program in pastoral counseling in Marin County, California. His books include the best-selling *Meeting the Shadow; The Shadow in America; Reclaiming the Inner Child;* and *Living from Inside Out.* Jeremiah can be reached c/o Mt. Vision Institute, P.O. Box 1042, Woodacre, California 94973-1042.

**Carol Tisch Allen** is a professional Vedic astrologer living in the forest in northern New Mexico with her new husband, Bill. She is finishing a book of short stories entitled *Pet Sitting Chronicles: The Trials and Tribulations of a Hollywood Dog Walker.* Carol can be reached at (505) 737-2398.

**Allen** and **Linda Anderson** coedit the Angel Animals newsletter, a collection of stories and poems from people around the world who share how to create a better life using the spiritual lessons animals teach us; and they are the authors of the book *Angel Animals: Exploring Our Spiritual Connections with Animals.* For a free sample of the newsletter, send your name and mailing address to Angel Animals, P.O. Box 26334, Minneapolis, Minnesota 55426, or e-mail AngAnimals@aol.com.

**Asandra** is an artist and has been a professional trance channel for fourteen years. She assists people to gain clarity so they can walk their higher life path. Her paintings are highly mystical, with a predominant focus on Goddess Archetypes. She resides in Miami Beach, Florida, and can be reached at (305) 672-5028.

**Carol Willette Bachofner** is an award-winning poet living in California. She teaches poetry workshops, and her poetry has been widely anthologized. Carol is married to Bill and is the mother of six and the grandmother to five grandsons. She can be reached at 7781 SVL Box, Victorville, California 92392, or at her website: www.linkLINE.com/personal/bbachofner/carolbachofner.htm.

**Jan Barron** is a respiratory therapist and works with an outreach program sponsored by hospitals for long-term care facilities. She lives with her husband, daughter, granddaughter, and two dogs named Maxine and Fluffy. She can be reached at 1017 E. Cleveland Venue, Hobar, Indiana 46342.

**Brent BecVar, M.S.**, has worked as a psychotherapist, healthcare administrator, and university administrator, and holds a master's degree in educational psychology. He has worked for Dr. Deepak Chopra since 1991 in both Massachusetts and California as an administrator and educator, is a certified yoga instructor, and was trained by Dr. Chopra as a teacher of Primordial Sound Meditation and the principles and techniques of Ayurvedic healing. He lives in La Jolla, where he can be reached by phone at (619) 551-0727, or by e-mail at brentbecva@aol.com.

**Anthony J. W. Benson** is a healer, respected producer, publicist, creativity consultant, writer, coach, and cofounder of injoi Productions. Anthony has guided the paths and careers of hundreds of people into success. His popular spiritual networking program, *Let's Connect,* is used internationally as a tool for building authentic communication in both personal and business relationships. He can be reached by e-mail at anthony@injoi.com.

**Jill Bruener** is a professional clairvoyant–spiritual counselor, a board-certified hypnotherapist specializing in past life regression, a licensed minister, and a Reiki master. She lives in the greater Cincinnati area with her family. Jill's work has been featured in the *Kentucky Post* and the *Enquirer*. She regularly hosts *Psychic Thursday* on WKRQ radio in Cincinnati, and has appeared on television. Jill also works on cases involving missing people and unsolved murders, and teaches meta-physical classes at Northern Kentucky Community College. She can be reached at P.O. Box 75164, Ft. Thomas, Kentucky 41075; (606) 441-1077.

**Victoria Bullis** has been doing psychic readings and spiritual counseling for seventeen years. She has been a guest on more than six thousand radio shows and has hosted her own talk show, with guests such as Deepak Chopra, Wayne Dyer, and Louise Hay. She is currently a regular on more than forty radio stations throughout the United States and in Hong Kong, New Zealand, Australia, and the United Kingdom. To schedule a phone appointment, contact Victoria at (415) 978-9947, or toll free at (888) 686-2200.

**Peggy Carter** is the author of several self-published books on horses and hunting. Her life has been spent volunteering. She ran A Big Brother's branch in Minnesota and, with her husband, a ski lodge in Wisconsin, a bed-and-breakfast in North Carolina, and a hunt in Mississippi. She still jumps horses at age seventy-eight.

**Scott Chesney** is a consultant with the Amelior Foundation, a philanthropic organization based in Morristown, New Jersey. During two years with the Miami Project, he raised more than one million dollars for spinal cord injury research. Today he works on programs involving inner-city youths and mentoring. He can be reached at his web address: www.d2motion.com.

**Rich Clark** is a professional medium whose clients include people from all walks of life. In addition to his private consultations, he gives readings at the Village Bookstore in Goshen,

New York, and New Spirit Books and Beyond in Nyack, New York, and leads workshops at the Madelyn Burns Studio in New York City.

**Eddie Conner** lives in the Los Angeles area and to date has been heard or seen on more than seventy-five radio and television shows across the United States. Empowering people to follow their hearts, Eddie is known as one of the nation's leading facilitators of well-being to thousands of clients. For more information about classes, products, or private sessions, call (818) 734-9392 or write P.O. Box 280718, Northridge, California 91328-0718.

**Nancy Cooke de Herrera** is the author of *Beyond Gurus*. As a Beverly Hills mother of four, she would have seemed an unlikely sponsor of transcendental meditation, which spread from the East to the West during the 1960s. However, a personal tragedy started her quest for spiritual knowledge in India. Captivated by its people and spiritual heritage, she returns there yearly. She can be reached by fax at (310) 274-7463.

**Rik Cooke**, a *National Geographic* photographer of many years, and his wife operate a unique retreat center located on seventy-seven acres of the beautiful and remote island of Molokai in Hawaii. This nonprofit center is dedicated to creativity, healing, and education through workshops. Rik can be contacted at (808) 567-6430.

**Sophie Woodson Coors** was born in Houston, Texas, in 1934 and has lived in Memphis, Tennessee, ever since. She is married to Giles A. Coors, and is the mother of two children and the grandmother of four. A painter, she studied at the Memphis Art Academy for forty years. Among her collectors are Johnny Cash, Perry Como, Tom Cruise and Nicole Kidman, and Debbie Reynolds.

**Sam Crespi** lives in Shepherdstown, West Virginia, where she is working on a novel, reads weekly to Mrs. Lee's sixth grade class, and does research for Peter Tompkins (*The Secret Life of Plants*).

She has traveled widely and speaks four languages. She is the single mother of a grown daughter who lives in California.

**Cyndi Dale** is the author of *New Chakra Healing*, a revolutionary book on energy healing. President of Life Systems Services and cofounder of injoi Productions, she assists individuals and organizations to apply the spiritual to meet their needs. Having earned her master's degree at the seminary, she now frequently appears in popular media to discuss healing, intuition, mysticism, and miracles. Cyndi can be reached at Life Systems Services, 121 West Franklin Avenue, Minneapolis, Minnesota 55404. Phone: (612) 871-7338.

**Lani DeFelice** lives in the Green Mountains with her son, Elijah Clearwater, her partner, Peter, and their Great Dane, Minnie. She grows organic vegetables, flowers, herbs, sprouts, and wheat grass, and is a graduate of Hippocrates Health Institute. Lani loves to take part in ceremony, and is a pipe holder in the Lakota tradition. You are welcome to reach her at RR1, Box 3303, Townshend, Vermont 05353.

**LaJeanne Doucet** is the creator of Sixth Scents, an herbal-based beauty line. To find out more about her products or place an order, call (800) 619-0893.

**Roger Drummer** is a practitioner of Chinese tonic herbalism. He learned this art through traditional Asian apprenticeship, and now teaches classes and gives lectures nationwide. He resides in Venice, California, with his wife, Laura, and daughter, Sarah, and is working on a book. He can be reached by e-mail at rdalchemy@earthlink.net.

**Micki East, M.A.,** is a mother, counselor, writer, teacher, and professional speaker. Her biggest joy in life is her son, Aleksei. She is the site coordinator for mental health services in an elementary school–based program for children with emotional and behavioral problems.

**Corinne Edwards** has traveled several life paths—from business owner to sales trainer, author, lecturer, poet, and TV producer.

She is the author of three books: *Low Pain Threshold, Love Waits on Welcome . . . and Other Miracles,* and *A Woman Without a Man.* She produces and hosts *Corinne Edwards Interviews* for the Wisdom Network. Write her at 1 East Delaware Place, Chicago, Illinois 60611; call her at (312) 642-7453; or e-mail her at miraclecor@aol.com.

**Monte Farber** is the author of thirteen major publishing projects in collaboration with his wife since 1975, the award-winning artist Amy Zerner. They are known as two of the world's foremost designers of interactive personal guidance systems, and their creations include *The Enchanted Tarot, Goddess Guide Me,* and *Karma Cards;* for kids, *Zen ABC, Scheherazade's Cat,* and *The Dream Quilt;* and an award-winning art book, *Paradise Found: The Visionary Art of Amy Zerner.* Contact Monte at P.O. Box 2299, East Hampton, New York 11937; telephone him at (800) 308-3578; e-mail him at Monte4Amy@Juno.com; or visit his website at www.Sun-Angel.com.

**Bruce Fields** is a professional photographer residing in Manhattan. He regularly shoots for major accounts, including cosmetics and jewelry. He has also recently shown portraits in a Soho gallery. He can be reached at bfields@mindspring.com.

**Anne Ford** is a native of Boston who now resides in Dallas, Texas, with her husband, Michael, three-year-old son, Logan, and two feline angels, Moshe and Golda. Her spiritual adviser Suzann Osborne can be reached at P.O. Box 1172, Novato, California 94948; phone (415) 393-9063.

**Judy Ford** is an attorney practicing employment law in Hollywood, Florida. You can reach her by e-mail at JSFord@worldnet. att.net.

**Montana Desiree Ford-Hilliard** is a thirteen-year-old Persian cat. She lives in La Jolla, California, with her parents and brother, J.B., a twenty-pound black-and-white-Maine coon. You can reach Dr. Gary Holz at (619) 275-8080.

**S. A. Forest** and **Alexandra Light Alba** and their Higher Selves, Glorious Light and Alimar, work together as a team to teach individuals, couples, and small groups how to access their own Higher Selves and utilize spirituality as the basis of a lifelong, loving relationship. Alexandra Light and Forest can be reached at (206) 217-0207 (phone and fax), or at P.O. Box 9634, Seattle, Washington 98109.

**Jacqueline Forsyth-Rubinstein**: Born in Singapore to Dutch parents, Jacqueline grew up traveling extensively and has lived in Denmark, Finland, New York, and Holland. She is happily married to Jerold Rubinstein, has three wonderful children, and resides in Santa Barbara, California.

**Stephen Freeman** lives on a small ranch in western Montana. **Shawna Mullane** is a painter who also works for a holistic health center in eastern Canada.

**Melissa Giovagnoli** has been a networking coach and a marketing, communications, and training consultant for sixteen years. She is the author of six books, including *Angels in the Workplace: Stories and Inspirations to Create a New World of Work*. You can contact Melissa at (847) 310-0571, or at Megnetwork@aol.com.

**Stephanie P. Gunning** is a freelance writer and book editor specializing in the categories of spirituality, psychology, and health. She lives in New York City. You can contact Stephanie by telephone at (323) 802-7856 or by e-mail at stephgun@aol.com.

**Mary Ann Halpin** is a fine-art and portrait photographer who lectures and leads seminars in creativity and Freedom of Vision. Her first book, *Pregnant Goddesshood: A Celebration of Life*, was released in 1997. She resides in Los Angeles. Contact her at Halpin-Croyle Photography, (213) 874-8500, or visit her website: www.Goddesshood.com.

**Julie Hill** is a literary agent, author, and astrologer with offices in La Jolla and Berkeley, California. She specializes in spiritual, psychological, and health books. She is the mother of three grown sons, the youngest of whom, Sutton Papanikolas, is the subject of the story "Mystical Child."

**Triana Jackie Hill** is an internationally respected lecturer and Beyond-Conception workshop teacher, a multitalented clairvoyant, and a spiritual and business counselor, and she has been honored in *Who's Who in American Women*. She's also a very popular radio personality. She can be reached at her company, Interlink Unlimited, P.O. Box 1988, Kihei, Hawaii 96753; phone (808) 874-1888; fax (808) 874-8777; e-mail link@mauigateway.com; website www.mauigateway.com/link.

**Dr. Gary Holz** is the owner and director of the Wellness Center in San Diego, California, specializing in alternative healing. He has a master's of science in immunology and nutrition and a doctorate of science in immunology from Westbrook University. In private practice, he concentrates on chronic and immune-deficiency disorders. You can reach him at (619) 275-8080.

**Barbara Horner** is an entrepreneurial consultant who resides in San Diego, California, with her best pal, a Pomeranian named Odie. Barbara can be contacted at bhorner@adnc.com.

**Celeste Huttes** has worked in business for ten years and is currently pursuing a master's degree in organizations and human development. Celeste lives with her cat, Pandora, in central Illinois.

**Gennica Ivey** is currently a resident of California, and plans to attend college in the near future. She enjoys being with family and friends, as well as writing and exercising.

**Gerald Jampolsky, M.D.,** is an internationally recognized authority in the fields of psychiatry, health, business, and education. In 1975, he cofounded the original Center for Attitudinal Healing in Tiburon, California. There are now more than 130 independent Centers for Attitudinal Healing in twenty countries. Dr. Jampolsky is the author of *Love is Letting Go of Fear*,

*Teach Only Love,* and *Out of Darkness, Into the Light,* among other books. He can be reached at The Center for Attitudinal Healing, 33 Buchanan Drive, Sausalito, California, (415) 331-6161.

**Jenny Jobson** grew up in a small town in Michigan, moved to New York City at the age of nineteen to pursue theater, and has since studied drama in both London and New York.

**Roberta Johnson** was born near Los Angeles, California, and raised in the Midwest. She is a practicing child life specialist in Arkansas Children's Hospital, providing emotional and developmental support to premature infants and hospitalized infants and toddlers through therapeutic play. She lives in Little Rock, Arkansas.

**Juliana**: This fifty-something author, born and raised in the coastal cities of California, moved in 1988 to Woodstock, New York, in order to devote the second half of her life to writing, painting, gardening, and designing a "healthy home." She can be reached via e-mail at juli.ana@ix.net.com or by mail at P.O. Box 51, Woodstock, New York 12498.

**Kathy Juline** is the coauthor of *You Are the One: Living Freely Through Affirmative Prayer,* and writes for *Science of Mind* magazine. Previously the editor of that magazine, she is also a librarian and a book editor, and she facilitates classes on creative writing. You can write to her at 530 South Madison, #10, Pasadena, California 91101.

**Laura Alden Kamm** is the founder and developer of Intuitive Therapeutics, a healing model and medical delivery system based on her work as a medical intuitive. Her healing gift has taken Laura across the United States and abroad, and she has private clients ranging from Singapore to Switzerland.

**Dharma Singh Khalsa, M.D.,** is president/medical director of the Alzheimer's Prevention Foundation (APF) in Tucson, Arizona. The APF is the world's leader in the integrated medical approach to the prevention and treatment of Alzheimer's disease. Dharma is the author of *Brain Longevity* and *The Pain Cure* (Warner Books). He can be reached at DrDharma@aol.com.

**Sri Harold Klemp** is the spiritual leader of Eckankar, the religion of the Light and Sound of God. As an inner and outer spiritual master, he teaches students of Eckankar through dreams, spiritual guidance, writings, and talks. He is an international lecturer and the author of more than thirty books. You can find out more by contacting Eckankar at P.O. Box 27300, Minneapolis, Minnesota 55427; calling (800) 568-3463; or visiting Eckankar's website at www.eckankar.org.

**Michele Kufner** is a housewife and mother. She can be reached through Dr. Eric Scott Pearl at (310) 659-9339; 8615 Santa Monica Boulevard, West Hollywood, California 90069.

**Lisa-Marie Lacroix** currently resides in a charmingly picturesque Canadian town with three profound and enlightened individuals, namely her radiant children, Kristy and Roque, and her sexy French husband, Roland. She has gone from singer/songwriter to wife/mother/composer of children's manuscripts. You may contact her by writing to P.O. Box 622, Rivers, Manitoba, Canada ROK 1XO.

**Wendy Lagerstrom** works as a writer, a designer of stained-glass windows, and a piano teacher to children. She self-published her book *She Dances on Waves*, practices the art of Reiki healing, and volunteers with hospice. Ms. Lagerstrom lives with her life partner, Ray, in the country, where they tend a large garden and seek a life of mindfulness and minimal stress. Please address any correspondence to Wendy Lagerstrom, P.O. Box 143, Penngrove, California 94951.

**Michael Peter Langevin** is the cofounder and publisher of *Magical Blend* magazine. He has contributed chapters to *A Magical Universe*, *Solstice Shift*, and *Hot Chocolate for the Mystical Soul* and consults, lectures, and teaches workshops on many spiritual subjects. He lives with his wife and two children on a farm in Chico, California. He can be contacted at P.O. Box 600, Chico, California 95927; via e-mail at magicalinreach.com; through the website www.magicalblend.com; or by calling (888) 296-2442.

**Kenny Loggins** has touched people for more than two decades as few musicians ever do. His body of work as an artist and songwriter is one of music's most distinguished, and he has sold more than twenty million albums over the course of his career. He and his wife, Julia, coauthored *The Unimaginable Life*, a celebration of their life and love. Kenny and Julia were married in 1992. The couple live in Southern California with their five children. Visit their website at www.kennyloggins.com.

**Susan Stroud Long** comes from a show-business family on both sides: her mother was a twin (the Brewster twins), and her father was a twin (the Stroud twins). The Brewster twins were contract players at Twentieth Century–Fox, and the Stroud twins started their career on Edgar Bergen's radio show. Susan resides in Castle Rock, Colorado, with her husband, Avery, and strange cat, Hedley. You may contact her at 7444 Norfolk Place, Castle Rock, Colorado 80104.

**Gerri Magee** is the director of advertising and public relations and the assistant to the editor of *phenomeNEWS*, the oldest metaphysical publication of its kind in the United States, based in Southfield, Michigan.

**Eugene C. Marotta** and his wife are human potential consultants and certified meditation instructors. Gene can be reached at 25051 Banbridge Court, #101, Bonita Spring, Florida 34134; phone (941) 498-1095; fax (941) 498-3797.

**Judy Martin** is an Emmy Award–winning reporter who has worked in television for fifteen years. For much of the last four years she handled community relations for Barnes & Noble bookstores in south Florida, promoting best-selling authors and events. Now, running her own production company, she produces television programs on solution-oriented health and socially conscious programming.

**Mariah Martin, M.S., M.A.,** is an intuitive channel and therapist. She is a single mother of three adopted children and the author of the forthcoming book *The Love Triad: Honoring the Adoptive Mother*.

**Pamela McGee** lives in a small mountain community seventy miles north of Los Angeles. As a mother of one, and a housewife, Pamela focuses her free time on being an artist and equestrian. Having performed in more than twenty-five theatrical productions as well as voice-over and television roles, Pamela is also gifted in the art of set design and construction. As a hobby and part-time business for more than twenty years, Pamela has produced hundreds of custom-quality stained-glass windows.

**Azita Milanian** is a clothing designer who uses her company, Stepping Out/Tosca Eveningwear and Dancewear, to host fashion shows four times a year to raise money for Save the Children around the world. You can reach Azita at (626) 797-5570 or by mail: SteppingOut/Tosca, P.O. Box 6135, Alta Dena, California 91003-6135.

**Catherine Miller** is the founder and publisher of the *Holistic Health Journal*, which is distributed internationally and has a circulation of fifty thousand.

**Bevey Miner** is the vice president of marketing at a high-technology research company based in La Jolla, California. She has worked in marketing, advertising, and public relations for more than twenty years in the high-tech and financial industries. She resides in San Diego, California, with her two children.

**Shawne Mitchell** is the author of *Soul Style: Creating a Home or Office Environment to Enhance Your Life and Your Spirit*. Shawne writes a regular column of tips and ideas to create a home for the soul, and gives workshops and private consultations. She also works for the premier real estate firm, Village Properties, in Santa Barbara, California, where she resides with her two sons, Travis and Austin. She can be reached at Soul Style, P.O. Box 5765, Santa Barbara, California 93150, or at soulstyle1@aol.com.

**Nancy E. Myer** is a psychic who has appeared on TV. She has also appeared on *Unsolved Mysteries, The Other Side, Attitudes, Sightings, 48 Hours,* and *Geraldo.* She has contributed information to the investigations of four hundred homicides in twenty-six years with 90 percent accuracy. Articles about Nancy have appeared in numerous publications. She is the author of *Silent Witness: The True Story of a Psychic Detective,* and her work is included in books such as Time-Life's *Mysteries of the Unknown, The Top Ten Psychics in America,* and *Who Killed My Daughter?* She lives in Pennsylvania and has her own column called "Nancy Myer's Psychic Tip of the Week" on the website www.OnTVPittsburgh.com.

**Yonah Offner** is a nationally known professional speaker and the C.O.O. and leader of The Offner Team, a consortium of health-care educators. He has been featured on TV and radio, and in magazines and newspapers coast to coast. Yonah is also a certified reflexologist, a certified yoga instructor, and a graduate of Laney College. You may contact Yonah by phone at (800) 655-6668, by fax at (760) 943-1081, or by e-mail at offner@earthlink.net.

**Ron Paul** has a degree in psychology from UCLA and worked for several years at UCLA developing The California Self-Help Center. A part-time actor and writer, he works full-time as the program director of The Learning Light Foundation in Anaheim, California. He is also a licensed clinical hypnotherapist and a certified spiritual counselor. He resides with his family in La Mirada, California.

**Charles Lewis Richards, Ph.D.,** is a psychotherapist residing in Del Mar, California, and a leading authority on nonhypnotic past-life therapy. As a spiritual adventurer his work has been featured on *Oprah* and NBC's *The Other Side*. He also conducts a variety of personal growth seminars and trainings, and can be reached by phone at (619) 755-5185 or via e-mail at Chaslr@aol.com.

**Elizabeth Russell** works in various aspects of the media and is also a freelance writer. She grew up in St. Paul, Minnesota, and has resided in California since 1979. You can write to her at 11684 Ventura Blvd. #672, Studio City, California 91604.

**Bobbie Sandoz, M.S.W.**, is the author of *Parachutes for Parents: 12 New Keys to Raising Children for a Better World* and *Swimming with Dolphins*. She is also a columnist for the *Honolulu Advertiser*, a professional speaker, and the president of Education for a Better World. Bobbie does not provide information on where to swim with dolphins. She can be contacted at SandozB@aol.com. or P.O. Box 22509, Honolulu, Hawaii 96823-2509.

**Jill Schneider** is a Shiatsu therapist and energy worker with twenty years in the field of holistic healing, also a performance artist, singer-songwriter-guitarist, mother of one son, teacher, and professional writer. She can be reached by phone at (561) 279-4801 or by e-mail at relief@gate.net.

**James David Seddon** is a poet and author who lives with his wife in southern Iowa. He can be reached at 708 West Washington, Centerville, Iowa 52544, or by e-mail at jseddon@lisco.net.

**Elizabeth Seely** is currently writing her first book based on personal spiritual experiences. She lives in central Ohio with her two lovely little girls. She also works for an international trading company. She can be contacted at elizseely@aol.com.

**Anne Wallace Sharp** is a registered nurse and freelance journalist who lives in Beavercreek, Ohio. She is the coauthor of the book *Gifts: Two Hospice Professionals Reveal Messages from Those Passing On*, which is a compilation of mystical stories involving her interaction with the terminally ill.

**Tracy L. Shaw**, a thirty-eight-year-old child on her spiritual path, lives in Carroll County, Maryland, works as a graphic production artist, and looks forward to the day she can exit the corporate world and help others with alternative healing methods.

**Linda Tisch Sivertsen** is an author who lives in the Southwest with her husband, Mark, and their seven-year-old son. She is the author of a book entitled *Lives Charmed: Intimate Conversations with Extraordinary People.*

**Modeste Slywka** is an actor and writer living in New York City.

**Jeanne Smearsoll** was born in 1938 and raised in Cleveland, Ohio. She graduated from Ohio University in 1961, taught elementary school for three years, then raised four children and worked a small farm in southwest Ohio. She is active in community theater: singing, acting, and producing shows. She is currently enjoying her four children and five grandchildren and recently became engaged. She plans to remarry in 1999.

**Allison Stillman** is a writer, teacher, and anointing practitioner. She teaches workshops nationwide on esoteric wisdom and spiritual practices, has taken groups on journeys to sacred sites, and facilitated wild dolphin swims. She is the author of *Romancing the Divine: The Sacred Art of Anointing* and has written articles for numerous publications. She resides in Ojai, California, and can be reached at (805) 640-0738.

**John Maxwell Taylor** is an actor acclaimed for his one-man drama *Forever Jung*, for which he received the Gradiva Award from the Association for the Advancement of Psychoanalysis.

**Eric Troup** lives in Costa Mesa, California, with his wife, Michelle, and his guide dog, Boomer. Eric is an aspiring writer and musician who is working on his degree in communications at National University. He can be e-mailed at lummox @ccinet.com.

**James F. Twyman** (a.k.a. The Peace Troubadour) has traveled the world performing The Peace Concert in areas most affected by violence and war, including Bosnia, Iraq, Northern Ireland, Israel, and India. He is also the author of the book *Emissary of Light*.

**Barbara Tse Tyler** was born in Manhattan, New York, in 1965 and later moved to Baldwin, Long Island, in 1972. She joined the Marine Corps in 1983 and married a fellow Marine in 1986. She has attended Palomar Community College in California, the University of Pittsburgh, and Suffolk Community College on Long Island, and has worked with mentally and physically disabled children and as a counselor to runaway teenagers. She currently lives with her husband and four children in Farmingville, New York.

**Doreen Virtue, Ph.D.** (yes, that is her real name), is a metaphysical doctor of psychology who works with the angelic realm. She is the author of *Angel Therapy*, *The Lightworker's Way*, and the audiotape *Chakra Clearing*. Doreen gives weekend workshops across the country about how to communicate with angels. For more information on her books, tapes, or workshop schedule, please call (800) 654-5126, ext. 0, or visit the conference room at the Internet site www.hayhouse.com.

**Ellen Lieberman Weil** is an internationally known psychic and psychotherapist. Her in-person and telephone consultations address personal, business, and relationship issues. She and her husband, Gunther, a management consultant, offer individual retreats for executives and other professionals that combine emotional healing, psychic work, Chi Kung, and executive coaching. Ellen also lectures and teaches psychic/intuitive development. You can contact Ellen at Aspen Consulting Associates, 4337 County Road #113, Carbondale, Colorado 81623; phone (970) 945-3078; fax (970) 928-8185; e-mail weil@aspenconsult.com.

**Ben Woodson** is a visionary businessman who created and developed the exclusive world-famous resort Little Palm Island in the Florida Keys. He can be reached by fax at (901) 685-2563.

**Jim Wright** is a former police officer with the Los Angeles Police Department who currently owns his own private investigation firm, Investigative Consultants, in Tacoma, Washington. He is listed in *Who's Who of Business* and has appeared on *Unsolved Mysteries* and *Paranormal Borderline* in addition to being featured in a *Reader's Digest* tape series on the mind and psychic phenomena. He can be contacted at P.O. Box 1281, Tacoma, Washington; (253) 383-0599 (office); (253) 383-0699 (fax); wrightpi@bigfoot.com (e-mail).

**Nancilee Wydra**, feng shui master and founder of the Feng Shui Institute of America, holds lectures and consultations, trains people to become professional feng shui consultants, and has authored four books on feng shui. Her latest book is *Look Before You Love*. She can be contacted at P.O. Box 488, Wabasso, Florida 32970; (888) 488-FSIA[3742]; e-mail windwater8@aol.com; or her website, www.windwater.com.

**Norma Jean Young** is a Reiki master and medical consultant. She has taught Reiki in nursing colleges, lectured at Planetree hospitals, and recently presented grand rounds at Massachusetts General Hospital. Trained as a nurse, Waldorf teacher, and family practice and music therapist, Norma Jean has been a Reiki practitioner for sixteen years and a member of the worldwide Reiki Alliance of Masters for twelve years. You can contact Norma Jean at the Center of Origins Reiki Foundation, (206) 706-7487.

**Tom Youngholm** is the author of the international best-selling visionary fiction *The Celestial Bar: A Spiritual Journey* and its sequel, *In the Shadow of the Sphere*. He has appeared on CNBC, PBS, and many other radio and television stations throughout the country. Tom presents workshops based on the various aspects of spirituality. You can contact Tom through Creative Information Concepts, P.O. Box 1504, Lemon Grove, California 91946; (619) 698-9462; e-mail: CreativeC@aol.com; website: www.celestialbar.com.

**Julie Zaslav, C.S.W., C.A.S.A.C.,** is an expert in the field of adolescent substance-abuse treatment. She is currently the director of an outpatient substance-abuse program for at-risk youth in downtown Brooklyn, New York. Ms. Zaslav is also a certified acupuncture detoxification specialist and implements auricular acupuncture to adolescents in the program. She loves to write short stories in her free time and maintains a private counseling/consulting practice focusing on teenage life. She can be reached at (718) 499-6992.

## Have You Had a Mystical Experience?

If you have had a personal mystical experience you'd like to share for a future volume of *Hot Chocolate for the Mystical Soul*, please send it to:

Arielle Ford
P.O. Box 8064
La Jolla, California 92038

or fax it to: 619-454-3319.

Please make sure to include your name, address and phone number!